INTRODUCTION
TO COMPUTING

Peter Greenfield

McGRAW-HILL BOOK COMPANY

London · New York · St Louis · San Francisco · Auckland · Bogotá · Caracas ·
Hamburg · Lisbon · Madrid · Mexico · Milan · Montreal · New Delhi ·
Panama · Paris · San Juan · São Paulo · Singapore · Sydney · Tokyo · Toronto

Published by
McGRAW-HILL Book Company Europe
Shoppenhangers Road, Maidenhead, Berkshire, SL6 2QL, England
Telephone 0628 23432 Fax 0628 770224

British Library Cataloguing in Publication Data
Greenfield, Peter
    Introduction to Computing
    I. Title
    004

    ISBN 0-07-707419-X

Library of Congress Cataloging-in-Publication Data
Greenfield, Peter
    Introduction to computing/Peter Greenfield.
        p.   cm.
    Includes bibliographical references and index.
    ISBN 0-07-707419-X :
    1. Computers. I. Title.
    QA76.G713 1992
    004--dc20   92-799
                                                                        CIP

1234 CUP 9432

Typeset by Keyword Publishing Services Ltd
and printed and bound in Great Britain at the University Press, Cambridge

To my parents

CONTENTS

PREFACE

This book is an introductory text on computing. Its principal goal is to equip the reader with the ability to recognize in a constructive manner the possible and actual uses, conditions and risks of the application of computers to a wide range of circumstances. The unifying theme employed is one of analysis and reduction, followed by synthesis and discussion. The book is organized into five parts that follow the theme: Introduction; Computing and Information Processing; Constructing Computer Applications; How Computers Work and Applying Computers. Concepts are introduced and then developed both within chapters and between chapters. The social ramifications of the concepts introduced in earlier chapters are introduced in the final part of the book.

The book is intended principally for the mature student at the outset of a masters degree conversion course in computer science or information technology, but also for arts students who are taking computing as a subsidiary subject. In all cases the expectation is that the student has little or no experience in computing. For the masters student, the book might be recommended as pre-course reading as well as being a useful background and unifying text for the whole course. For arts students, the book is intended to complement a practical course involving 'exposure to application packages that arts students are likely to encounter' with, it is hoped, a practical introduction to programming. By virtue of its principal goal, the intention is to provide an educationally more rewarding approach to the subject than the 'exposure' method on its own.

In order to fulfil the principal goal of the text, it is important that the reader becomes *computer literate*. This means acquiring not only an understanding of the current application and uses made of computers, but an ability to appreciate the effects of their application to new and unforeseen circumstances. This can only be done by introducing the principles behind the technology, and by illustrating the way computers can affect our way of life.

A frequent difficulty experienced by newcomers to computing is the plethora of jargon together with the apparently arbitrary way in which many of the concepts and the realities, such as computer equipment and uses, appear to be related (or unrelated). On the surface, unless one restricts one's horizons to one or a few packages such as word-processors, there appears to be little overall framework. At the theoretical level discrete mathematics is increasingly being used, and is important as a unifying framework in the specification and the understanding of computer applications (for example in the validation of safety-critical applications). However, such an approach is not really feasible as an underlying methodology for an introductory text such as this. It is also unfortunately the case that because computing has developed, and is continuing to develop rapidly and in a somewhat piecemeal fashion, some aspects of the subject do appear arbitrary in nature.

In this book I have attempted to steer a course between oversimplification on the one hand, and on the other, boggling the mind of the reader with the many complications that can arise from the totality of methodologies, programming languages and hardware capabilities currently in use. Thus limits have necessarily been placed on the applications, types of package, instances of programming languages, operating systems and information services to include. I have tried therefore to express the fundamental importance of abstraction in specification, design and programming, using and repeating simple examples. With the concept of abstraction understood, and an awareness of how abstract solutions can be effected, the student is in a better position to realize the potentials and the pitfalls of computing.

The book is organized into five parts: Introduction; Computing and Information Processing; Constructing Computer Applications; How Computers Work and Applying Computers. The first part introduces basic computing concepts and terminology. The second part deals with information, how it can be organized so it can be processed, and then how it can be processed and accessed. Applications from the apparently unstructured information in word-processing, through database and then to knowledge processing are described. The third part of the book explains, at an introductory level, how computer applications are specified, designed and built, together with both the underlying computing theory and practices. Part Four deals with the way the various parts of a computer are designed and organized, in terms of both hardware and software. The final part discusses how computers and computer-based solutions can be classified, how potential computer systems can be evaluated, and ethical considerations for their use in society.

The convention for spelling is British English. In computing, however, some technical words conventionally take the American form and this practice is followed where applicable. Indeed this is often imposed by computer software.

ACKNOWLEDGEMENTS

This book originated with lecture course material given by the author for various undergraduate courses in the University of Birmingham. Much material is from SE172 computer studies, a subsidiary course for arts students and social science students. Other contributions are from SE322(a) operating systems, from EE334 artificial intelligence and from SE207 logic programming. In addition to university teaching and research work, industrial experience in the systems software side of the computer manufacturing industry, and in scientific programming in the engineering industry has contributed much insight, material and glue.

I am grateful to IBM UK Limited for drawings of their equipment.

I am grateful to Mike Spivey for permission to use his LAT_EX macros for printing **Z** specifications.

I am grateful to Sylviane Cardey for permission to draw on her work in natural language morphology.

Although I take full responsibility for this book and any flaws it may contain, I acknowledge my gratitude to many colleagues. The following have in particular provided useful advice with various aspects of the book: Graham Allport, Tom Axford, Helder Coelho, Antoni Diller, Chris Hall, Nick Hall, Peter Jarratt, Sue Laflin, Dennis Parkyn, Angela Sasse, Dean Shumsheruddin, Jim Yandle.

Peter Greenfield
Birmingham

TRADEMARKS

PART
ONE

INTRODUCTION

ONE

WHAT IS COMPUTING?

The application of computers in current everyday life is legion. We find them applied to diverse uses. Their diversity of application is an indicator of their generality. In this book much attention will be directed at the flexibility of computers. All computers share two fundamental characteristics: the ability to process data to supply information, and the ability for humans to specify, by programming, the nature of the processing and the structure of the data to supply information. It is these abilities that distinguish the computer from other artifacts. The first characteristic, data processing, is concerned with how the computer behaves when servicing some application. The second characteristic, programming, involves the human in solving the problem generally, and being able to specify the problem solution by means of a program.

Computing, then, as covered in this book, involves knowing how a solution to a problem can be expressed generally, how the computer then solves the problem each time it is presented with particular data and, finally, knowing how to go about engineering computer-based solutions which have at their centre this problem-solving capability.

1.1 DIGITAL AND ANALOGUE COMPUTERS

In the same way as we may count whole numbers using our fingers (digits), in a *digital* computer the quantities that are processed have discrete, integral or whole values. If we want to deal with fractional quantities we can, but there may be a loss in accuracy. For fractional quantities, the degree of accuracy is dependent on the number of digits available. An *analogue* computer on the other hand is a physical representation of some real-world system, and when implemented, operates on continuously variable physical quantities. The accuracy of analogue computers depends on how accurately the quantities can be measured. The very great majority of computers are *digital* computers. The principal reasons for this are twofold. Firstly, they can be programmed to do a variety of tasks relatively easily, whilst

Digital   Analogue

Figure 1.1 Digital and analogue watch faces.

analogue computers are usually less flexible in terms of programming. Secondly, the accuracy of digital computers can, if necessary, be improved by providing more digits.

In computing, the quantities that are processed are called items of data. In a digital computer the data items processed have discrete, integral or whole values. An abacus is also an example of a digital calculating device; the range of values of the data items that represent particular numbers is limited by the number of counters. A digital watch is an example of a digital device employing electronic technology with a digital display (Fig. 1.1). The *output* data items are displayed as digits. Together, the digits and the various other punctuation marks and characters, supply *information*—the current time. A pocket calculator is another example of a digital device; the range of numbers it can process is finite. Both *input* data items, entered on a keyboard, and the information supplied by the output data items displayed as digits are discrete.

An analogue computer is an analogue of a real-world system, for example a river system with weirs and sluices, subjected to rainfall and other effects. Analogue computers are normally electrical analogues of the physical system; to program an analogue computer one builds the analogue in the form of a specific electrical circuit made up of electrical components which represent the various physical features (weirs, lengths of river, flood plains etc.). Within the circuit the values of electrical phenomena such as potentials (voltages) and currents are the analogues of, respectively, water levels and water flow rates. Analogue data can be displayed in an analogical manner; an analogue watch face displays time by means of pointers (the hands) to a graduated circle representing time (Fig. 1.1).

In the book we will be using the same example problem, that of finding the average of a collection of positive numbers, to illustrate various aspects of computing. (Throughout this book the word *collection* is used informally; there is no formal or mathematical meaning intended.)

Figure 1.2 illustrates an analogue computer devised to calculate the average of a collection of numbers. This analogue computer can be thought of as a physical analogue of the mathematical formula for calculating an average. It comprises a sequence of graduated vertical clear glass tubes, of the same height and based at the same horizontal level. The base of each of the tubes is connected to a common

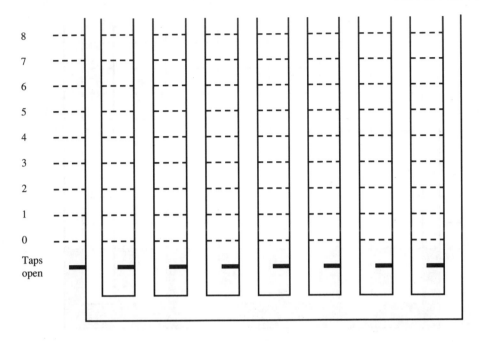

Figure 1.2 Analogue computer to find the average of a collection of numbers.

connecting tube by means of a tap. In Fig. 1.2 all the taps are shown in the open state. The analogue computer calculates the average by adding the heights (values of the numbers) of water together and dividing the result amongst the tubes (dividing by the number of numbers).

The computer is *initialized* by opening all the taps and adding or draining the water in the connecting tube until all the tubes have water to the zero mark, at which time all the taps are closed. The computer is shown initialized in Fig. 1.3.

The computer performs a program execution as follows. We first have to provide the computer with *input data*; for each value in the collection of values for which an average is required, an empty tube is selected. Water is poured into the top of the tube to a graduation mark appropriate to the value being simulated, and the tube removed from the set of candidate tubes (the value might have been zero). Assuming tubes are allocated left to right (which ones and which order does not in fact matter) then if the average of:

3, 2, 6, 0, 1, 2

is to be calculated, the state of the computer after this operation will be as illustrated in Fig. 1.4.

When there are no remaining input data values, we now have the computer *process* the data. To do this the taps of the selected tubes are opened and the water level is allowed to settle. We can now determine the *output* from the computer, the

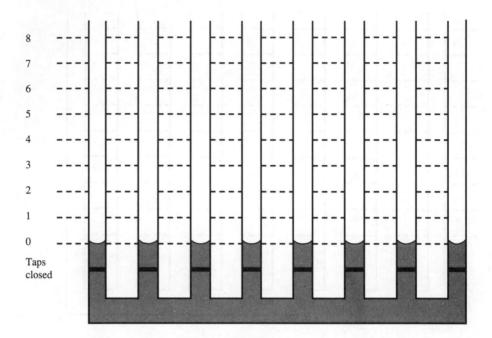

Figure 1.3 Analogue computer—initialized.

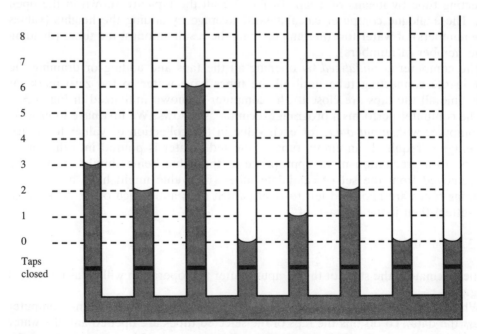

Figure 1.4 Analogue computer—set to find the average of 3, 2, 6, 0, 1, 2.

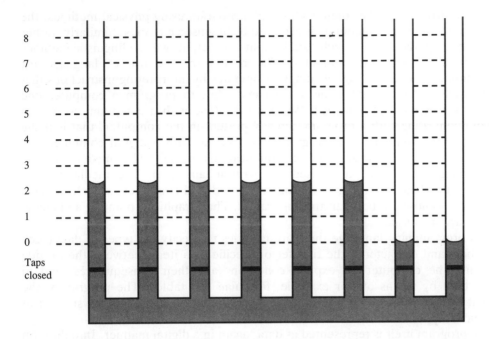

Figure 1.5   Analogue computer—the average computed.

average of the collection of numbers. We do this by observation. The average can be read off any of the selected tubes by reading the water level (Fig. 1.5). The average appears to be approximately 2.3. If we wanted to calculate the average of another collection of numbers, we would reinitialize the computer and carry on as explained.

The accuracy of analogue computers is dependent on the physical accuracy of the components, and the sensitivity of the measuring instruments. In the example analogue computer one has to consider, for instance, consistent bores, parallel tubes, accurate graduations, calibration of zeros, cleanliness of the bores (effect on the menisci), parallax and the consistent interpretation of physical phenomena, such as the menisci.

1.1.1 Digital computers

The very great majority of computers are *digital* computers (as distinct from *analogue* computers). In a digital computer the data items that are processed have discrete, integral or whole values, as opposed to the continuous values of data processed by an analogue computer. The digital nature of the data covers data supplied to the computer, input data, data supplied by the computer, output data, and data internal to the computer.

A digital computer that is to simulate a real-world system such as the river system, or be part of an artificial system such as a word-processor to aid in typing, editing, storing and retrieving a document, is also programmed as is an analogue computer. However, rather than 'setting up' a program using physical methods, the programming of digital computers is achieved by linguistic methods. Similarly, rather than 'setting up' the way in which data is input and output, we use linguistic methods to communicate with the computer. The reason for the use of language for programming is because a digital computer operates by interpreting instructions that are themselves represented using a language. Thus to program a computer one employs a *programming language*. When we dialogue with a computer, we are in fact communicating with a program, already present in the computer, that is being *executed* by the computer. To program and dialogue with a digital computer one uses a variety of languages and communications media. The media used in programming tends to be text-based (cf. written language). The media used to communicate when dialoguing with programs in a digital computer, as well as being text-based, is chosen to best suit the application. Thus graphical, pointing and tactile methods are also used.

In a programming language there are facilities to specify the types of data (such as numbers and characters), the transfer of specific data items between the outside world and the computer, to express conditions and their consequences, and to process data by means of, for example, formulae and tables. The program is the text that expresses, in the computer language, a model of a real-world system or of an artificial application.

The program itself is represented as data, again in a digital manner. Initialization of the computer requires that the program, in its digital data form, be input to and stored in the memory of the computer for the duration of the use of the program. The memory of a computer can have different data values stored in it at different times. For this reason, such digital computers that make up nearly all computers are known as *stored-program digital computers*. That a program is itself data is crucial to digital computers and fundamental to their flexibility and this in turn leads to their wide applicability. One may contrast the notion of a program stored as data and used to instruct the computer, with other devices (mostly historical) in which the program is fixed, such as a pianola and its separate rolls for each piece of music, and a musical box with its usually integral representation of a particular piece of music.

Some digital computer applications may have a fixed program, as in burglar alarms. However, it is usually economically advantageous to use a limited range of general-purpose components rather than design a new component for a specific purpose. Furthermore, such applications still require a program, and it is therefore sensible to be able to use the generally available programming techniques and capabilities that have been developed for stored-program digital computers for such single specific applications. Thus where a single specific application is required, the program is permanently fixed in memory, but otherwise a conventional stored-program digital computer is usually used.

For some applications the real-world types of data to be processed are discrete by nature, for example money values in business, and writing in the form of typeface characters. However, for other applications the types of data are continuously variable, for example the level of water at some point in a stretch of river. For such continuously variable quantities, where processed by a digital computer, there must be conversion between the real-world data (often called *analogue data*) and that used within the computer.

1.2 SOME APPLICATIONS OF COMPUTERS

The purpose of this section is to introduce basic concepts and terminology by means of describing and analysing a set of applications.

Word-processors Wherever people are composing or manipulating text, as in writing essays, books, letters, articles and so on, they may well be using, or contemplating the use of, a *word-processor*, a *tool* to assist them in their work. A word-processor is a computer-based *system* which allows the user to type, edit and file documents at a typewriter-like keyboard, view what has been typed on a screen, and subsequently cause a document to be printed. The screen normally also shows material other than the 'window' on the text currently being typed or edited. Figure 1.6 overleaf shows an example of a typical word-processor screen. Some of the other material displayed is for information purposes, whilst the rest indicates processing operations that the user can apply. Over and above an ordinary mechanical typewriter a word-processor gives the user the ability to *edit* a document, and to file the current state of the document and retrieve it at some later time—*information storage* and *retrieval*.

Not only are these basic document preparation procedures provided by the computing system, but without any additions to the physical equipment, many other typical document preparation needs are also provided. Thus the user might have several documents filed in a state of preparation at any particular time. A word-processor usually has *search* and *edit* facilities, the ability to merge another document or part document into the working document and a *spelling checker* (for the language of a given document). The word-processor will also provide assistance in that it can automate operations such as *pagination*, *word-wrap* and *layout* (such as forming neat paragraphs that are justified against the left and right margins) and possibly generate contents pages with page numbers.

The equipment used for word-processing, the computer *hardware*, can be used for other computer-based activities, for example to keep a file of names and addresses of a club's members, or to produce team game fixture lists. Each activity requires the use of a specific computer *application*. Applications may be used in an isolated manner but one often wishes to *import* or *export* data between applications. In the case of a word-processor there may be the need to access a separate *file* of names and addresses in order to generate 'personalized' mail by embedding individuals' names in the generated letters.

Applications, such as word-processing, that might be used by many people on their computer systems, are typically packaged—their various components are consolidated into a single *package*.

Applications require standard facilities, sub-applications, that are common to most other applications. Thus, just as in mechanical engineering where we find standardized components such as nuts and bolts, or in course timetabling where we use a standard template into which a department fits its lectures and seminars,

Microsoft Word - WP-DOC

☐ **File** **Edit** **View** **Insert** **Format** **Utilities** **Window** **Help**

Undo Formatting	Alt+BkSp
Repeat Character	F4
Cut	Shift+Del
Copy	Ctrl+Ins
Paste	Shift+Ins
Search...	
Replace...	
Go To...	F5
Header/Footer...	
Summary Info...	
Table...	

and su... ...e printed on paper by means of a printer. The screen
normal... ...e 'window' on the text currently being typed or edited.
Fig 1.6 ...rd-processor screen. Some of the other material
display ...t the rest indicates processing operations that the user
can ap...

Over a... ...pewriter a word-processor provides the user the ability
to edit ...tate of the document and retrieve it at some later time
– *infor...* ...only are these basic document preparation procedures
provide... ...out any additions to the physical equipment, many
other typical document preparation needs are provided. Thus the user might have several
documents filed in a state of preparation at any particular time.

A word-processor typically has *search* and *edit* facilities, the ability to merge another document
or part document into the working document, and a *spelling checker* (for the language of a given
document). The word processor will provide assistance in that it can automate for example
pagination, word-wrap and *layout* (such as forming neat paragraphs that are justified against the
left and right margins) and possibly generate Contents Pages with page numbers.

The equipment used for word-processing, the computer **hardware** can be used for other
computer based activities, for example to keep a file of names and addresses of a club's
members, or to produce team game fixture lists. Each such activity requires the use of a specific

On the screen, the user of a word-processor has a window into which text can be typed and edited.
Typically, the document is or grows to be longer than the window (as in the above illustration); the user
can move to any part of the document. The user uses a cursor as the point at which type will be placed
in the document, or to mark a point or area in the document to be manipulated in some manner (the
word 'hardware' is so marked above). To obtain access to extra functions such as filing the document
or editing it, 'drop-down' menus are typically used. In the above illustration the 'edit' menu has been
selected.

Figure 1.6   Typical word-processor screen display.

computers are normally provided with a base application called an *operating system*.
This base application must be present in the computer in order for other applications
to function.

The interface between an application and the base facilities provided by an
operating system (called operating system services) is complex; it is not at the level
of the electrical power plug and socket. This has meant that as computing has
developed, few operating systems have survived for new applications. In this book
we will have occasion to refer to only two, MS-DOS (DOS) and UNIX. The
personal computer uses MS-DOS, while UNIX was developed at Bell Laboratories
in the early 1970s for research purposes and in particular as a platform for software
development.

Commercial applications In commerce, computer systems are used to carry out
repetitive clerical duties in a *reliable* and *consistent* manner, for example invoicing,
balancing accounts and sales order processing. They are used where some problem,
often numerical, is tedious and prone to error when carried out by humans.

The problem itself is characterized by having a *procedure* laid down for its solution, and the procedure works on defined quantities, for example customer account numbers, cash balances, quantities of goods and dates, and precisely formulated facts such as customer names and addresses, and the names and identification numbers of stock items. We shall see that computer programming involves the specification of such procedures that operate on abstract quantities and facts, but expressed in a language that can be interpreted, directly or indirectly, by a computer. The procedure is subsequently applied to actual values each time the procedure is interpreted by a computer or computers. Computer programming is essentially the task of constructing a generalized solution to some problem. The actual values of these quantities and facts for a given enterprise are referred to as *data*, in their raw state as just numbers and sets of characters, and as *information*, when structured and interpreted by their type (for example customer balances, or a set of production quantities).

Information used and arising in one area of an enterprise usually has its uses elsewhere. For example a supermarket might use a computer system in which the point-of-sale units at the payment checkouts are connected, to allow the transfer of information to a stock reordering system. This system in turn might be connected in a similar manner to remote warehouses and suppliers. An attribute that a computer system may exhibit therefore is the ability to *communicate* not only with humans but with other computer systems.

As in computer-to-computer communications, users of commercial computer systems may themselves be remote from the bulk of the computer. For example a bank's cash dispenser machine is one of many identical *terminals* linked to a geographically distant computer system which has the customers' information on file. The terminal in this example comprises a specialized keyboard and screen so that the bank's customer can dialogue with the computer, together with a device which, under the computer system's control, dispenses cash. Information is transferred between the various components of the cash dispenser machine and the computer system by means of a communications network.

Scientific and engineering applications Organizations performing scientific and engineering functions such as structural engineering and meteorology use computers extensively to perform scientific calculations—for example design calculations for aircraft airframes and for producing weather forecasts. As in commerce, applied science and engineering are exact disciplines, and procedures exist for the solution of numerically oriented problems.

The computer is much more than a large pocket calculator; as well as performing the actual arithmetic calculations it typically has to manage large amounts of *data* and make decisions based on the values of data items. For example the computer system must manage the raw *input* data. In the case of meteorology this might comprise data supplied in real time from each of many meteorological stations, weather balloons and satellites. Data from a station might comprise the temperature, humidity, wind speed and time, together with the station's identifier. *Output* data may be information in the form of weather maps and weather forecasts for particular geographical areas.

The computer is often used to identify and warn of critical conditions. In a structural engineering application such as airframe design, if a critical value such as the stress limit of a component is exceeded, then there must be some consequential action; perhaps information is output to warn the design engineer.

As with previous examples, the need to manage data, to carry out calculations and to make decisions requires the availability of procedures and facilities to program these procedures in a manner that can be interpreted by a computer.

Embedded computer applications We often see and use artifacts which contain embedded computers, though we may be unconscious of the fact. Everyday examples include washing machines, household central heating controls and video recorders. We can suspect the use of embedded computers in such artifacts if they are programmable (as in a compact disc player or a washing machine), or if they provide functionality beyond the basic requirements (as in a fuel consumption display for a motor car). The reason for using embedded computers is to save costs and time by virtue of their *reliability*, *accuracy* and *consistency*, and by providing *extra functionality*. The medium used for communication with a human being is often tailored to the specific function and frequently resembles the traditional medium that the embedded computer system replaced. In some applications, embedded computers are not necessarily obvious; for example basic fuel management in modern motor cars where the computer-based solution is preferable to the traditional mechanically based equipment. In this case the medium used for communication with humans is identical to the traditional medium, the accelerator pedal.

In the last example there are direct and indirect advantages over the older mechanical systems. Direct advantages are those in respect of the principal function of the computer-based system—fuel management. Thus there are savings in fuel consumption because of the precision in terms of control offered by the computer, in addition to much simplified maintenance. Furthermore, embedded computers can provide indirect advantages that are extra to the mechanical systems they replace. Thus in the case of fuel management, the car servicing and repair mechanic can be provided with problem diagnoses using another computer temporarily linked to, and communicating with, the car's embedded computer.

1.3 DATA, INFORMATION AND KNOWLEDGE

The basic function of all computers is that of *processing* respectively *data*, *information* and *knowledge*. Data comprises one or more values, but these values alone have no sense or interpretation. Note that *data* are often treated in the singular rather than the plural in computing and one talks about '*a* data value', or, 'several data values'. A single data item is sometimes called a *datum*. A particular item of information comprises data for which there is a particular interpretation. Knowledge is information in a form that can be reasoned about and from which deductions can be made.

The numbers in the sequence shown in Fig. 1.7 are simply data values. There is no indication of sense—of what interpretation we can ascribe to the individual

16	13	13	15	14	15	16	19

Figure 1.7 Example data values.

numbers, or to the fact that they make up a sequence. They could be for example the sequence of data values that represent temperatures at one second time intervals in a reactor in a chemical plant. The sequence of data values becomes information when it is said to represent a sequence of temperatures. So, while in transit from the reactor to the computer, situated perhaps in the control room, and within the computer up to the interface with the application, the values are just data values. When the data values arrive at and are processed by the computer application controlling the chemical process, they are *information*.

Sequences of temperatures as in Fig. 1.7 are not in a form that can be reasoned about. However, suppose the following is also known:

    if Temperature at time T is greater than 19
        then signal alarm condition.

    if temperature at time T is greater than temperature at time T − 1 and
        temperature at time T − 1 is greater than temperature at time T − 2
        then register incipient problem.

A sequence of temperatures, together with the above *rules*, can be reasoned about. The rules represent *knowledge*, in this instance knowledge about recognition of incipient problems and alarm conditions in a chemical reactor. When the rules are applied to the information in Fig. 1.7 we can deduce that there is an incipient problem, but we cannot deduce that there is an alarm condition.

1.3.1 Software

Software, that is, computer programming and the consequent computer application, involves all the three concepts of data, information and knowledge. The term 'software' is used because it refers to something that is non-permanent, can be changed, and thus in some respects is ephemeral.

The computer programmer must describe in the program the knowledge in terms of rules and of *abstract* definitions of the *types* of information. When programming, the programmer does not know the *values* that will occur (for example the sequence of temperature values above) but will know the types, that is the ranges of values possible, and the ways these relate to one another. At some later time and typically on another computer, the sequence of data values, each value being derived from perhaps an electrical thermometer, supplies the information for the application. Normally the knowledge that the programmer has about a subject is reasoned about, but is used in a limited manner within the computer application. For example a chemical process application may simply signal alarm condition on encountering the condition:

    Temperature at time T is greater than 19

Information processing is characterized by the programmer applying the knowledge as defined by the specification of the application. The knowledge *per se* is not present in the application program which is executed; only an extract of it is needed to serve the functions of the application. In knowledge processing, the knowledge *is* explicitly available in the application program. Thus not only will the principal function of the application be handled (in the example, `signal alarm condition` and `register incipient problem`) but a variety of other functions might be provided. For example the chemical plant operator might want the application to justify why an alarm condition has been raised.

The particular processing function may be anything that can be *programmed*; the description of the processing that is to be done is carried out by people, computer *programmers*. The description of what the computer is to do is called a computer *program* (not program*me*). A computer program that serves a particular purpose is an *application*.

The historical development of computer applications has progressed from data processing to information processing (where knowledge has been used only in developing the application) and, more recently, aspects of knowledge processing have appeared within applications. For example early patient alarm systems were embedded data processing computer systems which individually monitored indicators, such as temperature and pulse rate, and could generate an alarm condition for each indicator. Patient alarm systems then developed to become information processing systems that could also allow medical staff to display the indicators' values over time segments on a screen. Interpretation in respect of detection of say morbidity indicator patterns over periods of time was the responsibility of the medical staff. Knowledge processing in this application might involve the computer application in *reasoning*, that is, employing knowledge comprising explicit theories supplied by medical specialists together with the current and historical indicator information. An example theory might cover early prognoses of possible complications and, under a request from the medical operator, provide a justification of the diagnosis.

Similarly, in commerce, the early data processing applications performed basic accounting procedures such as pay roll and sales order processing. Subsequently, information processing provided situation reports, for example lists of overdue customer accounts. More recently knowledge processing provides *decision support* facilities to resource control managers to provide diagnoses and forewarnings of problems and ranges of potential remedies, and to provide justifications for these. Knowledge processing is only feasible if the knowledge is explicitly available in the application that is run on the computer.

At the lowest level, computers process data. This usually means that the input data is used—processed—in calculations (if it is numerical data), or the input data is used symbolically, as is the case of a lending library catalogue enquiry system. The result of the processing is the output of data. Figure 1.8 represents in abstract form the notion of 'input → process → output'.

data input → process → data output

Figure 1.8 Data processing.

1.3.2 Hardware

The physical artifacts in a computer system are parts of its *hardware*. The term 'hardware' indicates something with physical substance and thus permanence (contrast software). Ancillary input and output *devices*, sometimes thought of as part of the computer *hardware*, are used in order to input and output the data from/to the relevant medium used to communicate with the real world, for the retention of data, or with other computers.

Data is transmitted between the external world and a computer in one of two directions, input or output. Thus one speaks of *input* data and *output* data, and the *interfaces* between the real world and the computer system. Input data enters a computer system from an input *device* such as a keyboard, a temperature sensor or a bar-code reader. Instances of output devices include screens (like television screens), printers and control valves (as used in the chemical industry). Computers themselves can be input and output devices to other computers, thus allowing computer *networks*. The data can be filed or transmitted on a variety of different *media* such as paper, for printed material used for invoices, and the electrical signals for alarm and control devices, as used in an oil refinery. When there is the need to retain data, the medium on which the data is filed is subject to both output and input; for example a computer *disk* on which one can save word-processing documents *and* subsequently edit a document, perhaps to make amendments.

A given computer comprises particular hardware functional units. At a minimum a computer requires:

- *Memory*. This hardware functional unit contains the current program and the current data values. The memory comprises a number of identically sized *locations*, each of which has a unique *address*.
- *Central processing unit (CPU)*. This interprets the instructions within the program (in the computer's memory). These instructions order the CPU to carry out arithmetic and logical operations on the data (also in the computer's memory) and to input and output data between locations in the memory and the 'outside world'. This is by far the most complex of the hardware units making up the computer.
- *Input/output interfaces*. The computer uses these hardware units to transfer data (which may be a program) between locations in its memory and the 'outside world'.
- *Bus*. This is the carrier of data and control signals between the other units of the computer.

Depending on the size of computer, various of the above hardware units may occur in multiple. Memory is often available in different sizes; this is usually achieved by being able to add extra memory units. The ability to have multiple input/output units is not uncommon. Multiple CPUs are, however, less common. To have multiple CPUs requires sophisticated software so that work can be coordinated between the various CPUs.

For example a personal computer (PC), see Fig. 1.9, typically comprises the basic hardware units of CPU, memory, an input/output interface and bus. In addition

IBM PS/2 model 30 286 with 85B colour monitor

Figure 1.9 Personal computer.

there will be a keyboard, screen, mouse (for pointing the cursor to and selecting items on the screen), disk drive and (usually) removable disks (a medium for filing programs and retained data), and printer (with paper as the medium) (see Figs 10.9 and 10.10). These hardware units and the way they are connected in respect of data flow are shown in diagrammatic form in Fig. 1.10.

Some of the hardware units, each of which serves a specific function, are packaged (boxed) together. One normally finds in the case of a personal computer, for example, that the central processing unit, memory, bus, and at least a single disk drive are boxed together. Figure 1.10 also shows the packaging of a personal computer in diagrammatic fashion.

A given *configuration* of computer hardware is typically capable of supporting quite varied applications provided it has the necessary hardware resources, for example a memory of sufficient size to hold the application's program and other necessary programs. Thus such a configuration of personal computer might be used for various *applications* such as word-processing, stock control, statistical analyses, graphical design and so on.

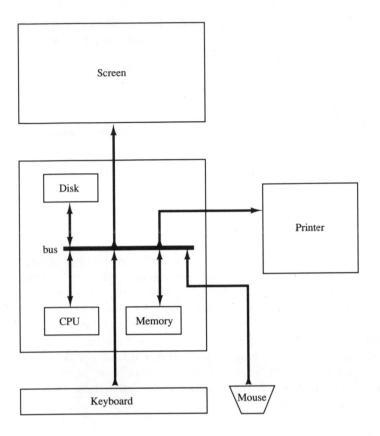

Figure 1.10 Typical personal computer hardware configuration in diagrammatic form.

1.3.3 Engineering computer based solutions

As in most human endeavours complex artifacts, such as buildings, are built from simpler components and interfaces between these, such as bricks and mortar (akin to computer hardware), from building design regulations and formulae (akin to computer software), and possibly from design catalogue books (akin to application packages). Standards are provided and these must be adhered to by both the builder and the architect.

Computer systems are similarly built from components, of both hardware (Fig. 1.10) and software (witness the various applications available on a personal computer). Applications themselves are built out of components, and so on. As with the design for a house, computer applications are normally designed to be *reusable* so that an application can be used as many times as one wishes.

Computer systems engineering is that branch of engineering involved with the hardware side of computers. *Software engineering* is the discipline of engineering applied to the design and implementation of computer software for particular applications. This book is principally concerned with the software aspects of computing, but, as this cannot be done in isolation from hardware, hardware is explained in the manner it is perceived by the software engineer.

1.4 CLASSIFYING COMPUTER SYSTEMS

Computers appear to have certain advantages over traditional methods of providing a solution to a problem. For example:

- Flexibility
- Repetitive working
- Consistency
- Reliability
- Speed

But what are the limitations of each of the above? For example flexibility (provided by programmability) can introduce error to a computer system, when it is being implemented, and this will compromise perceived advantages. Also, can we classify problems as to their suitability for solution by computer? Finally, what are the justifications for a computer-based solution? For all these questions both advantages and disadvantages become apparent and it is therefore important to realize the limitations of computer-based solutions. It is worthy of note that limitations are not necessarily of a technical nature but can be social and organizational as well. We address the underlying material in the text that follows and discuss these issues in particular in the final part of the book.

PART
TWO

COMPUTING AND
INFORMATION PROCESSING

TWO

COMPUTING AND INFORMATION

In this chapter we examine the application of computing to information. We commence by introducing the notions of structuring, processing and interfacing. We then examine the justification for structuring data to represent information; natural language is examined, followed by examples of artificial languages.

Next the important concept of *type* is introduced, as is the concept of type *instance*. We introduce the idea of abstract type, followed by built-in types—the basic building blocks that we use to build the representations of data which serve as information in computing. We then introduce structured types by way of examples, showing how basic types (and structured types) can be composed to build complex information structures.

The rest of the chapter is concerned with showing two ways in which data can be structured to provide information *processing*. The processing method chosen at this stage in the book is the *declarative* method. In the declarative method we can use the functional specification directly, as the specification of the processing to be done. In Chapter 5 we will see how to structure data when we use the *procedural* method for describing how information is to be processed, by specifying the steps that the computer must follow. The first way we structure data uses the *relational* method that is used in databases. Logic is used for the second method, specifically Horn clause logic, as used in *knowledge* processing applications.

2.1 STRUCTURING, PROCESSING AND INTERFACING

To enable the processing of information, we have to define the information in terms of its *structure* as well as the actual values of the data. The structure of the information is a property of the information itself. We may need a high degree of structure, as in a database of supermarket product lines, or little apparent structure, as in the initial text for an essay. Even the simplest items of information, such as individual temperature values, are represented as perhaps integer (whole) numbers. In all situations the lowest level types of the data structures must comply with the built-in types of the computer software and hardware that is to be used.

information input → process information → information output

Figure 2.1 Information processing.

In computing to deal with information, it is necessary to provide:

1. A means to *structure* the information.
2. The ability to *process* the information—that is to derive some useful 'processed information' from the information we already have.
3. *Interfaces*, both to and within the computer system, so that the structured and processed information can be accessed.

These three concepts, structuring, processing of, and interfacing to information are fundamental to computing and are applicable to all applications of computers.

In Chapter 1 the notion of 'input–process–output' was introduced (see Fig. 1.8). The three concepts of structure, processing of, and access to information, build on this basic notion with Fig. 2.1 being a development of Fig. 1.8. The term 'information' has replaced 'data', and 'process' has become 'process information'. The information may be in the real world, or may be contained within the computer system. The arrows thus represent the interfaces between the real world and the computer, or the interfaces between information residing within the computer system.

2.2 STRUCTURING DATA TO REPRESENT INFORMATION

In everyday life people structure raw data, both consciously and unconsciously. We consciously structure our days into work days and rest days, and within a day impose often complex structuring as for example a timetable for lectures. Organizations provide examples of conscious structures both externally, as in library catalogues, and internally, for example payroll information. Our use of natural language is an example of usually unconscious structuring, at least until many of us embark on writing material to be read by others. Natural languages appear to abound with such structures (for example the different parts of speech) and with rules for structuring sentences (syntax) and for composing words from perceived constituents (morphology). Grammarians study natural languages and formulate such rules of grammar (which have their uses as adjunctive functions in sophisticated word-processors). Natural languages are distinctive in that as well as being structured themselves, they can describe structures explicitly or in the abstract. With natural language we can describe in abstract or general terms the structure of our work day. We can be economical in such descriptions, using for example collective nouns and conditions such as 'lecturers' and 'provided fewer than 20 students'. Economy is useful because we can refer to complex structures with perhaps as little as a single word, and because we can reason using such words independently of the constituent data items. So, once we have elaborated a theory, we can refer to, and argue with concepts and hypothetical data values and conditions (such as 'provided fewer than 20 students').

We shall see that in computing, providing general structure definitions for data in which there is an economy of expression and a lack of ambiguity is an essential characteristic that pervades the way in which computer applications are devised, produced and assessed. Data instances that can be structured according to a given general structure definition are instances of information.

Though we might endeavour to describe definitions of information structures and meanings that we wish to impart using natural language, in most application areas more economical and precise languages have been devised. Examples include musical notation, logic, law, recipes, knitting patterns, choreography, and the applications of mathematics in the arts, sciences and engineering. Such languages are themselves artifacts, the result of human investigation and ingenuity; however they are usually restricted to applications in their respective domains.

Like natural languages, artificial languages also employ interface media. Often there may be more than one medium and more than one representation for presentation. For example, in music as well as the written stave method one can vocalize and write using the sol-fa or solmization method—doh, ray, me, fah, soh, lah, te, doh (C, D, E, F, G, A, B, C).

In computing we find that when we wish to apply the computer, we need a means to define information structures, to define actual data values, and to specify predicates, the relations that hold between information structures. We also need to be economical which requires abbreviations; that is being able to define structures in terms of constituent structures and data values. Furthermore in describing information structures we must be precise and unambiguous in terms of meaning. For these reasons techniques have been developed to enable description in an economical, precise and unambiguous manner.

2.3 TYPE

To enable economy of expression in computing, the notion of *type* is used. Mathematically a type is a set. When we define a structure to hold information, we must define the type of the information that can be contained, that is, the set of values within which the data items must fall. The notation used is the formal specification language **Z**, which is described in Chapter 6.

There are two approaches to defining types; by enumeration, or by abstraction.

2.3.1 Enumerated type definitions

In an *enumerated* type definition we explicitly provide the set of data item values. For example the set of courses which Dr. A. N. Other teaches is:

{SE207, SE172, SE322}

in which case:

*ANO*therTeaches = = {SE207, SE172, SE322}

defines '*ANO*therTeaches' as a type, in this instance an enumerated type. Thus SE172 is a valid instance of type '*ANO*therTeaches', whilst SE422 is not. Be careful to distinguish between types and instances of types.

2.3.2 Abstract type definitions

As we shall see, it is very useful to be able to have types that are abstract rather than enumerated. So for example we might have the abstract type '*N*' that stands for the infinite set of natural numbers (0,1,2,3, . . .). Indeed during the design of a computer system we may have necessarily abstract types which have not yet been completely specified (they may be partly specified). So we may have a type '*student*' in the design of a time-table application, but the details of students are either not yet known, or the package is to be used in different institutions with different definitions of '*student*'.

2.3.3 Built-in types

Types can be arbitrarily complex, as one can compose sets from sets. We need to use types for defining the data structures for use in information processing on digital computers. Computer programming languages and programmable applications typically provide a set of *built-in* types. These are also called simple, basic or fundamental types. Figure 2.2 illustrates typical built-in types which are all *scalar* (individual). One can also have types that are *structures* of types.

Built-in types are implemented by the computer's hardware (as explained in Chapter 9) or by special software. Because digital computers are limited to handling finite sets of data items, the built-in types are necessarily restricted. In Fig. 2.2 you

Type	Enumeration or explanation	Examples
Boolean	{1,0} — true or false	0, 1, `false`, `true`
integer	Whole numbers — range restricted	3975, 0, −2344196, −32768 to 32767
float	For real numbers that may not be whole — range restricted	0.5, −3.14159, 5.67 *E*41
enum	Enumeration — size restricted	{*red, yellow, blue, indigo*}
char	Keyboard characters	`0 1 2 3 . . . . A B C . . .` `a b c . . . + −`
string	Strings of keyboard characters — length restricted	`qwerty Q1W2E3r+t−y`

Figure 2.2 Typical built-in (scalar) types.

will see that there are restrictions in range, size and length (depending on the type). The restrictions for instances of types other than *Boolean* and *enum* can vary for different computer hardware and software.

You may wish to compare some of the types, and their restrictions to their nearest equivalents in a pocket calculator; for example number range and size of memory. Boolean type is named after the mathematician and logician George Boole. The implementation method used to simulate real numbers is usually by means of a *floating point* whereby a number is represented by a separate mantissa (which gives its precision) and an exponent (which gives its size). In Fig. 2.2, the number 5.67 *E*41 with type *float* is a representation for the number:

$$5.67 \times 10^{41}$$

where 5.67 is the mantissa, and 41 is the exponent. One sometimes sees the built in type *float* called *real*.

2.3.4 Structured types

Structured types are types that refer to the *structuring* of data, and often include within their definition the operations possible on instances of themselves. The data so structured may itself be structured, but eventually, the type of the simplest structure will be one of the built-in types of Fig. 2.2. In computing, there are some basic structured types which appear in many applications. The sections that follow illustrate in diagrammatic form instances of these basic data structure types.

In any given computer programming language, various data structure types may be provided as built-in facilities. If not, one would expect to be able to define a structured type in terms of at least the available built-in data structure types, or, with advanced programming languages, structured types that someone has already defined. If one does define a structured type in terms of other structured types, eventually the chain or chains of definitions must end at one or more of the built-in types provided in the programming language.

For a given structured type there is an associated set of basic operations on instances of the structured type. In some cases these are also illustrated. Instances of data types must be named. In computer programming languages, in whatever manner we name an instance of a data type, the actual name is that of the particular location in the memory of the computer in which the data instance is stored. Such names are called *memory addresses* or *pointers*. Instances of data types may occupy more than one location in the computer's memory (the size of all the locations is equal); however there will be a given location from which the other locations can be worked out. In the diagrams that follow, we indicate where a memory address points to by means of an arrow.

2.3.5 Scalar

Instances of some of the built-in types used in Fig. 2.2 may be shown:

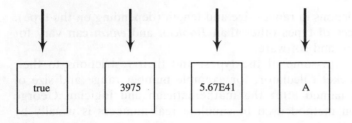

Each location containing an instance of a built-in type, must, if a scalar, have an individual name. Thus we show each instance with an arrow pointing to the location to indicate that it is named. Some built-in types have instances that cannot always be represented in a single location, or even a fixed number of locations. Examples of these are enumerations and strings of keyboard characters.

2.3.6 Array

An array comprises one or more instances of the *same* type of data, and each instance is stored in a particular location in the array. The locations are identified by an integer number called an *index*, usually starting from zero or one. For example, an array of integers:

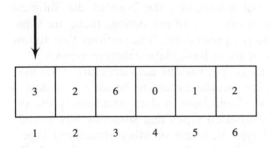

The name of the array corresponds to the memory address of the first location within it. The diagram shows the index value of each location in the array. See also Fig. 6.11.

2.3.7 Record

Where we want to group together a number of data items of different types, we use a record. For example:

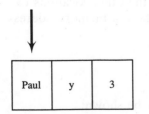

As well as naming the record, we will often want to access the *components* of a record, (see also Figs 2.6, 2.11, 6.9 and 6.11).

2.3.8 Tree

A tree is an hierarchical structure. Each *node* of a tree is implemented as a record, except the empty tree, which is shown in the examples as []. An empty tree:

↓

[]

A binary tree (*binary* because each node has two branches or arcs leading from it) containing a single leaf containing the value 3:

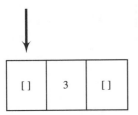

A binary tree employs a record of three data items. The data type of the node's value is in this case integer. The other two data items are either pointer values or the value used to represent a null tree. In the computer, pointer values will be the *addresses* of locations in the computer's memory. The data type of a complete node can be defined, using, for example, the computer programming language Pascal (introduced in Chapter 5) as:

```
type
    tree_node = record
                    left:   ^tree_node;
                    value:  integer;
                    right:  ^tree_node;
                end;
```

in which left, value and right are *component names*, and the ^ indicates a pointer. As the type definition tree_node refers to itself, it is *recursive*. Trees are examples of *recursive* data structures. The use of recursion is widespread in computing and will appear many times in this book. Normally, recursion must stop. As well as one or more recursive references in a recursive type, one would expect one or more references to *boundary* types. The boundary types for each of the left and right pointers, where either is an empty tree, are handled by using a null pointer. In this section we show a null pointer as []. Particular programming methods have their own ways to represent items such as a null pointer; in the case of Pascal, a null pointer is represented by the special instance nil.

An example of a non-empty binary tree:

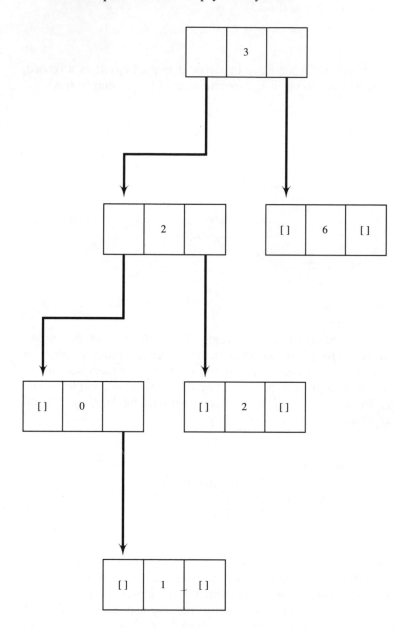

This tree has been built by adding nodes with the values 3, 2, 6, 0, 1, 2 to the empty tree in that order in such a manner that, if the tree is *traversed* left to right, the nodes are sorted in increasing value—i.e. 0, 1, 2, 2, 3, 6. Such a tree is called a *binary sorted* tree. (See also Figs 4.7, 8.6 and 11.2.)

2.3.9 List

A list is a special case of a tree in which there is a single data structure, usually of the same type, at each 'level'. At the last level, is a null data item (shown in this text as [ ]). The head of a list is the first item in the list, and the tail of a list is the rest of the list (itself a list or an empty list). An empty list:

⟶   [ ]

A non-empty list:

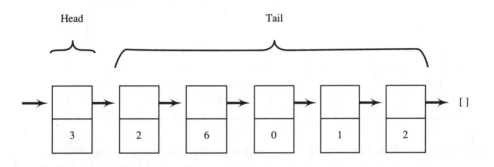

See also Figs 6.7, 6.8 and 6.23.

2.3.10 Queue

A *queue* is used to store data structure instances on a first-come-first-served basis. The *tail* of the queue is where data items are *enqueued*, that is, added to the queue. The *head* of the queue is where data items are *dequeued*, that is, removed. We illustrate queues using an auxiliary record containing the name of the tail and the head of the queue.

An empty queue:

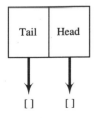

Queue items will be records in which one component names the previous item in the queue by pointing (and is sometimes called the *link* component), and the other item is the data instance. So, whenever a data item is to be enqueued, an associated queue item is required.

A non-empty queue:

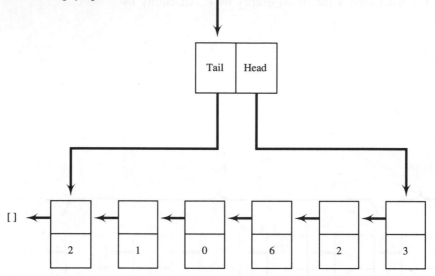

The data item 2 (on the left) is that most recently added (enqueued) to the queue. The data item 3 is the next item that will be removed (dequeued). See also Fig. 11.5 on page 216.

2.3.11 Stack

A stack is used to store and retrieve data structure instances on a first-in-last-out basis, like the spring-supported stacks of plates or trays one gets in self-service eating establishments.

One method of implementing a stack is to use an array to hold the data items, and a scalar to hold the current top of the stack (as an array index). An empty stack can be represented by having top of stack pointing to beneath the base of the stack:

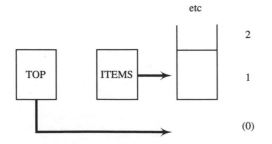

We can *push* a data item on a stack; for example, pushing the integer 3:

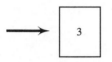

onto the empty stack results in:

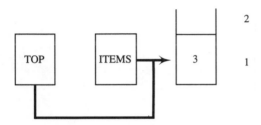

Continuing to push integer data items in the order 2, 6, 0, 1, 2 we get:

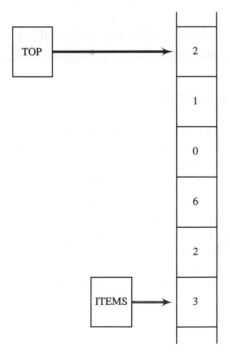

If we *pop* the top item from the stack, we get:

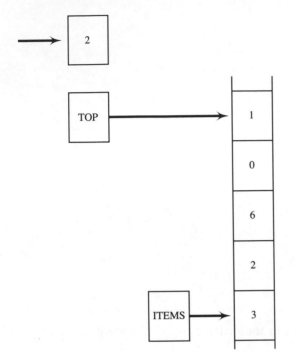

An example that appears in the book is Fig. 6.16 together with Fig. 6.15, and Fig. 6.17. Be careful to distinguish between queues and stacks.

2.4 DECLARATIVE INFORMATION PROCESSING

In this section we introduce approaches to data structures which rely on *declarative* means. A declarative method is one where we can use the specification of the problem directly as the specification of the processing to be done.

We will be looking at the following increasingly complex applications:

1. *Database*. Database packages allow users to define information structures, and then use the structures to store and to retrieve information. The processing functions are already defined as *built-in* facilities within the package. Typically they allow one to produce subsets of the information from the database, and to produce simple reports.

   In this text we restrict our interest to *relational* databases and the language SQL. The reason for this is that relational databases are formally underpinned by a mathematically sound definition.

- *Database with one entity type*. We commence with the requirements of a simple single file-based database system. The concept of data structuring employing entities and attributes is introduced.
- *Database with more than one entity type*. The next step in complexity is a database system where there is the requirement to structure data for more than a single entity type. Because more than one entity type is involved, there is a need to model the entities and the relationships between them, a task called entity-relationship (ER) modelling.

2. *Horn clause logic and Prolog*. The next stage is the representation of data structures that can be used with a processing capability that can express more complex relationships which embody constraints using a restricted form of the predicate logic called Horn clause logic. In fact, a restricted form of Horn clause logic is used in which the clauses are called *definite* clauses. We shall use just the term 'clause'. The language used in this case to express the processing is Prolog. For example, in the case of a family tree we can express conceptual and self-referencing relationships like ancestor and descendant, independent of any particular family. We can then use these relationships with the data representing any particular family.

We defer describing a general purpose method of data structuring, suitable for applications programmed with general purpose (procedural) languages to Chapter 5.

2.5 DATABASE SYSTEMS

2.5.1 Database with one entity type

Take for example a membership list for a whist club. The entities are the club's members. Entities are, by definition, unique, and are identified by a name (which must also be unique). An entity type is a set of information occurrences that share some property in the real world. In database terminology, an *information occurrence*, when it is a member of an entity type, will be an *instance* of that type.

The requirements are for a database consisting of a set of *records*, with a single record for each club member. Thus for each entity (club member), there is a corresponding record. The application involves a set of member records, each record being uniquely identified by a member's name. Each record will have the same structure comprising a set of *fields*. The fields include the member's name, whether their subscription has been paid, and the points they have accumulated during the year. An individual record might therefore be:

Leslie	y	2

The boxing lines are solely for the purpose of exposition. Figure 2.3 shows an example of a *table* named MEMBERSHIP. The table has a set of three *columns*, each column having a heading called an *attribute type*, for example NAME. The table has six *rows* (also called *tuples*), each row corresponding to a record, and a column within a row or record corresponding to a field. Each of the eighteen (6 rows × 3 columns) values in the table is called an *attribute value*. Note that in computing the term 'value' is used for any item of information, numeric or otherwise. The table MEMBERSHIP is a *base* or *real* table since it has a name and it is part of the database *per se*.

In Fig. 2.3 all the values of the attribute MEMBER are the names of members and are formed from alphabetic characters. Furthermore, whist club members, being entities, are unique. Thus their MEMBER value is unique. The value of a SUBSCRIPTION attribute is a single character, either a y or an n, indicating 'yes' or 'no'. POINTS have whole number values, of integer type.

MEMBERSHIP is a *base table*; it actually exists. Before a base table can be used, and data placed in it, it is necessary to *define* the table. Creation of the MEMBERSHIP table, see Fig. 2.4, uses a CREATE TABLE statement in structured query language (SQL). SQL is an example of an artificial language (as distinct from a natural language such as English) devised so that humans can communicate with computers. It is a comparatively simple language in which one can request the creation of base tables, and specify queries and other processing on tables. (We shall have more to say about SQL in this chapter, and, in later chapters, about such artificial specification and programming languages in general.) For the moment, the CREATE TABLE statement in Fig. 2.4 defines a type, not by enumeration (the table is empty on creation), but by composition of and restrictions on basic built-in types. The CREATE TABLE statement is an abstract type definition. The CREATE TABLE statement defines the set of possible records or rows, by stating the type of each column or attribute, and by requiring that no two rows are identical. For example the value of a POINTS data item must be an integer.

As regards records being unique, this accords with the definition of an entity. In the CREATE TABLE statement, the entities are identified by the PRIMARY KEY, whose name is MEMBER. In SQL, the primary key of a table is a unique identifier

Base Table:

MEMBERSHIP

MEMBER	SUBSCRIPTION	POINTS
Paul	y	3
Leslie	y	2
Anne	n	6
Justine	y	0
Patrick	y	2
Rachel	n	1

Figure 2.3 Single table example.

```
CREATE TABLE MEMBERSHIP
      (MEMBER          CHAR(15)   NOT NULL,
       SUBSCRIPTIONCHAR(1)        NOT NULL,
       POINTS          INTEGER    NOT NULL,
       PRIMARY KEY( MEMBER ) );
```

Figure 2.4 Create the base table MEMBERSHIP.

for the rows in the table. In other words, no two rows can have the same MEMBER value. In any case we often wish to access a table by its primary key; for example we may wish to know how many points Patrick has. In this case the MEMBER attribute is a *key*, and it is the table's primary key (there may be other keys). Thus:

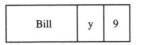

| Bill | y | 9 |

is an allowed row, but the following rows are not:

| Archie | n | zero |

| Annabelle-Josephine | y | 3 |

There are certain restrictions that apply to tables. The reason for these restrictions is that the structuring and consequential processing of the data can be very much simplified. Put another way, a technique based on a branch of mathematical logic, the relational calculus, can be applied to tables of a particular and simple form. A further advantage of the technique is that it can be programmed independently of any particular table definitions. Databases comprising tables that are structured according to the necessary restrictions stated in Fig. 2.5 are called *relational* databases. The word *relational* is used because *relation* is the mathematical term for a table. The table MEMBERSHIP (in Fig. 2.3) conforms to these restrictions. The relational model for databases was developed by E. F. Codd.

1. The ordering of rows is not significant.
2. The ordering of columns is not significant.
3. There can be only one value for a given row and column.
4. No two rows can be identical.

Figure 2.5 Relational table restrictions.

2.5.2 SQL—a relational language

*S*tructured *Q*uery *L*anguage (SQL) is used to solve queries against the relations in relational databases. The formal framework used by SQL and the relational databases it operates on is based on a branch of mathematical logic; SQL itself is a form of the relational calculus. SQL typically has an associated programming and program execution system. SQL is extensively used in commerce, because much of the data encountered in commercial applications tends to be organized in *tables* of like records. The relations correspond to the *tables* shown in Figs 2.6 and 2.12. SQL is a declarative language; an SQL query specifies only what is required, not how to carry out the query. A good book encompassing databases and SQL is by C. J. Date (1990). SQL (originally spelt SEQUEL and sometimes pronounced as such), was first defined by D. D. Chamberlin and others at IBM, in the early 1970s.

Our initial example is to show SQL applied to the (single) whist club table MEMBERSHIP. The base table MEMBERSHIP is reproduced in Fig. 2.6 together with examples of the SQL statements SELECT, INSERT, UPDATE and DELETE, applied in sequence to table MEMBERSHIP.

The SELECT operation can be paraphrased in English as 'produce a table with the names and points of members who have overdue subscriptions'. Thus the input comprises the attribute values in MEMBERSHIP, the processing is specified by the SQL *query* together with the table definitions (the attribute definitions and the association of attribute definition with tables), and the output is in the form of attribute values in the table 'Result Table'. The output of a SELECT operation is itself a table, distinct from being a base table, in that it is a *virtual table*, also known as a *view*. Both the input and the output data are structured according to the restrictions applying to relational tables. In this form the structure and the actual values of each table comprise the information processed by the computer system (in computing a complex collection of information can have a value as well as a simple item of information).

2.5.3 Database with more than one entity type

Suppose we wish to have a database in which there is more than one entity type: that is, more than one set of information occurrences that share some property in the real world.

The first step in deriving an information structure is that of *data modelling*. Essentially this consists of identifying the various entity types and the relationships between them, hence the term 'entity-relationship' (ER) modelling. In the top-down approach to design, in which we start at the most abstract level, our interest is identifying entity types. On completion of the information structure design we will have specified a set of table definitions (table names and for each table the attribute types) upon which SQL queries can be specified. At an intermediate stage in the design process it is necessary to assign particular attribute types to the tables being developed.

Take, for example, a simple database comprising information on faculties, lecturers, students and courses. Individual occurrences of faculties, lecturers, students

Base Table:

MEMBERSHIP

MEMBER	SUBSCRIPTION	POINTS
Paul	y	3
Leslie	y	2
Anne	n	6
Justine	y	0
Patrick	y	2
Rachel	n	1

1. Retrieval:

```
SELECT MEMBER, POINTS
FROM MEMBERSHIP
WHERE SUBSCRIPTION = 'n' ;
```

Result Table:

MEMBER	POINTS
Anne	6
Rachel	2

2. Inserting new data:

```
INSERT
INTO MEMBERSHIP
VALUES ('Frances', 'y', 0) ;
```

3. Updating existing data:

```
UPDATE MEMBERSHIP
SET SUBSCRIPTION = 'y'
WHERE MEMBER = 'Anne' ;
```

4. Deleting existing data:

```
DELETE
FROM MEMBERSHIP
WHERE MEMBER = 'Rachel' ;
```

Base Table now is:

MEMBERSHIP

MEMBER	SUBSCRIPTION	POINTS
Paul	y	3
Leslie	y	2
Frances	y	0
Anne	y	6
Justine	y	0
Patrick	y	1

Figure 2.6 Single base table and a sequence of SQL example operations.

faculty	lecturer	student	course	year
Science	W. Bloggs	Paul	SE322	1
Engineering	A.N. Other	Leslie	SE172	2
Arts		Anne	SE422	3
Social Science		Justine	EE334	4
		Rachel	SE207	
		Patrick		

Figure 2.7 Example of entity occurrences.

and courses are entities, and examples of entity occurrences, grouped under appropriate headings, are shown in Fig. 2.7. To be useful in respect of the database we identify properties that the entities share. There are evidently four such properties, entity types, namely `faculty`, `lecturer`, `student`, and `course`. There are also compound entities, relationships, that exist in the real world between, and within, the entities. We can thus derive compound entity types, or relationship types. For example there may be a compound entity:

Arts	Rachel	2

signifying the fact that the Arts Faculty has Rachel registered as a second-year student.

Examples of relationship types are: `attends`, in 'a student attends a course' (the compound entity above is thus of type `attends`); `teaches`, in 'a lecturer teaches a course'; `recognized` in 'a faculty recognizes a lecturer'; `instructs`, in 'a lecturer instructs a student' and `registers`, in 'the faculty registers a student for a degree'. Notice that, being entities, compound entities or relationships are unique. We can use a diagrammatic technique to show the entity types and the relationship types between them (Fig. 2.8). The names of entity types usually turn out to be nouns, as in `faculty` and `student`. Relation names tend to be verbs, as in `teaches`.

To carry the example further, depending on the teaching institution there may be policy constraints that dictate the *degree* of a relationship. In the example, a given lecturer may teach *one or more* courses; whilst a given course may be taught by *only one* lecturer. In general, there are four possible degrees of relationship: one-to-one, one-to-many, many-to-one, and many-to-many. One or more students attending one or more courses is an example of a many-to-many relationship. The degree of a relationship is normally shown on ER-type diagrams. For example Fig. 2.9(i) states that the degree registration relationship between a faculty and a student is one-to-many. This is shown by a 1 and an N. Figure 2.9 (ii) shows that the recognized staff relationship between faculties and lecturers is many-to-many. This is shown by an M and an N. ER-type diagrams may be combined or decomposed to

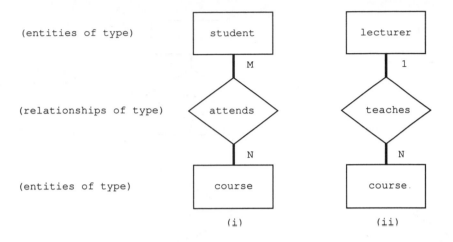

The significance of the M, N's and 1 is explained later in the text.

Figure 2.8 ER-type diagrams.

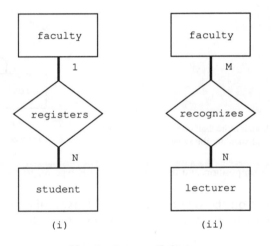

Note that the Ns are distinct.

Figure 2.9 ER-type diagrams showing the degree of the relationship.

suit the requirements of the eventual computer database application (see Fig. 2.10).
Note that Fig. 2.10 (ii) corresponds to Fig. 2.9 (ii).

Having determined the entity types and the relationship types that are to be
modelled it is necessary to derive table definitions.

Suppose that we want a limited database in which is stored course information
associated with students and lecturers. As a result of our data analysis we might
derive the ER-type diagram shown in Fig. 2.10 (ii) and the following three base

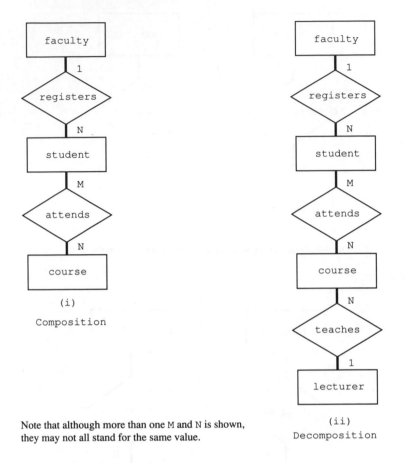

(i)

Composition

Note that although more than one M and N is shown,
they may not all stand for the same value.

(ii)

Decomposition

Figure 2.10 Composition and decomposition of ER-type diagrams.

tables, based on the one-to-many the ER-type diagram `registers` and `teaches` and the many-to-many ER-type diagram `attends`:

1. REGISTERS—to hold information on which faculty has registered which student and (as an extra attribute) which year the student is in.
2. ATTENDS—to hold information on student names, faculty and courses which a student attends.
3. TEACHES—to hold information on lecturer names and courses taught by the lecturer.

The CREATE TABLE statements for the base tables REGISTERS, ATTENDS and TEACHES are illustrated in Fig. 2.11. Note that the definition of the (unique) primary key ATTENDS is *composite*; it corresponds to the compound entity type because two attribute names make up the primary key. The CREATE TABLE statement for the base table ATTENDS also defines the foreign keys STUDENT and COURSE. This is necessary because the attribute values in column STUDENT in the table ATTENDS are constrained to be the values of the primary key STUDENT in

```
CREATE TABLE REGISTERS
      ( FACULTY              CHAR(15)     NOT NULL,
        STUDENT              CHAR(15)     NOT NULL,
        YEAR                 INTEGER      NOT NULL,
      PRIMARY KEY  ( STUDENT ) ) ;

CREATE TABLE ATTENDS
      ( STUDENT              CHAR(15)     NOT NULL,
        COURSE               CHAR(5)      NOT NULL,
      PRIMARY KEY  ( STUDENT, COURSE ),
      FOREIGN KEY  ( STUDENT )    REFERENCES REGISTERS ),
      FOREIGN KEY  ( COURSE )     REFERENCESTEACHES ) ) ;

CREATE TABLE TEACHES
      ( LECTURER             CHAR(15)     NOT NULL,
        COURSE               CHAR(5)      NOT NULL,
      PRIMARY KEY  ( COURSE ) ) ;
```

Figure 2.11   Create the base tables REGISTERS, ATTENDS and TEACHES.

the table REGISTERS. Similar reasoning applies to COURSE. Foreign keys are necessary to ensure the database's *referential integrity* under insert, update and delete.

The tables are shown in Fig. 2.12. The tables contain example attribute values. Inspection of the values confirms the degree of each relationship. To be of use as a database, that is to provide information by processing the contents of the tables, we want to be able to express *queries* over more than one table as well as over a single table. For example in natural language we might want to 'find all the second year students registered in the Arts Faculty who attend courses taught by Dr A. N. Other'. We wish to derive a new relationship, based on the existing relationships tables REGISTERS, ATTENDS and TEACHES, and which has as attributes STUDENT, TEACHER and COURSE. The SQL for this query is shown in Fig. 2.12 which also shows the result of the query in 'Result Table'.

The formal framework used by SQL and the relational databases it operates on is the mathematics of relations. The relations correspond to the tables in Fig. 2.12. For example the table ATTENDS relates students' names with their course. The SQL SELECT statement requests the (anonymous) relation between arts students and the lecturers whose courses they are attending. It does this by using the select operation.

The tasks of deriving ER-type diagrams and relational tables are in fact considerably more complex than may be apparent as described here. These two sections have introduced at a rudimentary level the basic concepts of Entity-Relationship modelling, and also at a very basic level an introduction to relational data organization in tables, and the associated specification of processing by means of SQL. For any person embarking on a data analysis and database design exercise, a rigorous approach is required; if this is not undertaken, the result is likely to be very unsatisfactory. For example, it is important that the restrictions applying to a table are met, as given in Fig. 2.5. Producing a set of table definitions that together satisfy these restrictions (called a *normalized* set of definitions) is only the first task.

SQL Base Tables:

REGISTERS

FACULTY	STUDENT	YEAR
Science	Paul	3
Arts	Leslie	3
Social Science	Anne	2
Engineering	Justine	3
Arts	Rachel	2
Arts	Patrick	3

ATTENDS

STUDENT	COURSE
Patrick	SE172
Paul	SE322
Justine	EE334
Leslie	SE207
Rachel	SE207
Paul	EE334
Leslie	SE322
Anne	SE172
Justine	SE322

TEACHES

LECTURER	COURSE
W. Bloggs	SE422
A. N. Other	SE207
W. Bloggs	EE334
A. N. Other	SE172
A. N. Other	SE322

SQL:

```
SELECT    ATTENDS.STUDENT, TEACHES.LECTURER, ATTENDS.COURSE
FROM      REGISTERS, ATTENDS, TEACHES
WHERE     ATTENDS.COURSE=TEACHES.COURSE
AND       REGISTERS.FACULTY='Arts'
AND       TEACHES.LECTURER='A.N.Other'
AND       REGISTERS.YEAR=3 ;
```

Result Table:

ATTENDS.STUDENT	TEACHES.LECTURER	ATTENDS.COURSE
Leslie	A.N. Other	SE322
Patrick	A.N. Other	SE172
Leslie	A.N. Other	SE207

Figure 2.12 Structured Query Language SQL example.

Because the language SQL can also be used to change the data content of a database (by inserting, updating or deleting), the table definitions must embrace further restrictions. If there are redundant attribute values, for example the same logical attribute instance appearing in more than one table (as can occur in a non-normalized database), then the database can be rendered inconsistent upon a change; for example on an update not all instances are updated. Furthermore, the database management system (DBMS), the software system that provides the database facilities, may not implement referential integrity. Methodologies have been developed to remove redundancies and to apply yet other restrictions which, if not applied, cause other highly undesirable results. These techniques, a full description of the relational model and also of ER modelling needed to produce database applications, are beyond the scope of this book. For a good text describing these topics see Howe (1989).

2.5.4 Database transactions

Suppose, as is frequently the case, we have a database comprising several tables and the data contained is to be changed (by inserting, updating or deleting) or presented (by selection). If the database is to be used in a simple application by (usually) just one individual, then it might be feasible for that person to make *ad hoc* queries (including changes) to the database.

Often, however, the queries that are to be made can be predicted. The result of a system design will be these query definitions, which are called *transaction definitions*. The execution of a transaction definition applied to a database containing data is called a *transaction*.

To derive the transaction definitions for an application we first need to identify them. A transaction definition is associated with a processing operation on data associated with entities. *Prior* to the design activity that resulted in the ER-type diagrams, another design activity will have been conducted, to produce the set of transaction definitions required of the application.

Consider the teaching institution database. An application using this might be that for enrolling a student on a course. The *data flow diagram* in Fig. 2.13 illustrates

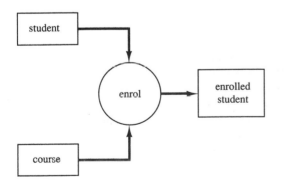

Figure 2.13 Data flow diagram—course enrolment application—top level.

```
INSERT         INTO ATTENDS
VALUES         ('Paul', 'SE207')
WHERE          EXISTS
               (SELECT *
               FROM            REGISTERS
               WHERE           STUDENT = 'Paul'
               AND             FACULTY = 'Science')
AND            NOT EXISTS
               (SELECT *
               FROM            ATTENDS
               WHERE           STUDENT = 'Paul'
               AND             COURSE = 'SE207')
AND            50 >
               (SELECT         COUNT (DISTINCT COURSE)
               FROM            ATTENDS
               WHERE           COURSE = 'SE207');
```

Figure 2.14 Course enrolment—Insert Query.

the top-level design of the student enrolment application. The input data items are student and course, the process is enrol and the data output is the enrolled student. In data flow diagrams data sources are conventionally shown in rectangular boxes, whilst processes are shown in circles.

The transaction description for enrol is developed as follows. Assume there is a maximum size that a class can be—say 50.

SQL includes *aggregate functions* such as COUNT, SUM, AVG (average), MAX (maximum) and MIN (minimum) to perform arithmetic on tables. These functions are used in effect as if they were attributes.

Suppose Paul, a Science Faculty student, wishes to enrol in course SE207, then the SQL query shown in Fig. 2.14 could be manually entered. The query works as follows. The tuple:

Paul	SE207

is inserted into the table ATTENDS provided Paul is a registered student in the science faculty, provided he is not already registered on the course and provided that the count of the existing attendees of SE207 is less than 50. To evaluate the count, the query uses a conjunction of WHERE conditions, that is, conditions separated by ANDs. Each of these conditions involves a *subquery*. The first condition, starting with the EXISTS, evaluates to true if and only if the result of the first subquery is a non-empty table—the '*' is a shorthand for a list of all the attribute names of the table named in the FROM clause; that is, there is in the table REGISTERS a tuple:

Science	Paul

The second condition uses NOT EXISTS with a subquery to ensure the non-existence of the tuple to be inserted. The final condition involves a subquery that returns a result table comprising a single integer value being the number of distinct tuples with course equal to SE207.

Queries such as INSERT will in practice be repeated many times, but for different students registered with different faculties enrolling for different courses, and perhaps for different maximum class sizes. To be of general use as a transaction definition, SQL queries such as Fig. 2.14 need to be *parameterized*. This involves replacing the literal values that differ for each usage (for example Paul and SE207) with variable names, and the parameterized version used with the actual values needed for a particular transaction.

Transaction definitions in isolation are not necessarily satisfactory on two accounts; first finding the transaction definition appropriate for the task to be done, and second knowing how to set parameter values for a given transaction to be performed. It is not uncommon to find the use of *front-end* software which assists the user to identify the particular transaction definition needed (for example via a sequence of menus on the computer's screen). Having located the transaction definition, the user is then prompted on the screen for the given transaction definition's parameter values. Where a transaction involves presentation of a result table, the front-end software allows the user to browse through this.

The design approach that one would use to derive the transaction definitions for an application is based on *functional decomposition*, sometimes called *stepwise refinement*. One starts with the notion of the application as a single whole process together with input and output data (as for example in the top-level data flow diagram in Fig. 2.13), and by means of one or more design steps arrives at the set of individual transaction definitions. The next step in decomposition of Fig. 2.13 is illustrated later, in Fig. 7.3.

2.5.5 Database management system

A database management system (DBMS) is the software application package that allows users to define information structures, and then use the structures to store information, and to retrieve information.

The systems analyst, a human being, initially defines the information structures for a given application. The systems analyst is guided in defining the *input* of the information structures to the computer, by the nature of the application. The result of this task is an information structure containing, as data, attribute definitions, and is called a *data dictionary*, see Fig. 2.15.

DATA DICTIONARY

ATTRIBUTE	TYPE
FACULTY	CHAR(15) NOT NULL
STUDENT	CHAR(15) NOT NULL
YEAR	INTEGER NOT NULL
COURSE	CHAR(5) NOT NULL
LECTURER	CHAR(15) NOT NULL

Figure 2.15 Data dictionary example.

The purpose of a data dictionary is to have in a single store the definitions of all the attributes used in the database. The data dictionary is subsequently referred to by the systems analyst when deriving the ER model for the database, when specifying the CREATE TABLE SQL queries for the base tables, and when defining the transaction definitions. The data dictionary will be used by the database administrator, another human being, during the use of the database, and when changes to it (both additions and alterations) are deemed necessary.

At its most primitive, a data dictionary is a table with the attributes' names as the primary key, and other attributes of the data dictionary will include, for example, the type definition of the subject attribute. For example, in Fig. 2.15, TYPE is a data dictionary attribute and the type definition of STUDENT is character data of 15 characters in length and must be present (NOT NULL).

The database administrator will normally register the different users of the database system, including themselves, and the users' *access rights*. Different users may have different rights of access to the SQL query commands themselves (CREATE, SELECT, INSERT and UPDATE). Furthermore different users may have different rights of access to SQL query commands as applied to different tables, and to attribute values in tables (either to columns, or, more complex, to rows).

The database management system usually provides a basic SQL user interface to its facilities, employing a screen and a keyboard. As well as accepting SQL queries, results tables of SELECT queries will typically be presented on the screen or printer. The DBMS may provide menu and screen forms facilities and in this way the user can access and use predefined queries; that is queries that have been previously devised as part of a transaction definition by the systems analyst.

As well as providing the SQL query facilities, the DBMS must provide the systems analyst and the database administrator with data definition (e.g. data dictionary), and administration (e.g. user registration) facilities, as have been described. One way that these can be implemented is by treating the definition data as a database in its own right. This definition database holds as data (in tables) the data dictionary containing the attribute definitions, the base table definitions (as defined by CREATE queries), the set of users and their access rights. In effect we have a *definition dictionary* which can contain all the data definition items which make up the application database. The use of *software tools* (here a DBMS) to support themselves in this manner is not uncommon in computing.

2.6 HORN CLAUSE LOGIC AND PROLOG

In Sec. 2.5 we have described a particular method of structuring data, into tables, so that we can use the relational language SQL to specify queries. In this section we introduce a more powerful data structuring method in which we can express data structures in terms of *Horn clauses*, named after the logician Alfred Horn.

Suppose we want to model the family relationships *parent, ancestor* and *descendant*. We take the following family tree as an example:

```
George = Elizabeth (Queen Mother)
       |
   Elizabeth = Philip
           |
      Charles = Diana
           |
     ┌─────┴─────┐
  William      Harry
```

Individuals are entities:

```
elizabeth     george       queen_mother    charles
philip        diana        william         harry
```

When we name entities and relationships (family or otherwise) in this representation, the lexical rules dictate that we start with lower case letters, and replace a space with, for example, an underscore _. Thus the Queen Mother is represented as queen_mother. Using ER modelling, we first establish that there is a single simple entity type, person. There are relationships (in the family meaning of the word) between instances of entity type person. We name the relationships as has_parent, has_ancestor and has_descendant.

Horn clauses allow us to represent concrete relationships, that is with data values, and relationships with various levels of abstraction. Figure 2.16 illustrates

Horn Clauses

Family Relationships:

```
/*      Clauses relating specific individuals:   */

/*
has_parent(Person,Parent) :-
        Person has parent Parent.
*/
has_parent(elizabeth,george).
has_parent(elizabeth,queen_mother).
has_parent(charles,elizabeth).
has_parent(charles,philip).
has_parent(william,charles).
has_parent(william,diana).
has_parent(harry,charles).
has_parent(harry,diana).


/*      Clauses defining general relationships: */

/*
has_ancestor(Person,Ancestor) :-
        Person has ancestor Ancestor.
*/
has_ancestor(Person,Parent) :-
        has_parent(Person,Parent).
has_ancestor(Person,Ancestor) :-
        has_parent(Person,Parent),
        has_ancestor(Parent,Ancestor).

/*
has_descendant(Person,Descendant) :-
        Person has descendant Descendant.
*/
has_descendant(Person,Descendant) :-
        has_ancestor(Descendant,Person).
```

Figure 2.16 Horn clauses to define family relationships.

the use of Horn clauses to represent the parent relationship in a wholly concrete manner; for example the following Horn clauses, called *facts*, correspond to rows in a fictitious SQL table called HAS_PARENT:

```
    has_parent(elizabeth,george).
    has_parent(elizabeth,queen_mother).
    has_parent(charles,elizabeth).
    has_parent(charles,philip).
    has_parent(william,charles).
    has_parent(william,diana).
    has_parent(harry,charles).
    has_parent(harry,diana).
```

We have in fact defined the type has_parent by enumeration; in the specification language **Z** we could write:

```
has_parent ==
{(elizabeth,george), (elizabeth,queen_mother),
 (charles,elizabeth), (charles,philip),
 (william,charles), (william,diana),
 (harry,charles), (harry,diana)}
```

Conventionally a set of such clauses with the same relationship name, has_parent and *arguments* (two in number, corresponding to the fictitious attribute names PERSON and PARENT) is called a *procedure*. Procedures are named by their relationship name, followed by a slash '/' followed by the number of arguments—thus has_parent/2. Figure 2.16 contains two other procedures, has_ancestor/2 and has_descendant/2. Both these other procedures have two arguments. Conventionally, a procedure is immediately prefixed by a comment, for example:

```
/*
has_parent(Person,Parent) :-
    Person has parent Parent.
*/
```

that describes the relationship in natural language terms. Comments are not interpreted as part of the program *per se*; they are intended to aid human interpretation.

The two other procedures in Fig. 2.16, has_ancestor/2 and has_descendant/2, specify the ancestor and descendant relationships in an abstract manner. has_parent/2 is an enumerated type definition *and* a relation, whilst has_ancestor/2 and has_descendant/2 are abstract type definitions, *and* relations. So, unlike a relational database in which we have a base table for each relation, using Horn clauses our relations can refer to other relations. The references to the other relationships appear on the right hand side of the :- symbols. These references may be thought of as equivalent to foreign keys in SQL.

We shall now discuss Fig. 2.16 in logical terms; we can use the clauses in the procedures to make inferences in order to deduce conclusions. The technical name for a relationship name with a given number of arguments in Horn clause logic is a *predicate*. Indeed, Horn clause logic is a subset of *predicate* logic (cf. the term predicate in natural language grammar). Thus a procedure is the definition of a predicate.

Clauses without a :- are called *facts*. Thus in Fig. 2.16,

```
has_parent(elizabeth,george).
```

and

```
has_parent(william,charles).
```

are facts. Facts are true. Clauses with ':-' in them are called rules, for example,

```
has_descendant(Person,Descendant) :-
    has_ancestor(Descendant,Person).
```

is a rule. The :- in rules is paraphrased in English as 'is true if'. Names starting with an uppercase letter, e.g. `Person` and `Descendant` are *variables*, place holders for entities. A paraphrase of the above rule is:

> Any person has a descendant *is true if* the person is an ancestor of the descendant.

The English paraphrase of `has_ancestor/2` is:

> any person has as ancestor a parent *is true if* the person has a parent
> *or*
> any person has an ancestor *is true if* the person has a parent *and* the parent has an ancestor.

'is true if', 'or' and 'and' correspond to the logical operations reverse–implication, disjunction and conjunction respectively.

- Reverse-implication—if
  When we say A *is true if* B, this means that if B is *true*, A must be *true*.
- Disjunction—or
  When we say A *or* B, this means that if either A is *true*, or B is *true*, or both A and B are *true*, the result is *true*.
- Conjunction—and
  When we say A *and* B is true, this means that the result is *true* if, and only if, both A and B are *true*.

Logical operations are met again when the binary system is explained in Chapter 9.

It is the facility to express rules, that may be self referencing (as in the second `has_ancestor/2` clause), that provides Horn clause logic with an advantage in terms of expressiveness compared with relational tables. As well as relationships based on tables, which is possible using just Horn clause facts, one can express constraints involving the same, or other relationships, in an arbitrary fashion. With rules one can express generalizations over facts that contain the specific data instances. When a procedure contains a rule that is self referencing, as in `has_ancestor/2`, we say that the procedure is *recursive*. Normally, as with structured data (such as a tree), as well as a recursive rule one expects to find a *boundary* clause or clauses in a recursive procedure. This is indeed the case with `has_ancestor/2`, where the first clause is the boundary clause. Computer programming involving Horn clause logic is usually called *logic programming* and a good text on this topic is Nilsson and Małuszyński (1990).

To provide information processing using Horn clause logic, we need to define the particular inputs, processing and outputs that are required. We do this by means

```
?-has_parent(charles,Parent).
Parent=elizabeth ;
Parent=philip ;
no
?-has_ancestor(harry,Ancestor).
Ancestor=charles ;
Ancestor=diana ;
Ancestor=elizabeth ;
Ancestor=philip ;
Ancestor=george ;
Ancestor=queen_mother ;
no
?-has_descendant(philip,Descendant).
Descendant=charles ;
Descendant=william ;
Descendant=harry ;
no
?-has_parent(george,Parent).
no
```

Figure 2.17 Query and processing of Horn clauses using Prolog.

of an hypothesis which is presented in a *query*. Figure 2.17 shows a series of queries and outputs. The outputs are the values of the entities for each instance of the relationship named by the query's predicate. For example the query:

```
?- has_parent(charles,Parent).
```

can be paraphrased in English as:

Is it true that Charles has a parent? If so what is the parent's name?

From Fig. 2.17 we can see that the following two theorems have been deduced from the Horn clauses in Fig. 2.16:

```
has_parent(charles,elizabeth).
has_parent(charles,philip).
```

Use of the query:

```
?- has_descendant(philip,Descendant).
```

has enabled the following theorems to be deduced from the Horn clauses:

```
has_descendant(philip,charles).
has_descendant(philip,william).
has_descendant(philip,harry).
```

However the query:

```
?- has_parent(george,Parent).
```

fails, and shows that this hypothesis is false, and is therefore not a theorem. This last query illustrates the *closed-world assumption*; that is, the set of clauses (in Fig. 2.16) represents all the information from which theorems can be deduced. In input–process–output terms the query can be paraphrased as:

> charles is input, the processing to be done is that defined by the procedure has_parent/2 and the output is a value of Parent. As the relationship has_parent/2 is many to many for Person to Parent, the set of parent values is provided:
>
> ```
> Parent=elizabeth ;
> Parent=philip ;
> no
> ```

where the ';' is typed by the user to obtain another solution. When there are no more solutions, 'no' is output.

In terms of information processing, we can view the information processing at two levels, either as an application (a system for family relationships), or as information processed by a *Prolog* system. A Prolog system is a computer system that processes Horn clause representations of information and the associated queries typed by the user. The language used in this case to express the Horn clauses and the processing is also called Prolog, which stands for *programming* and *logic*. Prolog was devised by Alain Colmerauer at the University of Marseilles in 1972, for use in the computer analysis of natural languages. Sterling and Shapiro (1986) is a good text on the language.

The two levels of information processing are:

1. Application
   - Input—entity values in the query;
   - Processing—entity values as constrained by the application's procedures;
   - Output—entity values of variables in the query.
2. Prolog system
   - Input—the Horn clauses comprising the facts, rules, and the query;
   - Processing—Prolog is a 'mechanical' theorem prover;
   - Output—the theorem comprising the predicate and the values of variables.

Notice that the clauses making up the data structure are either specific to particular individuals—the has_parent relationship, or are generally applicable to *any* individuals—the has_ancestor and has_descendant relationships. When developing data structures, and in programming, we always strive to construct solutions which are as general as is possible; the has_ancestor and has_descend-ant relationships are applicable to all individuals related by has_parent clauses.

THREE

THE USER INTERFACE

In this chapter we discuss the interfaces between the human user and the computer by means of the general purpose interface provided by a screen and typewriter-like keyboard. Other methods and media for communication between the user and computer are discussed in Sec. 10.4.

Fundamentally, all information, whatever its external form, be it text, pictures, sound, the temperature of a chemical process, is represented within the computer hardware in a numeric manner. Interfaces are present between the world and the computer. As computer users, we need information that is presented to us by the computer to be in a representation to suit the problem to be solved. When data is input to the computer, we need means to both physically input the data, and logically to indicate in what way the data is structured. To present information in a meaningful way, and to input data into the computer, we need a means of translation between the external form of the information and its internal representation within the computer. To do this, we use hardware and software, and often do so unaware of the translations being effected. Thus the hardware and software is used to translate key strokes on a keyboard, or the temperature in a chemical reactor, to numerical data within the computer, and to represent as output on a screen characters or a picture that is present in numeric form within the computer. When information is to be presented for human consumption, there may be alternatives, for example numbers or diagrams. Software and hardware can provide the translations necessary for these different presentation methods.

3.1 PHYSICAL AND LOGICAL INPUT/OUTPUT DEVICES

Input and output interfaces between the real world and the computer are by means of devices and these can be *physical* or *logical*. A physical device corresponds to that provided by the computer hardware. A keyboard modelled on the 'Qwerty' keyboard of a typewriter (Fig. 3.1) is an example of a physical input device, as is

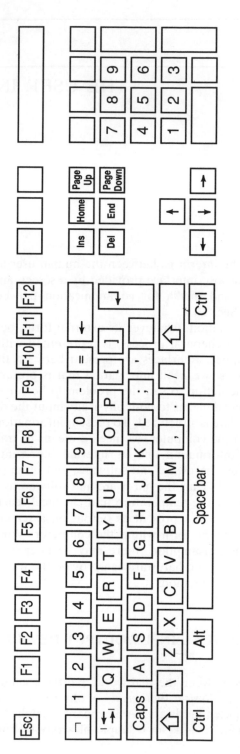

Figure 3.1 Keyboard modelled on the typewriter's keyboard.

54

the interface between a thermometer and a computer. Logical devices are those associated with software—the applications.

As an example, some keyboards have a set of keys extra to those found on a typewriter keyboard, usually called *function keys*. In Fig. 3.1, the function keys are named F1 to F12. However, pressing a particular function key might cause a particular effect in a given software application; that is the pressing of a function key causes a particular datum to be input to the computer and for this to be interpreted by the application to cause a particular logical output. For example the function key F1, when pressed, may cause the application software to print specific and possibly contextual 'help' text on the screen of the computer. Function key F1 acts as the 'help requested' logical input device in conjunction with the particular software application currently present within the computer.

3.2 INTERACTIVE INTERFACES WITH HUMANS

The screen-based user interface to modern software systems frequently uses *graphical* methods for presenting data in various different ways. As well as using characters (letters, numbers and so on), pictorial representations such as diagrams, graphs and the mimicking of real world objects are used. Such human–computer interfaces are called graphical user interfaces (GUIs). GUIs employ a set of techniques to provide dialogue between the user and the computer. Some of these techniques are collectively called by the acronym *WIMP* (window, icon, menus, pointing). Figure 3.2 shows an example of a GUI screen interface showing windows, icons, menus,

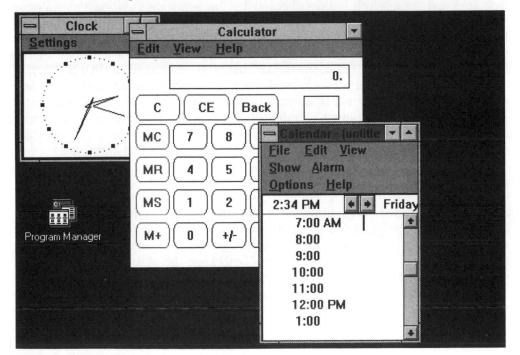

Figure 3.2 Screen using a Graphical User Interface.

forms and dialogue boxes with buttons. The various features are accessed by the user pointing to them, usually with a mouse. For screens used in public areas or in environments where a keyboard (or a mouse) is inappropriate, other physical input devices may be used which have the same logical effect; for example a remote control device (as used for remote control of televisions) or a touch sensitive screen.

3.2.1 Syntax-directed and syntax-free user interfaces

The user interface between the user and the computer comprises the physical and logical devices provided by the computer and the software present within the computer. Use of physical and logical devices can provide user interfaces that are *syntax-directed*, *syntax-analysed* or *syntax-free*. All computer applications have syntactic requirements for their input data; that is the input data must conform to particular application-specific types.

Some computer applications dialogue directly with the user. By using a syntax-directed user interface, it is thus possible for an application to ensure that the user can only present for input, data of the correct type at the particular point in their dialogue with the application. In a syntax-directed user interface, *cue* output data is first presented to the user, and the user can only make choices from the sets provided or implied by the cues. In the sections that follow we will see that features such as icons, menus, forms and buttons are devices used by applications employing syntax-directed user interfaces. These features in effect are external views of the internal types used in the application.

In the case of a syntax-analysed user interface, the user can provide input data in a free-text form which is then checked by the application during the dialogue with the user. An example of a syntax-analysed user interface is that of a command language in which the user in effect converses with the computer application; within the dialogue the user inputs a command which is analysed and acted upon by the application. (Commands and command languages are described in Chapter 11.)

Syntax-free user interfaces are used when the onus is on the user to present data to the computer in either a syntactically correct form, or where no syntax applies, in which case the input is in the form of *free text*. One example is the input of free text using a word-processor. Another example of a syntax-free user interface might be input of a computer program or test data in free text form using a *text editor*. A text editor is a program that is used by computer personnel, such as programmers, to input free text into the computer. A text editor is similar to a word-processor but without a word-processor's sophisticated formatting facilities. Some syntax-directed text editors will recognize the syntax of the programming language of the program being input, and control and advise the programmer inputting the program accordingly. In any case, input of syntax-free data is often followed at some later stage by syntactic checking, be it by a word-processor performing layout and paragraphing, or during the subsequent translation of a computer program to the internal representation needed for it to be executed by the computer.

3.2.2 Window

A *window* presents output data from the computer and is a 'virtual' or logical screen which appears on the physical screen. Figure 3.2 shows a physical screen with three windows: a clock, a calculator and a calendar. It is often the case that the user can move windows about on the screen, and can sometimes vary the size of the window, or the magnification of its contents. It may be the case that a single application uses several windows because that makes for a sensible interface to the user; or the user is concurrently using more than one application. Thus a word-processor package may include a 'help' window; it may allow more than one typing window at a time, or a window(s) on another file(s) from which one can 'cut and paste' into the typing window. Alternatively, the user may be using a word-processor package at the same time as an electronic mail package. Screen-based user interfaces without windows can be thought of as having the physical screen as a single window.

The *window system* is the software system that manages how the various windows are displayed on the single screen, to channel a given application's output data to its window, and to associate the pointing device with the application associated with the window being pointed at. An example of a window system is the *X-Window* system.

Windows may contain various features. For general purpose usage one typically finds the analogue of an unfurling scroll of paper which is typed into at its 'end', and on which previous data can be viewed by *scrolling*, that is, by analogically moving the window with respect to the scroll. The 'end' of the scroll, that is where the next character is to be typed, is represented on the screen by a *cursor*, a characteristic mark. In the case of a word-processor's input window, where text is typed by the user, the cursor can be positioned within existing text (by means described below), allowing the user to insert or overwrite text; see Fig. 1.6.

Windows can contain other screen features such as icons, menus, forms and dialogue boxes with buttons. An ambitious window system would allow windows to contain windows. The *window manager* is the software system that is used to manipulate windows themselves and their features.

3.2.3 Icon

An *icon* is a small pictorial representation of an object such as a window, a menu, form, dialogue box or an operation that might be performed. The screen shown in Fig. 3.2 contains an icon for the window of the application 'Program Manager'. The meaning of a particular icon should be self-explanatory. The user can 'hide' windows as icons, as in the case of the program manager window, (perhaps when the screen gets too cluttered), and restore them. Typically, if the user points at an icon and possibly confirms the placement by some further input of data, then the object, be it a window, menu, form or dialogue box is revealed by being *pulled-down*, or some operation occurs.

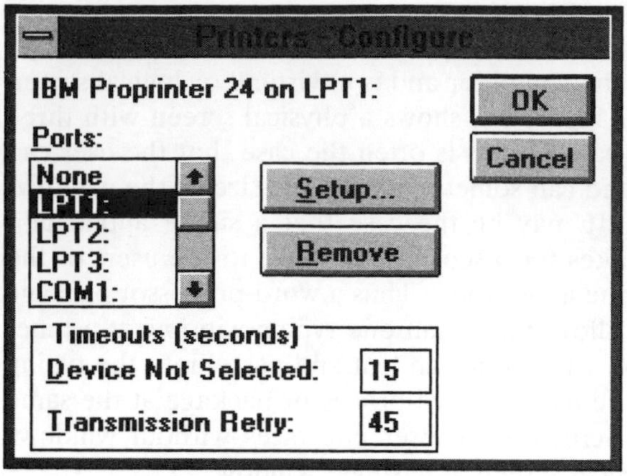

Figure 3.3   Window illustrating a menu and buttons.

3.2.4 Menu

A *menu* is a set of individual choices displayed in a window on the screen, one of which may be selected by the user. A menu in computing is an analogue of the à la carte menu found in restaurants. Thus a menu provides output data from the computer (the choices) and input data to the computer (the selected item). Choice selection may be by pointing to the appropriate item as shown in Fig. 3.3, which illustrates a window containing a menu of printer ports. Port LPT1 is the choice that is currently being pointed at. An alternative technique is shown in Fig. 3.4 where each menu item is labelled, and the choice selection is done by keying the label value (in this case a number) on the computer's keyboard.

Each choice in a menu should be self-explanatory to the user of the application. A menu choice may lead to another menu, in which case the terms 'menu hierarchy' or 'menu tree' are used to describe the relationship between the menus. For space limitation reasons dictated by the size of the menu window, icons can be used as an alternative presentation method for the text of menu items.

Because the user is constrained to follow menu choices, menus are syntax-directed user interfaces.

3.2.5 Form

A *form* is the analogue of a paper form (Fig. 3.5). The form is presented on the screen, within a window. The user normally uses a form for *data entry*, i.e. to input data to an application, in a syntax-directed manner. Sometimes the form method is used for making a query; that is, the user having input data, this is used to construct a query (cf. SQL SELECT), to output information that the user is seeking.

In the form there are *fields*. A field is either an *output* field, for example a prompt to the user (e.g. Member's name) or a current data value (e.g. Paula, which here also serves as a *prompt*), or the field is an *input* field (e.g. the fields in

```
1        a  a word of a syllable of form Consonant-Vowel-Consonant
2        b  a word terminated by Consonant-Vowel-Consonant or by
            Consonant-Vowel(pronounced)-Vowel(pronounced)-Consonant
3        j  "wool"
4           others
?
```

Each line specifies a choice. The number identifies the choice, the letter (a, b, j) is extra data for the user of this application, and the text explains the choice. If the user selects 2, this leads to another menu:

```
1        c  last syllable accented
2        d  terminated by -l or -m
3        g  "handicap, humbug"
4        h  "worship, kidnap"
5        i  terminated with -ic
6           others
? 2.
```

If there is just one choice, a question and answer method can be used:

```
        e  Is the word used in England (y/n) ? y.
        f  Is the word "(un)paralleled" (y/n) ? n.
```

Figure 3.4 Menu example—choice is by selection of choice identifier, in this case a number. The letters a, b, j etc. are specific to the application.

Acme Whist Club

Whist Club Drive

Date 29/02/1992

Venue _____

Member's name	Points
Paula	——
Leslie	——
Frances	——
Anne	——
Justine	——
Patrick	——

Figure 3.5 Form example.
The form as first presented on the screen.

the Points column). Input fields can have attributes such as 'must-enter' (e.g. for the field to the right of Venue, type (for example alphabetic, numeric, only y or n, date format—as in the field to the right of Date), and default value (if data is not input by the user). Default values may be existing data values (e.g. 'today' being 29/02/1992 when the form is used, this is shown to the user as the default) that the user can change. An input field is also an output field if a default or current data value is present when the form is first displayed (e.g. 29/02/1992).

A user might use the same form (Fig. 3.5) for either data entry, whence the current club members (those who have paid their subscriptions, see Fig. 2.6), are displayed, or for making a query, say to find the results of a match on a previous data (requiring the user to enter that date in the date field).

3.2.6 Dialogue boxes and buttons

The concept of the dialogue box, with its data displays and buttons as used to control equipment, is used in computing as a vehicle for syntax-directed user interfaces (see Fig. 3.3). The visual aspects of the 'box' are displayed on the screen (including the simulated buttons). Such screen-based software dialogue boxes may be cost-effective compared with their physical control panel counterparts. The 'equipment' accessed by the dialogue box has neither to exist in reality nor have any physical significance. One uses the dialogue box concept in the same way as the menu concept—an analogue of an approach to access data and to control the application, whatever that application might be. Thus the dialogue box in Fig. 3.3 presents a control panel approach to configuring the printer attached to a computer.

Dialogue boxes are so displayed that they appear to have depth; this is achieved by shading the 'edges' of the buttons and display areas. Thus display areas can appear inset, and buttons can appear proud and may 'move' when 'pressed'. A *button* is the analogue of the type of button used to control equipment. The button is presented on the screen, within a window, on a simulated dialogue box. Figure 3.3 has buttons labelled Setup, Remove, OK and Cancel. A button, if 'pressed' as will be explained below, causes the application to perform a function.

In comparing icons and buttons, icons represent concepts whilst buttons mimic physical dialogue box buttons; an icon has significance in isolation whilst a button has significance in the context of its dialogue box.

3.2.7 Pointing and the mouse

Pointing involves the user pointing to a feature such as an icon, a menu item, or a button that is displayed on the screen. Thus pointing provides input data to the computer in the form of a position on the screen which allows the computer to identify the feature. Pointing often also allows the selection of an action (because of the nature of the feature; for example making a menu choice by pointing rather than typing in a number as in Fig. 3.4). Pointing can be achieved in various ways. The keyboard may have cursor keys, often arranged together; see the group of keys labelled with arrows in Fig. 3.1. Use of these keys will cause the cursor to traverse either within its associated window, or, in the case of a screen-wide cursor, the screen.

In addition to the keyboard as a physical input data device, there may be a *mouse*; Figs 1.9 and 1.10 show a mouse on the right side of the illustrations. A mouse is a physical input data device that is used to move the cursor over the screen by moving the mouse over a flat surface. The mouse senses the motion and the resultant motion data is input to the window system software in the computer. The mouse has on its top one or more physical buttons (not to be confused with the screen dialogue box buttons explained above). Pressing a button causes a data item to be input to the window system software.

Pointing works in the following manner. The window system software knows firstly the absolute position of the cursor on the screen. It also knows the absolute position of icons, menus and their choices, buttons and so on. It knows this information because the various applications using these features have requested the window system to provide them, the applications, with the features. We have more to say on this matter of 'what-does-what', in Sec. 3.4.

One selects a particular icon, menu item, button or piece of text (for example in a 'cut' operation) or place on the screen (for example in a 'paste' operation) by positioning the cursor using the mouse and by pressing a particular button on the mouse. The mouse is thus used as a pointer to make selections (by pointing at a menu item with the cursor and pressing a mouse button).

In the case of windows that accept free text (those not under syntax-directed control), the window to which typed data will be input can itself be selected by pointing at it with the cursor.

3.2.8 WYSIWYG

What you see is what you get (*WYSIWYG*) is used in screen-based user interfaces for applications in which the user is using the computer to interactively construct some artifact, for example a document or in desk-top publishing. The idea is that a graphical representation of the artifact is constructed and amended 'immediately' by the computer, rather than first input all the data and then run a program to produce the artifact.

3.3 PRESENTING INFORMATION

Information has inherent structure dependent on the information's type. For some structures, various presentation methods have been devised over the years (and often prior to the advent of computers). We will limit our discussion to tabular data (as for example the whist club database) but various presentation methods have also been devised for more complex data structures (for example menu hierarchies), and these appear at appropriate places, later in the text.

For numerical tabular data, which can be difficult to comprehend at a glance, information can be displayed in other ways appropriate to the nature of the information and the user's needs. Long before the advent of computers, statisticians

Sequence of temperature values at one second intervals:

16   13   13   15   14   15   16   19

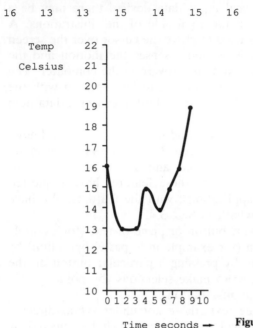

Time seconds ➔   **Figure 3.6** Diagrammatic presentation methods—graph.

and others devised pictorial and diagrammatic methods of presentation. Figure 3.6 shows a graph of the temperature values already met in Fig. 1.7 plotted against time. The points have been joined by a smooth curve generated by software using the technique called *spline fitting*. Figure 3.7 shows a histogram and a 'pie' chart representation for the points obtained by individual members (in alphabetic order) of the whist club (see Fig. 2.3).

Such display techniques often use apparently continuous (e.g. Fig. 3.6) rather than discrete methods. Physical output devices such as computer screens and computer printers, in conjunction with the appropriate software, can provide alternative *presentations* of some given information, independent of the application that generated that information.

3.4 STANDARDIZED USER INTERFACES

With the facilities provided by graphical user interfaces together with the possibility of multiple concurrent applications each with one or more windows, there is the need for *standardization* of the user interface. There are good reasons for using as much as possible that is common between the various user interfaces used by applications such as a word-processor, an electronic mail system, a database system, a diary, and access to other applications packages a user might require.

Tabular Representation:

MEMBERSHIP

MEMBER	SUBSCRIPTION	POINTS
Paula	y	3
Leslie	y	2
Anne	n	6
Justine	y	0
Patrick	y	1
Rachel	n	2

Histogram:

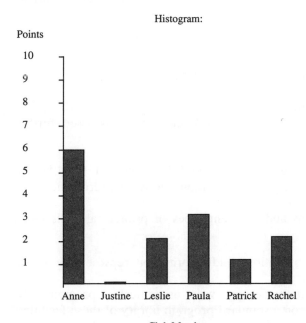

Pie Chart:

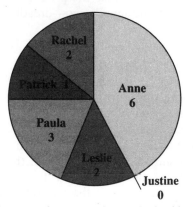

Figure 3.7 Diagrammatic presentation methods—histogram and 'pie' chart.

The following sections discuss the reasons for providing commonality and describe how this commonality manifests itself.

3.4.1 Consistency—the need for the software engineering approach

We first address the consistency issue between different applications using graphical user interfaces, and then discuss the ramifications of this for the software designer.

Rather than a plethora of different conventions and protocols to do essentially similar things, such as:

- Which mouse buttons do what.
- How to invoke the help system.
- Which colours signify what information (red = danger?).
- Where pull-down menus appear.
- How to delete the data just entered.
- How to deal with users with different natural languages (discussed further below).
- Currency symbols and usage.
- Ways of representing numbers (e.g. 1,234.56 and 1.234,56 and 12,34.56 are different national methods for representing one thousand two hundred and thirty four decimal point five six).
- Cope with different size screens and different types of printer (also discussed further below).

The interface is uniform for the operations and information representations are common across applications.

Instead of having every applications designer write user interface programs, the designer makes the application call on a standard program library of these facilities. Thus an application does not normally contain programs to variously manipulate the screen, handle icons, menus, forms, dialogue boxes and buttons, provide diagrammatic presentation methods, deal with the layouts, program colours explicitly and so on. This approach not only saves costs; it avoids the production of interfaces which are individualized—good perhaps for the designer's ego—dreadful for the user.

3.4.2 Natural language independence

An application may be used by people with different natural languages. Figure 3.8 is the French equivalent of Fig. 3.4. Notice that input (the o. and n. standing for 'oui' and 'non' respectively) must also be catered for. Furthermore, there is the requirement to provide diacritics, e.g. the accents on é and è. All the dialogue text that is output or input by the application should be separate from the application's program. This means that when translating the application for another natural language, one is only concerned with the translation of the natural language text— the application's program remains the same.

```
1       a  un mot d'une syllabe formée de Consonne-Voyelle-Consonne
2       b  un mot terminé par Consonne-Voyelle-Consonne ou par
           Consonne-Voyelle(prononcée)-Voyelle(prononcée)-Consonne
3       j  "wool"
4          autres
? 2.

1       c  avec la dernière syllabe est-elle accentuée
2       d  terminé par -l ou -m
3       g  "handicap, humbug"
4       h  "worship, kidnap"
5       i  se termine-t-il par -ic
6          autres

? 2.
e       Le mot est-il en Angleterre (o/n) ? o.
f       Le mot est-il "(un)paralleled" (o/n) ? n.
```

Figure 3.8 Menu example—French is the dialogue language.

3.4.3 Alternative presentational methods and output devices

Physical output devices such as computer screens and computer printers, in conjunction with the appropriate, preferably standardized, software, can provide alternative *presentations* of the same information, independent of the application that generated that information (as shown in Fig. 3.7).

The application should be independent of the type of physical device; for example the size of the screen, the use of a monochrome screen for an application using colour, the use of a printer rather than a screen, and the saving of screens to a computer disk.

Thus a given presentation method should be independent of a particular physical output device, and a given device should be independent of the different presentation methods. Software can provide the mapping between the data as internally represented in the computer (as numbers) and a presentation method, and again between the presentation method and the device.

3.4.4 Psychology and user interfaces

The design of good user interfaces is *not* easy. Care is needed to manage consistency and uniformity, and to properly use visual cues (such as dialogue boxes). There are prescriptive methods that can help in the design process. This design discipline that involves both psychology and computer science is commonly called *human–computer interaction*—HCI.

3.4.5 Separation of the user interface and the application

The previous sections have presented reasons why the design of user interfaces needs to clearly separate the application from the implementation of the features of, in particular, the graphical user interface. This separation makes good sense too when it concerns the actual application program. In Chapters 11 and 12 we shall see that the screen may be attached to a computer other than that where the application program is executed. With the separation of functions between the application and the user interface features, we can place the latter with the local computer, or indeed with an embedded computer packaged with the screen (this last is described in Chapter 10).

The X-Window system, which deals with windows in conjunction with a window manager, enables the separation of application from the graphical user interface to be done in a standard manner.

FOUR

COMPUTING AND KNOWLEDGE

When software is produced, it is usually the case that much of the knowledge used in its production is not accessible in the application. One can ask the software package neither 'why' nor 'how' it has produced particular output for a given input. In conventional software, neither the specification of the program, nor the program as represented by the programmer, is available for reasoning with when the software is run. One would have recourse to consulting the people involved in producing the software system to get an answer to these questions. These people would have to interpret the specification, the design documentation and the programs, in conjunction with the data input.

In this chapter we will examine applications where a richer method of representing and interpreting information is needed; ones where it is necessary that the software is self-explaining.

Consider how we might try and represent the intricacies of natural language morphology. For example, in a teaching environment, is the word composed from 'model' and the suffix 'ing' spelt 'modelling' or 'modeling', and if one or the other, under what circumstances and why? There is a need for a system that uses such information to *reason* with, and to provide explanations and justifications of its reasoning in solving a problem; in other words, to mimic a human expert. To perform such reasoning requires a deductive capability. The information used to represent the problem domain can therefore be considered to be knowledge.

The data structuring and information processing methods we have seen so far, with the exception of the Horn clause example in Fig. 2.16, do not *per se* support reasoning by computer. Nor do the methods (including that using Horn clauses) provide explanations as to why they processed their data as they did; that is, provide reasons. We need some way to firstly represent *knowledge* and secondly to *reason* with, and provide explanations of how the knowledge is used. Natural language would seem the obvious candidate as a representation method, but it is prone to imprecision, ambiguity and inconsistency.

Knowledge processing is the processing of knowledge by computer. *Knowledge engineering* is producing knowledge processing applications—cf. software engineering.

Knowledge engineers are practitioners of knowledge engineering. Software engineers require representation methods such as programming languages, and software tools such as the programming systems that implement programs written in programming languages. Knowledge engineers need similar methods for representing knowledge, and similar tools to build *knowledge-based systems* (cf. database systems). Much of the knowledge engineer's work can involve 'standard software' tools, but knowledge representation and processing usually necessitates rather different software. We shall see examples in this chapter.

4.1 KNOWLEDGE PROCESSING APPLICATION AREAS

Knowledge is a form of information which can be reasoned about. To enable such reasoning to be done, and in a mechanical manner by computer, we require representations for knowledge that are conducive to 'mechanical' reasoning. The information to be reasoned with can be represented by, or supplemented with, a *model*, that is, a computer simulation of the domain under investigation; in this case *model-based* reasoning is used.

Examples of application areas in which knowledge processing techniques are used include:

- *Natural language processing.* This encompasses both understanding (including parsing and semantic analysis) and generation of natural language. Applications include translation to other natural languages or as a 'front-end' to an existing computer system, for example to enable natural language queries to, and answers from, a database. Such an application might translate natural language queries to SQL, and translate output tables to a natural-language version.
- *Expert systems.* Computer programs that simulate human expertise in some limited domain; for example fault diagnosis in motor car engines. A model-based expert system for fault diagnosis in motor car engines would include a computer simulation of the car's engine.
- *Computer-aided learning.* Knowledge processing can be applied to applications in computer-aided learning in two ways:

  1. *Model-based reasoning.* Systems which reason using a model of the domain being learned, in order to provide explanations.

  2. *Pedagogy.* Systems which reason about the student's current perceived knowledge of the domain, to assist in the construction of exercises, and the diagnosis and remedy of the student's difficulties. These systems, sometimes called *intelligent tutoring systems* (ITS), can diagnose and remedy the student's difficulties. They typically incorporate models of the domain being learned.

- *Pattern recognition.* The principal areas are in visual recognition and speech recognition. In the case of a robot that is assembling some artifact, the robot must be able to recognize different components and then select the correct one at a particular stage in the assembly process.

Speech recognition may be limited to single words, or it may involve sentences being a 'front-end' to natural language processing. An example of such an application might be to the natural language example above, allowing spoken dialogue with a database.

- *Planning*. Humans are frequently involved in planning tasks, for example the 'best' way to get from London to Rome, and how to plan a course of study for a student.
- *Systems that learn*. Systems that, in being able to learn, effectively program themselves to perform subsequent functions. For example in an intelligent tutoring system, the pedagogue component of the system endeavours to learn the student's abilities and weaknesses, so that the didactics component can plan the material to be presented and the method of delivery.

When the needs of the various knowledge processing application areas are examined it is found that in many cases the information and the processing required cannot easily be handled by the rather 'static' techniques described in Chapter 2. We find we need to codify and process *knowledge*. Hence the term *knowledge processing*.

For the rest of this chapter we confine ourselves to examples drawn from natural language processing, expert systems and computer aided learning, using a model in each as follows:

1. *Natural language processing*. The application is confined to the syntax analysis of very simple English sentences.
2. *Expert systems*. As well as providing dialogue in the form of questions to the user constructed from a separate domain description, the expert system can provide explanations of its reasoning, both during the dialogue with a user, and, on completion, a reasoned justification of its advice.
3. *Computer-aided learning using a model*. In the final example we demonstrate the ability of a separate software tool to use a domain description method (in the general area of natural language morphology) which models the expert linguist's rules, in order to provide the student with instructive dialogue for a particular problem area in the morphology of a language.

4.2 NATURAL LANGUAGE PROCESSING

Natural language processing is concerned with *understanding* and *generating* natural language. The approach used in this text relies on a grammatical method. Thus morphological analysis of individual words and the syntax concerned with the way words can be combined to form grammatically correct sentences is undertaken. Semantic analysis is performed to find the meaning of an input sentence. Such an analysis is used to control the application. An example is a natural language front-end to a database—users, instead of using a computer-oriented query language such as SQL, might instead use natural language. Other examples include natural language translation, and controlling a device using speech, in which natural language

Grammar and Lexicon:

```
/*          Definite Clause Grammar Example.          */
/*          Grammar:              */
```

sentence → subject, predicate.

subject → noun_phrase.

predicate → intransitive_verb.
predicate → transitive_verb, complement.

complement → direct_object.

direct_object → noun_phrase.

noun_phrase → determiner, countable_noun.
noun_phrase → uncountable_noun.

```
/*          Lexicon:          */
```

determiner → [the].

countable_noun → [lecturer].
countable_noun → [student].

uncountable_noun → [computing].

intransitive_verb → [learns].

transitive_verb → [teaches].

Examples of use:

```
?- sentence([the,What,learns],[]).
        What=lecturer ;
        What=student ;
no
?- sentence(Sentence,[]).
        Sentence=[the,lecturer,learns] ;
        Sentence=[the,lecturer,teaches,the,lecturer] ;
        Sentence=[the,lecturer,teaches,the,student] ;
        Sentence=[the,lecturer,teaches,computing] ;
        Sentence=[the,student,learns] ;
        Sentence=[the,student,teaches,the,lecturer] ;
        Sentence=[the,student,teaches,the,student] ;
        Sentence=[the,student,teaches,computing] ;
        Sentence=[computing,learns] ;
        Sentence=[computing,teaches,the,lecturer] ;
        Sentence=[computing,teaches,the,student] ;
        Sentence=[computing,teaches,computing] ;
no
```

Figure 4.1 Natural Language example using a definite clause grammar.

processing is integrated with speech processing. Natural language processing relies on a knowledge of both linguistics and computer science and is a subject within the field of *computational linguistics*.

To give an idea of one aspect of natural language processing, Fig. 4.1 shows an example of a (very simple) grammar for a very small subset of English, together with a small lexicon, and examples of use. The grammar comprises rules of syntax that relate parts of speech (such as nouns and verbs) and constructions (such as noun phrase, predicate and sentence). The lexicon comprises the actual words and what part of speech each is (such as 'teaches' is a transitive verb).

Prolog systems will normally accept such a grammar, called a *definite clause grammar* (DCG), as a program. Definite clauses are Horn clauses adapted for expressing grammar rules (also called productions). There is a simple translation between a DCG and the equivalent Horn clause representation and this is typically done by the Prolog system. The grammar, as a program, will parse a sentence and generate sentences. In Fig. 4.1, the 'Examples of use' show two queries. The first query illustrates successful parsing of a sentence in which the word What happens to be variable; the possible words that might appear in a particular part of a sentence are output. The second query illustrates sentence generation, all the possible sentences derivable from the grammar and lexicon being produced.

Figure 4.1 shows the potential complexity of real natural language processing systems by reason of its deficiencies. For example, not dealing with semantics, sentences that do not have a meaning can be processed (for instance 'computing learns'). To be able to do semantic processing, there is the need to construct a structural representation of the sentence in terms of its constituent parts of speech and constructions; this is often called a parse tree. For an example of a parse tree, admittedly of an artificial language sentence (Prolog Horn clause), see Fig. 8.6. Natural language grammars are far more complex than this simple example implies— consider morpho-syntax (*adult* → *adults*, but *child* → *children*) and lexical morphology (*model* → *modelling* (British), but *modeling* (US)).

A further and fundamentally serious defect of the grammar in Fig. 4.1 is that this grammar is limited to a language with a finite number of sentences. Natural language is distinguished in that there is an infinite number of sentences possible, even with a finite-sized lexicon and grammar. Grammars in which an infinite number of sentences are possible have *recursive* grammar rules. An example of recursion is a grammar that handles sentences with zero or more relative clauses, as for example in the following sentences:

> The lecturer who teaches the student learns.
> The lecturer who teaches the student who learns learns.

Such sentences can be handled by the grammar in Fig. 4.1 to which have been added the following grammar rules. To the existing grammar rules headed by noun_phrase add:

> noun_phrase → determiner, countable_noun, relative_clause.

together with the grammar rules:

    relative_clause → relative_pronoun, predicate.
    relative_clause → relative_pronoun, predicate, relative_clause.

and to the lexicon:

    relative_pronoun → [who].

The recursion is handled by the two grammar rules headed by `relative_clause`. Logically, a relative clause is either a single relative clause in the form of a relative pronoun (in this case the lexicon contains just who) followed by a predicate, or it is a relative pronoun and predicate followed by another relative clause. Figure 4.2 illustrates the grammar in Fig. 4.1 to which have been added the above grammar rules. The first example of use illustrates the application of the recursive grammar rule for relative clauses by means of generating ever longer sentences. The second example illustrates the generation of all syntactically correct sentences of eight words starting with 'The' and ending with 'learns'.

Programming languages require grammars (also with recursive grammar rules to enable an infinite number of possible programs); this matter is discussed in Chapter 8.

4.3 EXPERT SYSTEMS

An expert system is a computer program that behaves like a *human* expert for some problem domain. It *must* exhibit the following attributes:

1. Problem-solving capability.
2. Explanation capability.
3. Ability to cope with incomplete and/or uncertain knowledge.

An expert system is an example of a knowledge-based system, but it is distinguished by having an *explanation* facility—it can explain *why* it is behaving in a particular fashion and *how* it has reached a conclusion. Thus, as well as being able to reason, an expert system has to justify its reasoning to the user. Expert systems can be classified by the problem domain to which they are applicable. The problem domain defines the application area; for example medical, electronics and career counselling. However, it is also possible to classify expert systems according to the *types* of problems that are independent of the problem domain. Examples of problem types are classification, diagnosis, advice, design and repair.

Expert systems are usually *interactive*, a computing term that means that users interact with them directly (word-processors are thus interactive). However, expert systems may be embedded within a computer system. An example of an embedded expert system is one that monitors aircraft movements in order to assist air traffic controllers by predicting flight collisions. Interactive expert systems emulate a *consultation* between an expert and a user. A person may be an expert in operating

Recursive Grammar and Lexicon:

```
/*        Definite Clause Grammar with Recursion Example.        */

/*        Grammar:        */

sentence → subject, predicate.

subject → noun_phrase.

predicate → intransitive_verb.
predicate → transitive_verb, complement.

complement → direct_object.

direct_object → noun_phrase.

noun_phrase → determiner, countable_noun.
noun_phrase → uncountable_noun.
noun_phrase → determiner, countable noun, relative_clause.

relative_clause → relative_pronoun, predicate.
relative_clause → relative_pronoun, predicate, relative_clause.

/*        Lexicon:        */

determiner → [the].

countable_noun → [lecturer].
countable_noun → [student].

uncountable_noun → [computing].

intransitive_verb → [learns].

transitive_verb → [teaches].

relative_pronoun → [who].
```

Example of use:

```
?- sentence (Sentence, []).
    Sentence=[the,lecturer,learns] ;
    Sentence=[the,lecturer,teaches,the,lecturer] ;
    Sentence=[the,lecturer,teaches,the,student] ;
    Sentence=[the,lecturer,teaches,computing] ;
    Sentence=[the,lecturer,teaches,the,lecturer,who,learns] ;
    Sentence=[the,lecturer,teaches,the,lecturer,who,teaches,the,
    lecturer] ;
    Sentence=[the,lecturer,teaches,the,lecturer,who,teaches,the,
    student] ;
    Sentence=[the,lecturer,teaches,the,lecturer,who,teaches,computing] ;
    Sentence=[the,lecturer,teaches,the,lecturer,who,teaches,the,
    lecturer,who, learns]
yes
?- Sentence = [the,_,_,_,_,_,_,learns], sentence(Sentence [ ]).
    Sentence=[the,lecturer,who,learns,who,teaches,computing,learns] ;
    Sentence=[the,lecturer,who,teaches,computing,who,learns,learns] ;
    Sentence=[the,student,who,learns,who,teaches,computing,learns] ;
    Sentence=[the,student,who,teaches,computing,who,learns,learns] ;
no
```

Figure 4.2 Natural Language example using a recursive grammar rule headed by relative_clause.

an artifact—for example a complex or difficult to use application package; in this case the expert system could be a 'front-end', sandwiched between the user (perhaps a trainee) and the application package, able to give advice and possibly fore-warnings.

4.3.1 Expert system architecture

Expert systems architecture is concerned with the organization of expert systems and the components that make them up.

A typical expert system comprises three components: a *knowledge base*, an *inference engine* and a *user interface*, Fig. 4.3. An expert system *shell* is a package comprising an inference engine and a user interface. This architecture allows a shell to be used with different knowledge bases represented in the form that can be interpreted by the shell. This is analogous to the way in which a programming language can be used for different programs in that language.

4.3.2 Knowledge base

The knowledge base is problem-domain specific. An expert system can normally only work in a small and very specific domain. If the domain is more general, the expert system is usually limited to a coarse classification task. The knowledge must first be acquired, a task called *knowledge acquisition*, normally done by the knowledge engineer. There are various knowledge acquisition techniques and these are summarized in Fig. 4.4. The knowledge base has the task of representing the acquired knowledge in a form that can be processed so as to provide reasoning and explanation capabilities. There are various *knowledge representation* methods, and

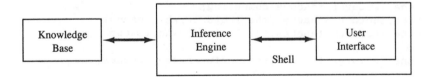

Figure 4.3 Expert system architecture.

- *Interviewing* an expert in order to elicit the rules — perhaps *ad hoc*, and empirical — that the expert uses to reason with, together with the methods of reasoning used.

- *Observation* of an expert in the work-place.

- *Protocol Analysis* — a term meaning the analysis of the dialogue between the expert and the user(s) during a consultation, or between an expert operator and an artifact.

Figure 4.4 Knowledge acquisition techniques.

in this book we limit the discussion to one of these, *production rules*. Conventionally production rules take the form:

if *condition* then *conclusion*

where the condition can be made up of conditions related by the logical operators and, or and not. In the example expert system we restrict the production rules to a simple form; for example we shall ignore *uncertainty*. Figure 4.5 shows the knowledge base of a (very naïve) 'Garden Earth Physician' expert system. Production rules and facts of this form can be directly represented as Horn clauses. For example:

```
if
    earth_texture(crumbly) and
    earth_colour(dark)
then
    peat.

fact sand_colour(yellow).
```

can be represented as:

```
peat :-
    earth_texture(crumbly),
    earth_colour(dark).

sand_colour(yellow).
```

4.3.3 Inference engine

The *inference engine* is the part of an expert system that provides the problem-solving capability. Furthermore, it provides the information for explanations, and it handles situations where there is incomplete or uncertain knowledge. The inference engine is a program which, given the knowledge base and the ability to use the knowledge representation method used, employs a reasoning technique to infer conclusions from the knowledge represented and the answers to questions made on the user via the user interface. Logic is the reasoning technique used for the example expert system.

Questions to the user of the expert system are to be constructed from the knowledge representation and the current state of the dialogue with the user. For example, in attempting to infer if the earth is wet, and if this information is not in the knowledge base, the inference engine can construct the question:

```
earth_moisture(wet)?
```

The inference engine *learns* the user's answer, affirmative or negative, to prevent the same question being repeated later in the consultation.

```
/*          Garden Earth Physician Expert System Knowledge Base.          */
if
        peat
then
        treat_earth('add quicklime').

if
        sandy
then
        treat_earth('add compost and potash').

if
        clay and
        clay_treatment(Treatment)
then
        treat_earth(Treatment).

if
        earth_texture(crumbly) and
        earth_colour(dark)
then
        peat.

if
        earth_moisture(wet) and
        earth_texture(gritty)
then
        sandy.

if
        sand_colour(Colour) and
        earth_colour(Colour)
then
        sandy.

if
        earth_moisture(wet) and
        earth_texture(sticky)
        or
        earth_moisture(dry) and
        earth_texture(hard) and
        weather(drought)
then
        clay.

if
        Treatment equals 'dig drainage channels' and
        drainage(bad)
        or
        Treatment equals 'add lime' and
        not drainage(bad)
then
        clay_treatment(Treatment).

fact sand_colour(yellow).
fact sand_colour(white).
```

Figure 4.5 Example knowledge base—production rules.

4.3.4 User interface

The user interface is the part of the expert system with which the user who is seeking a consultation dialogues. Thus a question constructed by the inference engine is presented to the user and the user interface accepts the answer, passing it back to the inference engine. Similarly the user may question the expert system 'why am I being asked this question' and expect the expert system to answer for its part.

Questions asked by the expert system are necessary when the knowledge in the knowledge base is *incomplete*. For example, in Fig. 4.5, the fact:

```
fact    earth_moisture(wet).
```

is not in the knowledge base. Indeed, as we would expect the expert system to be general purpose (abstract), we would rather it questioned the user as to the state of the earth moisture in the problematical area of the garden. The user interface also handles *why* questions posed by the user. The user interface displays *how* the expert system arrived at a particular solution. This is provided after the last question asked by the expert system. All these aspects are illustrated in the example user/expert system dialogue in Fig. 4.6.

In Fig. 4.6 the user first poses the query `solve treat_earth(Treatment)`. On being asked by the expert system `earth_texture(gritty)?` the user wants to know why this question is being asked, and responds by typing why. The expert system responds with its current line of reasoning—it is endeavouring to find out if the earth is sandy. If the earth is wet and it is gritty it can conclude that it is sandy, and it prints this rule. The user is not satisfied with this amount of explanation and responds why, a second time, and again a third time, but this exhausts the expert system's current line of reasoning. When the expert system has solved the problem, it prints its reasoning, starting with `treat_earth('add compost and potash')` `is proved using rule`.

In order that questions can be formulated from the knowledge base, to be able to answer 'why' questions, and to be able to print a 'how' justification—a *proof*—we require firstly that the knowledge base is available for interpretation whilst the expert system executes and secondly that during execution the expert system builds a history of the decisions it made and why these were taken. The history-building is done as an adjunct to the inference engine.

4.3.5 Expert system shell

The inference engine and user interface are typically packaged together because these components of an expert system are of a general nature. The package is called an *expert system shell* as it provides the user interface and the ability to process arbitrary knowledge bases. Thus we can construct an expert system in a domain other than advising on garden earth condition problems, provided the domain

```
?- solve treat_earth(Treatment).
earth_texture(crumbly)? no.
earth_moisture(wet)? yes.
earth_texture(gritty)? why.
if
            earth_moisture(wet) and
            earth_texture(gritty)
then
            sandy.
earth_texture(gritty)? why.
if
            sandy
then
            treat_earth('add compost and potash').
earth_texture(gritty)? why.
No more explanation possible
earth_texture(gritty)? yes.
treat_earth('add compost and potash') is proved using rule
if
            sandy
then
            treat_earth('add compost and potash').
sandy is proved using rule
if
            earth_moisture(wet) and
            earth_texture(gritty)
then
            sandy.
earth_moisture(wet) has been learnt
earth_texture(dry) has been learnt

            Treatment=add compost and potash
yes
?-
```

Figure 4.6 Expert system—example of dialogue.

knowledge can be expressed using the same knowledge representation method—by the production rules.

The expert system shell illustrated in this section is based on the approach described by Sterling and Shapiro (1986).

4.4 COMPUTER-AIDED LEARNING USING A MODEL

Taught domains are attractive as computer-aided learning applications if they are expressed in a formal manner, in a way that they can be modelled. This is because, as the formal representation can be reasoned with in a mechanical manner, we can provide the student with useful dialogue which better explains the material being learnt.

In this section we show how grammatical rules in natural language morphology can be represented formally, and how the representation can be used to guide the student in solving particular grammatical problems. The ideas and material presented are drawn from the work of Sylviane Cardey (1990). We will now deal with the example problem in lexical morphology posed at the beginning of the chapter—is the word composed from 'model' and the suffix 'ing' spelt 'modelling' or 'modeling', and if one or the other, why? To solve such problems, we generalize. We require knowledge in the form of grammatical rules that deal in general with the doubling or not of the consonant in English before a final -ed, -ing, -er, -est, -en. Figure 4.7 shows a representation of such rules. The meaning and usage of the material in the diagram will become apparent.

The method for solving such a problem is as follows. Starting at the top or root of the (inverted) *binary decision tree* (Fig. 4.7), if the *condition* is true, the left branch is followed, and if false, the right branch is taken. Eventually a *leaf* is arrived at. At the leaf there is an *operator* that describes whether doubling occurs or not, or whether the special case for words ending in -ic applies. Examples of words with the relevant operation applied are also shown at each leaf. The words are shown with their stressed syllable marked with a preceding ', for example dis'tiller and 'modeling.

The description of the problem area that governs the step-by-step process by which we solve a particular problem is called an *algorithm*. We shall be examining the topic of algorithms in more detail in Chapter 5. The decision tree in Fig. 4.7 therefore represents an algorithm, in this case to solve a particular grammatical problem. However, the linguist who is preparing the grammatical material for a given grammatical problem, needs to specify the algorithm that they have derived in a compact manner which is acceptable to the instructional software that the student will use. Figure 4.8 shows two different but functionally equivalent ways of specifying the algorithm to solve the problem of doubling of the consonant in English before the final -ed, -ing, -er, -est, -en. Alternative representation methods for the input of information can be helpful to the human user (in this case the linguist), just as we have seen is the case for output of information (eg. the sets of illustrations Figs 3.6 and 3.7).

The input information in this case is the algorithm and it is input to the instructional software prior to the student solving grammatical problems. In effect, the algorithm is a computer program in its own right. In the case of the algorithm represented by means of a string of characters (like a sentence), the instructional software, in effect, interprets the algorithm, when solving a student's problem, by traversing the algorithm from left to right. An up arrow ˆ represents *true* and always follows a condition. A down arrow ˇ represents *false* and always follows an operator. The arrows are numbered with integers that identify the application of the condition. By inspection, one can see that the condition tree and the algorithm as a string of characters are functionally equivalent. For example the numbers in the algorithm correspond to the *node* numbers in the condition tree.

By following the algorithm, the instructional software can guide the student through the solution to the original question, constructing the relevant questions to be asked of the student from the applicable condition's text, and responding to the student's answers with either the appropriate next condition text or, eventually, the answer to the original question in the form of the text of the appropriate operator.

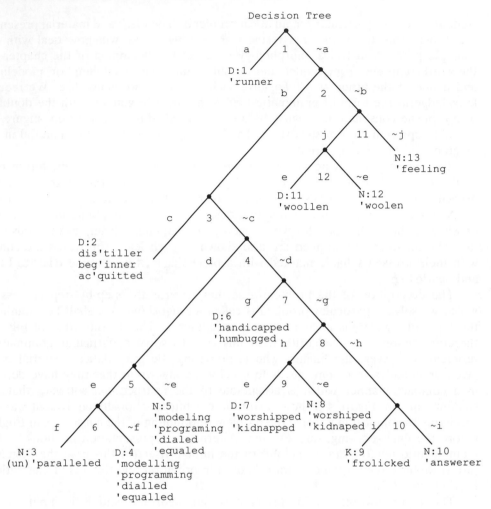

Conditions:
```
a = word of a syllable of form Consonant-Vowel-Consonant
b = word terminated by Consonant-Vowel-Consonant or by
    Consonant-Vowel(pronounced)-Vowel(pronounced)-Consonant
c = last syllable accented
d = word terminated by -l or -m
e = in England
f = the word is "(un)paralleled"
g = the word is "handicap, humbug"
h = the word is "worship, kidnap"
i = the word is terminated with -ic
j = the word is "wool"
```

Operators:
```
D = Doubling of the consonant
N = No doubling of the consonant
K = The words terminated by -ic take -ck
```

Figure 4.7 Lexical morphology example—doubling of the consonant in English before the final -ed, -ing, -er, -est, -en;—decision tree representation.

Algorithm as a string of characters

```
a ^ 1 D. v 1 b ^ 2 c ^ 3 D. v 3 d ^ 4 e ^ 5 f ^ 6 N. v 6 D. v 5 N.
v 4 g ^ 7 D v 7 h ^ 8 e ^ 9 D. v 9 N. v 8 i ^ 10 K. v 10 N.
v 2 j ^ 11 e ^ 12 D. v 12 N. v 11 N.
```

Algorithm as a flow diagram

```
1. a -- D
1. b -- N
   2. c -- D
   2. d -- N
      3. e -- D
         4. f -- N
   2. g -- D
   2. h -- N
      3. e -- D
   2. i -- K
1. j -- N
   2. e -- D
1. N
```

Figure 4.8 Lexical morphology example—algorithm representations.

The notion of one computer program (in this example the instructional software) interpreting another (the grammatical rules for doubling the last consonant) may at first seem strange. It is, in fact, a technique that is very widely used in computing. It enables one to build software systems on the basis that other systems will interpret them, rather than having to build a given system from scratch. It also enables one to have more easily programmable systems in which the programming representation methods are at the user's conceptual level (here the linguist's notion of grammar rules), rather than the computer's own level (usually low and very different).

An example of the instructional program in use follows. The problem concerns whether a word such as 'model', with the ending -ing, is spelt 'modelling' or 'modeling'. The student is presented with a series of menus of potentially applicable conditions. These can be generated from the algorithm. You may wish to compare each of the menus that follow with the decision tree in Fig. 4.7 to see how this can be done. The first menu is that from the 'root' of the decision tree and subsequent ones depend on choices (of conditions) from previous menus.

```
1  a  a word of a syllable of form Consonant-Vowel-Consonant
2  b  a word terminated by Consonant-Vowel-Consonant or by
      Consonant-Vowel(pronounced)-Vowel(pronounced)-
      Consonant
3  j  "wool"
4     others
```

Each applicable condition is identified by its name and its associated text. The student chooses in this instance condition 'b' by selecting menu item '2':

```
? 2.
1  c  last syllable accented
2  d  terminated by -l or -m
3  g  "handicap, humbug"
4  h  "worship, kidnap"
5  i  terminated with -ic
6     others
? 2.
```

If there is just one condition, the instructional program uses a question and answer method rather than a menu:

```
e    Is the word used in England (y/n) ? y.
f    Is the word " (un)paralleled" (y/n) ? n.
```

A leaf has been arrived at, leaf number 4, for which the operator is 'D'—'Doubling of the consonant':

```
Operation to apply:
D:4    Doubling of the consonant—for example:
       'modelling, 'programming, 'dialled, 'equalled
```

The instructional program has kept a trace of the steps by which the problem was solved, and these are now printed:

```
Steps:
˜a, b, ˜c, d, e, ˉf, D:4
```

Under the conditions that the student has stated apply, 'model' with an 'ing' suffix is spelt 'modelling'.

The student is offered the choice of another exercise:

```
Another exercise (y/n) ? y.
  1  a  a word of a syllable of form Consonant-Vowel-Consonant
  2  b  a word terminated by Consonant-Vowel-Consonant or by
        Consonant-Vowel(pronounced)-Vowel(pronounced)-
        Consonant
  3  j  "wool"
  4     others
  ? 2.
  1  c  last syllable accented
  2  d  terminated by -l or -m
  3  g  "handicap, humbug"
  4  h  "worship, kidnap"
  5  i  terminated with -ic
  6     others
  ? 2.
  e  Is the word used in England (y/n) ? n.
```

In this exercise, unlike the previous one, the student has selected 'no' to the 'Is the word used in England' question. A leaf has been arrived at, leaf number 5, for which the operator is 'N'—'No doubling of the consonant':

```
Operation to apply:
N:5      No doubling of the consonant—for example:
         'modeling, 'programing, 'dialed, 'equaled
Steps:
˜a, b, ˜c, d, ˜e, N:5
```

Under the conditions that the student has stated apply, 'model' with an 'ing' suffix is spelt 'modeling' (rather than 'modelling' as determined in the first exercise).

The student not only has two solutions to the problem, but also has been involved, in the same way as the linguist who devised the algorithm, in applying the relevant conditions to the problem word in the correct sequence in order to arrive at the solutions.

PART
THREE

CONSTRUCTING COMPUTER APPLICATIONS

CHAPTER FIVE

PROBLEM SOLVING AND PROGRAMMING

This chapter is concerned with problem solving and then expressing the solution as a computer program.

The problem specification has to be translated, by a programmer, into a program. This requires that the programmer translates the specification into an algorithm, that is, a sequence of steps. The programmer then expresses this sequence of steps as a procedure that the computer will follow, using a programming language. The resulting procedure is the computer program. The translation from specification to program involves 'what' (is specified) being translated into 'how' (the specification is to be realized).

In Chapter 2 we have seen examples, using SQL and Prolog, where the specification of the problem is also the solution. The specification is sufficient for the computer to work out how the specified problem is to be solved. The reason for this is that both SQL and Prolog are based on formal mathematical representations and calculi. The crucial point is that the calculus to solve a problem, specified in one of these representations, can be *separately* programmed from the specification of the problem itself. These separate programs appear as, respectively, the relational database system that accepts SQL queries, and the Prolog system that accepts Horn clauses.

This chapter introduces a different method of problem solving in which the resulting program specifies *how* the computer is to solve the problem. Thus the programmer translates the specification of the problem, expressed in a specification language, to the 'how' form in a programming language. Such programming languages are currently in use for programming the great majority of problems that cannot be solved with the relatively simple and restricted facilities of languages such as SQL.

These programming languages are called *procedural* programming languages because the program represents the step-by-step procedure that the computer follows. In this type of programming language the programmer, a human being, as well as deriving the input and output data structures, has to derive the step-by-step procedure that satisfies the problem specification. Some of the steps may have to be carried out prior to others, the result of one step being needed by a subsequent step. For a given problem, we call the sequence of steps, an *algorithm* (named after Al-Khowârizmî, a Persian mathematician of *circa* 825). The programmer then expresses the algorithm in the form of a program using a suitable programming language. We say suitable because there are many programming languages; some are suitable for particular types of application—for example for business-oriented problems, or for scientifically oriented problems.

Given that there are problems that can be solved by just specifying what they are, you may wonder if there is any need for algorithmic programming. Surely it should be possible to devise a universal algorithm which will solve any problem that can be specified? It can be proved that this is not possible. For a readable account of algorithms, algorithmic solvability and unsolvability see Trakhtenbrot (1963).

5.1 BACKGROUND

In applying computers to a new application we must break the project down into a series of steps, starting with a *requirements study* and finishing with *maintenance*. In Chapter 7 we will examine these steps and the relationships between them in more detail. Our interest at this stage is to assume that we already have the requirements and that we have to devise a computer *program* that will meet the functional aspects of the requirements. By functional we mean the relationship between the data inputs and outputs; we do not include, for example, the choice of processing speed or what input and output devices we require.

In general, a computer will not solve the problem by itself—it needs to be *programmed*. When a computer is purchased for a particular application, for example word-processing, both the *hardware*, and the *software* (comprising computer programs) will be supplied. In this chapter we assume that no such program exists for the problem in question. The problem therefore has to be *specified* and solved by human means, and the solution specified to the computer in the form of a program. The solution should be as *abstract* as possible; the more abstract, the more *general purpose* is the program. A program that sorts a collection of numbers into ascending order is not as useful as one that will *also* sort a collection of character strings into alphabetic order.

The essential idea behind programming is to solve a problem *once* only, and in as abstract a manner as possible. The program that results from an abstract solution can be used as *many* times as is desired by having the computer execute the program with the relevant input data. When the computer executes a program it is mechanically going through the steps of the problem solution prescribed by the programmer. A program is therefore an abstract solution to a problem.

The way we express the solution, in the form of a computer program, is through *language*. Just as we use natural language in human discourse, we employ programming language (but perforce artificial language) to dictate to the computer how it is to operate. Because we require concepts like abstraction and the ability to express complex solutions we need the power of *language*. Language gives us this power because we can devise grammars to ensure we have the required facilities. To this end *programming languages* have been devised. As with natural languages, programming languages have grammars that allow an unlimited number of programs to be devised. However, unlike natural languages, computer programs (the equivalent of natural language sentences in this respect) are *unambiguous* and *precise* in their meaning.

The data processing operations that a computer is capable of are very primitive. For example, it may take several instructions for a computer to move a single character of data between two locations in the computer's memory, to add two numbers in the computer's memory together, or to input a number from outside the computer and place it in a specific location in the computer's memory. The data items operated on are at the level of the primitive built-in types shown in Fig. 2.2. In order to process complex data, such as a payroll or as occurs in a package that allows one to input and edit musical notation, aggregates of data organizations must be built up, from the primitive data objects available (such as numbers and characters). Similarly the processing that we require has to be built up from the very simple primitive operations. The primitive operations are still there in the computer application, as are the simple individual data objects—the point is that they are organized, *structured*, into structures of operations (that define the processing), and structures of data objects (that define the information).

When it comes to being asked to produce a computer program, and our only way of causing the computer to process information is by means of the very simple operations and data objects, what do we do? There are two approaches, top-down (analysis) and bottom-up (synthesis). Applying the top-down approach, we start with the *specification* of the application; this comprises a top-level description of the input and output information, and the process to be applied. Then, by a process of decomposition, we split the specification into sub-specifications, and so on, until we get to the primitive operations and data objects. Rather than produce a design in which we explicitly make concrete all the data and program representations, it is much more sensible to keep these abstract, and have separate designs which have progressively more concrete representations until we get to the primitive data and processing capabilities of the raw computer. The other method, bottom-up, involves building groups of operations and data objects, using these groups to build more sophisticated ones, and so on until (hopefully) we reduce the groups to a single one, representing the application's specification.

The approach we take in this book is the top-down method; indeed this is the preferred method of designing computer applications as these typically commence life as a high level specification with little or no notion of how the system is to be structured in terms of either the information structure, or the processing to be applied. In reality, both methods are usually used for a given application because one wants to reuse existing common software components, where these exist. Some parts of an application may therefore be built of components from a library whilst other parts are programmed down to the primitive operations provided by the programming language.

5.2 PROBLEM SPECIFICATION

Before we look at problem solving and programming we need to be clear as to what the term *problem specification* means.

5.2.1 Informal and formal specifications

In the specification of a problem, we must unambiguously state *what* the problem *is* and this includes what the input and output data are; we do *not* state *how* to solve the problem. Using the notion of input → process → output, some informal examples of specifications are:

- Sort a deck of playing cards into suits and values in suits.

    unsorted deck → sort into suits → sorted deck

- In a given piece of text, produce a concordance on a given word.

    text, word → generate concordance → concordance

- For a point-of-sale unit in, for example, a supermarket, read the bar code on the item of merchandise, and use this code to find the price and description of the item.

    bar code → find price, description → price, description

The last of the above examples, involving a point-of-sale unit, might be part of a larger specification. The larger specification might involve producing the total value payable for all the customer's merchandise. Stock control processing, the adjustment of stock levels and the ordering of stock could also be included by the customer. This larger specification in turn might be related to a stock reordering specification. There may be related specifications—for example to determine stock turnover, 'best-before' date expiry of stock, sales performance of stock lines and so on.

As with data structuring, we use a top-down or analytical approach to developing the specification. Thus in producing a specification for the overall problem we break this down into smaller components which fit together, and by analysis we make the whole specification. Sometimes the smaller components of the specification have inputs and outputs with the real world, in other instances such inputs and outputs are wholly internal to the particular problem's sub-components—as for example in the case of how we might sort a deck of cards into suits. When we perform this breaking down process we find that the elemental components—often called *objects* or *modules*—have *interfaces* with the other objects, just like the interfaces between the system and the real world. In the supermarket example a particular interface may be the way we organize the stock *file* so that the different modules all have the *same* view of the stock file and the stock lines it contains.

5.2.2 Formal specification

Natural language is usually employed for specifying a problem, together with any associated diagrams and tables to assist the specification; for example the layouts for the screens in a car-hire reservation system or the layout of a gas bill. If there is a calculation to be done the specification would include the formulae, and how the calculation relates to the inputs and outputs; for example the amount of gas used, the price tariff applicable to the customer and the resultant price for a unit of gas. However, due to the possibility of ambiguity, natural language for specification of a problem can be unsatisfactory.

In this chapter we will use an informal specification. In Chapter 6 we describe the formal specification language **Z**. We specify there the same example problem, in **Z**, and also provide example programs, derived from the **Z** specification by hand.

5.3 DERIVING DATA STRUCTURES

The programming techniques that have been described so far in the book, SQL and Horn clauses, have been specialized in that their effect is to express the information processing required by means of using, respectively, a particular mathematics and a particular logic. SQL is a computer realization of the relational calculus, and Prolog of the Horn clause subset of the predicate calculus. (A calculus is a particular method of calculation; an SQL system and Prolog represent such methods). The data structures that they respectively process are computer realizations of mathematical and logic structures, respectively, relational tables and Horn clauses.

Procedural programming languages typically do not have semantics which are mathematically and logically simple, such as is the case with declarative programming languages such as SQL (relational programming), Prolog (logic programming) and functional programming languages (introduced in Chapter 6). Rather, procedural languages have evolved an approach to defining data structures and program structures in terms of three basic constructions, *sequence*, *selection* and *iteration*. Whilst these structures are in themselves simple, the semantics of a given program (other than a trivial one) turns out to be complex and thus difficult to validate.

The term 'sequence' used in this program structure context is not to be confused with the mathematical term 'sequence'. We shall see that the same three basic constructions are also used in structuring procedural programs themselves. This association between data structure and procedure structure is of particular importance in computing; such associations between data and procedure are not confined to procedural programming.

The order of items in a sequence is defined by their relative placements. This is to be distinguished from the restriction in relational tables that the order of attribute columns is not significant, and in Horn clauses that the order of arguments in a relation is not significant. That the order of items in a sequence is significant conforms to the notion of procedural programming.

We take as an example a report to be produced for a whist club (Fig. 5.1). The computer representations we are interested in are the data items in the boxes represented in `typewriter font`, for example `Paula` and `2.333`.

Acme Whist Club

Monthly Report February 1992

Member's name	Subscription paid	Points
Paula	y	3
Leslie	y	2
Andrew	n	6
Justine	y	0
Patrick	y	1
Rachel	n	2
Average Points		2.333

Figure 5.1 Example monthly report of a whist club.

It is convenient to use a specific representation method to define structures, which, in holding data, provide information. The method we employ is based on M. A. Jackson's structured programming methodology (Jackson, 1975). As with other representation methods (in computing as well as in other disciplines such as music, geometry and choreography), there are alternative ways of notating a given *canonical* representation. In the case of information structure definitions, both text and diagrammatic presentations are popular. The three elements, *sequence*, *selection*, and *iteration*, of the Jackson Structured Programming (JSP) methodology are shown in text and diagrammatic notation in each of Figs 5.2, 5.3 and 5.4 respectively.

```
a1    seq
      a21;
      a22;
      a23;
a1    end
```

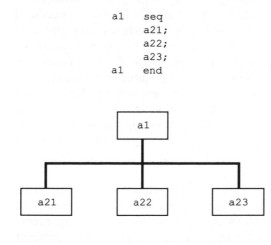

Sequence:

The sequence a1 is a21 followed by a22 followed by a23

Figure 5.2 Sequence notation—JSP based.

```
a1    select
      a21;
      or
      a22;
      or
      a23;
a1    end
```

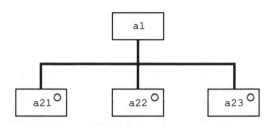

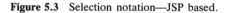

Selection:

The selection a1 is a21 or a22 or a23

Figure 5.3   Selection notation—JSP based.

```
a1    iter
      a21;
a1    end
```

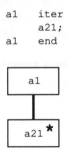

Iteration:

The iteration a1 is a21 repeated zero or more times

Figure 5.4   Iteration notation—JSP based.

Initially we start with the top level, report, as shown in Fig. 5.5.

We now proceed to define report. Notice that our approach is one of *analysis*; we started off with the *abstract* concept of a report. Our first step has been to realize that a concrete report comprises principal areas and we represent this concept accordingly. As we proceed with the analysis, we *refine* our structure definition; we

Figure 5.5 Top level of the whist club report structure.

make it eventually wholly *concrete* as opposed to our initial, wholly abstract definition, in this example just the *identifier* report. Note that it is the eventual structure definition that defines how data items are to be organized that is concrete, *not* a given information structure as this would include actual data items. Analysis of abstract definitions structure in this manner is variously described as *stepwise refinement*, *functional decomposition* and just plain *analysis*. Proceeding with the analysis, each individual principal area on the report should have a name. The areas are evidently the name of the club, the date (month and year) of the report, the members' details and the average points. We ascribe these to a *sequence* as shown in Fig. 5.6.

Consider the identifiers in the sequence report. Each of these is analysed to form its definition. For example a club's name cannot be further decomposed, except into individual characters. Thus club is of a built-in string type. A date is a sequence of a month followed by a year. The month is a character string, whilst a year is four digits; again, data items in these structural positions will be instances of an alphabetic character string built-in type and a digit string built-in type. The date sequence is shown in Fig. 5.7.

We now take the members' details. We have an iteration of the details for each member, as shown in Fig. 5.8. Each member's details has the definition shown in Fig. 5.9, where the member's name is a character string, and the number of points is an integer, another built-in type.

A subscription is either paid or not; this is represented by a selection, Fig. 5.10. The value of paid is therefore true or false. We might represent the state of

```
report   seq
         club;
         date;
         details;
         average;
report   end
```

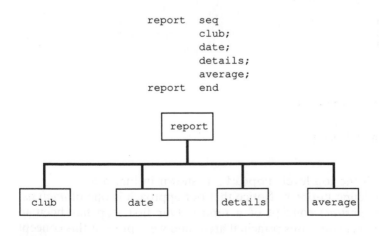

Figure 5.6 Decomposition (i).

```
date    seq
        month;
        year;
date    end
```

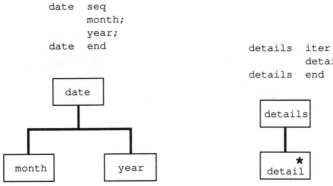

Figure 5.7 Decomposition (ii).

```
details  iter
         detail;
details  end
```

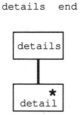

Figure 5.8 Decomposition (iii).

```
detail  seq
        member;
        paid;
        points;
detail  end
```

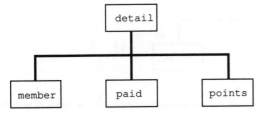

Figure 5.9 Decomposition (iv).

```
paid    select
        yes;
        or
        no;
paid    end
```

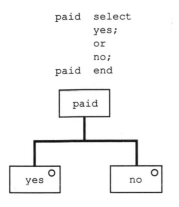

Figure 5.10 Decomposition (v).

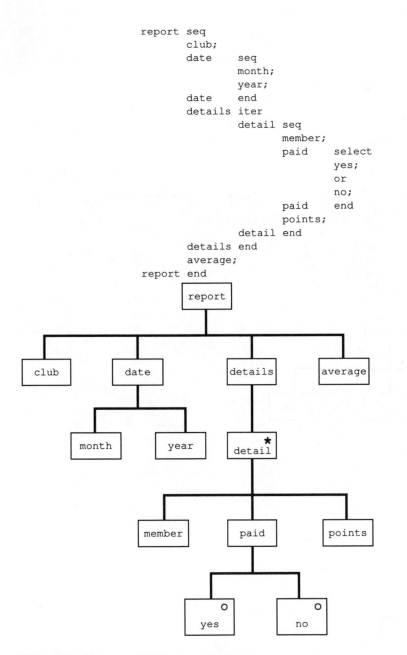

```
report seq
        club;
        date    seq
                month;
                year;
        date    end
        details iter
                detail seq
                        member;
                        paid    select
                                yes;
                                or
                                no;
                        paid    end
                        points;
                detail end
        details end
        average;
report end
```

Figure 5.11 Structure definitions combined.

payment on the report with a y or n. In a programming language we might declare the type of paid as Boolean (see Fig. 2.2).

Structure definitions can be combined as shown in Fig. 5.11. At the lowest level of decomposition we get down to built-in data types that can and must be represented by the computer's internal representation of data, binary representation, as described in Chapter 9. We can exploit types, both hardware supported ones (such as integer) and constructed ones (such as characters that can be either y or n). For example we can use the definitions to validate input data—e.g. attempting to input an alphabetic character into a number. Furthermore we can have the computer system that handles the input to an application do this for us, rather than have to program the validation explicitly. *Introspective* software is a good practice; it increases the degree of abstraction, and it reduces the amount of programming.

In the section that follows we will be using the JSP approach, both for data structure definition, as in this section, and also to develop the structure of an algorithm and thus procedure structure. The algorithm is involved with finding an average, as required in the whist club report (see Fig. 5.1).

5.4 DERIVING AN EXPLICIT PROBLEM-SOLVING ALGORITHM

For our example the *requirement* is for a program to calculate the average of a collection of numbers. At this stage we will use an informal specification; our current interest is to develop the approach to problem solving and then show how the solution is represented by a computer program.

To solve such a problem we use the algorithmic approach; an algorithm is *how* a particular problem is to be solved. An algorithm consists of a *sequence* of steps that solves a problem. Some steps operate on data. Other steps might decide what to do next; such decisions are called *selections*. A given step may be one that must be repeated, an *iteration*. The data may be defined in the problem specification (the input or output information as structured data), or it may be data internal to the algorithm.

An example of the basic procedural programming operations used in implementing algorithms is given in Fig. 5.12. Notice that the three types of operations that are used to construct an algorithm correspond to those used to describe information as data structures. In respect of data operations, the elementary operations are on data items of the built-in types (see Fig. 2.2).

An algorithm is made up of *steps* comprising the operations *sequence*, *selection* and *iteration*, if necessary in a *nested* fashion. A sequence of operations can be grouped together into a single composite operation. As with forming data structures, the human process of producing an algorithm can also be assisted using diagrammatic means; for example by using JSP notation (Figs 5.2, 5.3 and 5.4).

Selection, the ability to make decisions based on data values, is one of the important properties which distinguishes computers from other artifacts.

When an algorithm is to be applied to structured information then it is usually found that the structure of the algorithm matches the structure of the information.

1. *Sequential* operations
   - Data transfer—for example moving a value from one memory location to another.
   - Arithmetic operations—for example add, subtract, multiply, divide.
   - Logical operations—comparisons—for example equal, not equal, greater than.
   - Input or output of data.
   - Whole selection operation.
   - Whole iteration operation.

2. *Selection* operations
   These involve a comparison. If the comparison is true (that is it holds good) then a consequential operation is done. For example:
   'if balance = 0 then warn customer'.

3. *Iterative* operations
   These involve the iteration of one or more other operations. For example:
   'while items still to find on order list, price item, decrement stock level and remove item from order list'.

Figure 5.12 Examples of elementary procedural programming operations.

The example algorithm that is developed is to calculate the average of a collection of numbers. Computer programs should be as general as possible. Thus the algorithm, from which the program is to be derived, should be as general as possible. In the case of an algorithm to find an average, it should handle *any* collection of numbers. This means that neither the values of individual numbers, nor the count of the numbers, is known when devising the algorithm. As in algebra, we use variables to represent unknown quantities. Rather than use variable names like X, Y, and Z we will use *mnemonics* such as *average* and *count*. If we use such mnemonic names as *identifiers* of the corresponding computer memory locations in the program, such as average and count, the program will be easier to understand (when read by a human being). This is important. The programmer may forget the reasoning used in deriving the program. Furthermore, the program may subsequently be checked, maintained or upgraded by someone other than the programmer.

A first draft of the algorithm for the average of a collection of numbers is given in natural language text in Fig. 5.13. If we examine this algorithm in detail we find assumptions are present. For example, how is the count of numbers found? Thus the algorithm requires further refinement. A more refined version is shown in Fig. 5.14; this version *initializes* the *variables* used in the algorithm. We need to break the English statements down into the individual algorithmic operations and the result of doing this is shown in JSP text notation in Fig. 5.15. A JSP diagram version of the algorithm at this stage of refinement is shown in Fig. 5.16. Figures 5.15 and 5.16 each have two corresponding structures, a data structure data and a procedure structure (the algorithm) Average. In documenting designs it can be useful to be

1. While there is a number, get it and add it to the sum of the numbers so far.
2. If the count of numbers is greater than zero divide the sum by the count of numbers to give the average.

Figure 5.13 Algorithm to find the average of a collection of numbers—natural language text.

1. Set the count and sum of numbers to zero.
2. While there is a number, get it and add to the sum of the numbers so far, and increment the count of numbers by one.
3. If the count of numbers is greater than zero, divide the sum by the count of numbers to give the average.

Figure 5.14 Algorithm to find the average of a collection of numbers—refined.

```
data      seq
          sum       integer;
          count     integer;
          numbers   iter

                    number    integer;
          numbers   end
          average   real;
data      end


Average   seq
          init      seq
                    set the sum of numbers to zero;
                    set the count of numbers to zero;
          init      end
          compsum   iter while there is a number
                    input the number;
                    add the number to the sum of the numbers so far;
                    increment the count of numbers by one;
          compsum   end
          gt_zero   select the count of numbers is greater than zero
                    comp_out seq
                    divide the sum by the count to give the average;
                    output average;
                    comp_out end
          gt_zero   end
Average   end
```

Figure 5.15 Data structures and algorithm to find the average of a collection of numbers—JSP text notation.

able to identify uniquely items in the design. An identification method is shown by means of example in the Average structure in Fig. 5.16.

You may wish to compare:

1. The data structure and the procedure structure in Fig. 5.16. You will see that the procedure structure shares aspects of the data structure. This is typical in

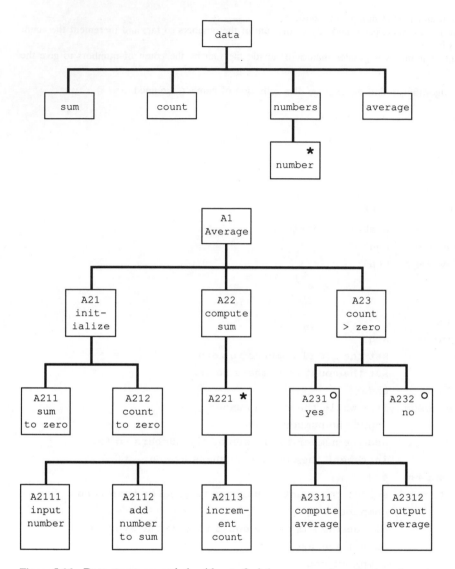

Figure 5.16 Data structures and algorithm to find the average of a collection of numbers—JSP diagram notation.

programming in general; it is not just applicable to procedural programming;
2. The structures in Fig. 5.16 with the previous data structure developed for the report shown in Fig. 5.11.

There are typically many algorithms that will solve a given problem. For example, the count and the sum of the numbers could be calculated separately. Each method has its advantages and disadvantages, usually related to speed and the amount of space in the computer's memory needed to store the data items, and to input and output the relevant data items.

5.5 PROGRAMMING

Programming involves translating the algorithm into a program, 'written' in the relevant computer programming language. This process is performed by a person, a *programmer*. A translation of the algorithm (in Fig. 5.15), to find the average of a collection of numbers, into the functionally *equivalent* program is given in Fig. 5.17. The programming language used is Pascal, named after the French

Pascal Program

```
program Average(input,output);
{ Finds the average of a collection of integer numbers. }
var    sum, count, number : integer;    { declare sum, count, number }
       average: real;                   { declare average }
begin
   sum : = 0;                           { initialize sum of numbers }
   count : = 0;                         { initialize count of numbers }
   writeln('Enternumbers: ');
   while not eof do                     { compute sum }
   begin
      readln(number);                   { input number }
      sum : = sum + number;             { add number to sum }
      count : = count + 1               { increment count }
   end;
   if count > 0 then                    { count > zero? }
      begin                             { yes: }
         average : = sum / count;       {    compute average }
         write('Average = ');
         writeln(average:5:3)           {    output average }
      end
   else writeln('No numbers')           { no: }
end {Average}.
```

Example of program execution:

```
average
Enter numbers:
3
2
6
0
1
2
Average = 2.333
```

Figure 5.17 Program in the programming language Pascal to find the average of a collection of numbers.

mathematician Blaise Pascal. Pascal (Jensen and Wirth, 1985) was devised by Niklaus Wirth in the late 1960s as a programming language for teaching programming.

You may wish to compare the Pascal program in Fig. 5.17 with the final refined version of the algorithm shown in Fig. 5.15. The numbers iteration in Fig. 5.15 is not represented explicitly within the program; rather it is represented by reading from the sequence of data items within the compsum iteration. In some of the later examples of programs for the same problem (in Chapter 6) the numbers iteration is represented using the relevant high level language data structures suited for collections of data.

There are several things to note in Fig. 5.17:

- As with the SQL and Prolog examples in Chapter 2, the language used bears some resemblance to natural language, in this case English. One can use mathematical formulae, albeit in a restricted form. Comments in Pascal are *enclosed* between { and } brackets; e.g.:

```
count : = 0; { initialize count of numbers }
```

The comments correspond to text in Fig. 5.15.

- Only a limited character set and layout is available. For example the formula:

$$average = \frac{sum}{count}$$

is *coded* in Pascal with

```
average : = sum / count;
```

- It is *good programming practice* to use *mnemonics* such as average rather than a; it simplifies the understanding of programs by others.
- Extra information is required over and above a formula—for example:
  - to specify that this is a program—program Average;
  - to declare the *identifiers* of the memory locations in the computer such as sum, count, number and average and how the data in these are to be represented by *specifying* their types integer and real. Variables in formulae are represented in the programming language by the identifiers of the memory locations which will contain the variables' data values;
  - to delineate the part of the program that is *executed*—the begin and end, to act as punctuation—the ';' between *statements* and also the begin and end;
  - to input the numbers for which an average is to be computed and output the average using readln and write statements respectively.
- With just this brief example and the previous Prolog example (Fig. 2.16), it is clear that computer programming is a precise discipline; it is also evident that errors can occur, and in a variety of ways. For example the specification of the program might be faulty—perhaps the program specification should have stated that the program is to calculate the average of just the positive numbers input; or the programmer introduced an error called a *bug* by, say, incorrectly specifying the statement for the formula as:

```
    average : = sum * count;
```

(* is the Pascal symbol for ×, arithmetic multiply.)

- The statements between the begin and the end are executed by the computer in the order in which they appear in the text. This is called *sequence* as previously explained in Section 5.4. Statements themselves are either simple—for example:

```
    readln(number);
```

or compound—for example a block of statements enclosed by a begin and an end makes up a compound statement. The statement beginning with while is an *iteration* statement (repeating the execution of a statement—in this case a compound statement delineated by a begin and an end).

The great majority of computer programming languages work by executing the statements as they appear, one after the other in the sequence in which they actually occur, or as directed by selection or iteration. Such programming languages are called *procedural* (or *imperative*). The reason for introducing this concept of sequencing and designing it into procedural programming languages is twofold. Firstly because the vast majority of computers themselves work in this fashion when they *execute* programs. Secondly, when we produce an *algorithm* to solve a problem, in many cases we express this in terms of sequence, selection and iteration. We shall have more to say on this matter later, particularly in Chapters 6 and 9.

- The layout of the statements in respect of their *indentation* corresponds to the *nested* structure of the program. This layout is usually not mandatory but it does ease both the programmer's job and the job of anyone else who must read the program, for example a quality assurance person or a maintenance person. The layout style may therefore be a mandatory *standard practice*.

For the moment we can say that programs written in programming languages such as Prolog and Pascal may not in fact be executed directly, but are translated (by another program!) to another language, *machine language*, which can be directly *executed* by the computer's hardware. The development of programs that can be executed directly by the computer is discussed in Chapter 8.

CHAPTER SIX

SPECIFICATION AND PROGRAMMING LANGUAGES

In this chapter we introduce the concepts of the specification language and the programming language, and why such artificial languages have been devised. Particular specification and programming languages are introduced, using in many cases the same small example problem (finding the average of a collection of numbers) as an illustration. The languages are compared, in particular as to their method of expression, their ability to support decomposable and reusable designs and programs, and their domain of applicability.

We need at the outset to be clear what we mean by a language, as far as its use in computing is concerned. A language is a method to convey meaning unambiguously, and the meaning must be both *correct* (does not state what we do not want) and *complete* (states everything that we do want). In computing we wish to convey the meaning of our problem to a computer. We do this by expressing our problem in a language, and the actual expression is called a *program*. Because programming languages are not necessarily the best means to initially specify our problem in a straightforward manner, we can do this using a *specification language*. We subsequently translate our specification to a program that expresses the same problem; that is, has the same meaning. With this definition of language in mind we omit in this chapter requirement and design notations which fail to meet the above criteria. This is not to decry their use as an aid in the design step in the software life-cycle, but we must be aware of not placing trust where it cannot reasonably be lodged.

We have already been introduced to the languages SQL, Prolog and Pascal in Chapters 2 and 5. We saw that in the case of SQL and Prolog we could specify a problem directly, provided we could express the problem given the syntax (structural capabilities of the language) and the semantic capabilities provided (what the meaning of the program is when expressed in the language). We also saw that in all three languages, we could use our description, either the specification, or the algorithm (in the case of Pascal) as a program acceptable to a computer. A program *written* in a language such as SQL, Prolog or Pascal cannot be interpreted directly by the computer hardware's Central Processing Unit (CPU), since the CPU is only capable of executing programs in machine language representation. Programs in the form written by the programmer are called *source* programs. In Chapter 8 we will see how a source program is translated to its functionally equivalent machine language form. Programs produced in this manner are called *object* programs (not to be confused with the word 'object' standing for something in its own right). In Chapter 9 we will see how machine language programs are interpreted, i.e. *executed*, by the CPU.

Languages for specification and programming can be characterized in three different ways: by level (high to low), by method of expression (declarative to procedural) and lastly by method of decomposition (object-oriented to fusion):

1. *Level*. High-level languages are specification or programming languages that for the human simplify the production of a solution to a problem. The converse is a low-level language that is near to or is the computer's own language, machine language. An example of a low-level language is assembly language in which the programmer uses symbolic names that correspond one-to-one with machine language structures.

    Figure 6.1 presents examples of the same programming problem expressed in the high-level programming language Pascal, an assembly language and a machine language (these two latter being for a very simple hypothetical computer). The problem involves adding two numbers together that are already in the computer's memory, and storing the result in the computer's memory. In respect of the Pascal high-level language fragment, Pascal has already been introduced (see Fig. 5.17). The assembly language and machine language contents of this figure are repeated and explained at later stages in the text, but for the moment compare the three representations for this same problem. High-level language is 'human friendly' in some area of human discourse (in the example one needs to know basic algebra), whilst machine language is 'machine friendly' in as much as machines—computer hardware—can be feasibly constructed that will interpret programs expressed in such a language. Assembly language attempts to put a human friendly veneer on machine language. Real assembly and machine languages are usually more complex than the hypothetical pair illustrated, and thus appear even more arcane to the non-specialist.

    High-level languages endeavour to combine relevant methods of discourse, with facilities pertinent to some class of problems. Just as natural language enables us to describe problems and their solutions in a structured fashion, high-level languages enable us to express and structure our specifications and programs.

2. *Methods of expression*. When we have a problem we wish to specify or to program, two methods of expression are possible. Either we express a description of *what* the problem is or we express *how* the problem is to be solved. These two different methods of expression have resulted in two different types of language, called respectively *declarative* for the 'what' approach, and *procedural* (also called *imperative*) for the 'how' approach.

High-level Language (Pascal) program fragment:

```
var x, y, z : integer; { define data representation }

begin
                .
                .
        z : = x + y;
                .
                .
end.
```

Assembly language program fragment:

```
x           integer
y           integer
z           integer
                .
                .
        load    x
        add     y
        store   z
```

Machine language program fragment, shown in binary form, as it appears in the hypothetical computer's memory:

```
address         contents

. . 0 0 1 0     . . . . . . . . . .
. . 0 0 1 1     . . . . . . . . . .
. . 0 1 0 0     . . . . . . . . . .
. . . . . .     . . . . . . . . . .
. . . . . .     . . . . . . . . . .
. . . . . .     . . . . . . . . . .
. . 1 0 0 1     0 0 0 1 . . 0 0 1 0
. . 1 0 1 0     0 1 0 0 . . 0 0 1 1
. . 1 0 1 1     0 0 1 0 . . 0 1 0 0
```

Figure 6.1 Program fragment in a high-level, assembly and machine language.

In Chapter 5 the concept of the algorithm was explained in terms of a sequence of steps. A computer's machine language program is interpreted by the computer's hardware. The program is a sequence of steps, each step being an instruction. Procedural languages have, in part, developed from the notion of providing a more 'programmer friendly' method of writing algorithms that, once translated to machine language, can be interpreted directly by the computer. Indeed, the first high-level programming language devised so as to easily represent algorithms, Algol60 (algorithmic language 1960), had the two aims of being both a language to describe algorithms as well as a programming language. Algol60 is an 'ancestor' of the languages Pascal, C, Ada and C++ (the latter three to be described).

3. *Methods of Decomposition.* When we have a problem we wish to program, there are two extremes to the methods of decomposition. One extreme, *object-oriented*, condones the approach, and the other, *fusion*, assumes that the problem solution is a composite one-off. Most specification and programming languages provide some object or module structuring facilities which support and track the decomposition process, but these vary in the ease they provide for software reuse.

    Most languages support some form of modularization in which one can have self-contained program items that can be used by other parts of the program. These items can usually be placed in a software library. There is a plethora of terminology in use for this concept whose meanings somewhat overlap between the different languages; for example procedure, function, subroutine, sub-program. . . . The term *procedure* is the one we will adopt to cover the minimum modular unit that a language provides. (Do not confuse a procedure with procedural programming.) We have already seen procedures in Prolog; for example the procedure has_ancestor/2 in Fig. 2.16.

    At a coarser level of object, the more recent programming languages provide *abstract types* which normally can contain procedures. In an abstract type one can define data structures and sometimes the operations on these by means of procedures without having to define the data in terms of built-in types. One separately associates the abstract types with further refined abstract types or concrete types—ones that are built from built-in types. The notion of the abstract type is expanded in the section on the **Z** specification language. Such abstract types in the Ada programming language are called *packages*, and in C++ they are called *classes*.

    At a finer level, languages vary in the provision of structuring facilities. Procedural languages normally separate the statements that deal with data structuring from the specification of the procedural statements. *Block structured languages* are procedural languages that directly support, by means of language constructs, the sequence, selection and iteration of at least the procedural statements, and in the newer languages also data structuring statements. Algol60 was the progenitor of block structured languages such as Pascal, Ada, C and C++.

These three ways in which to characterize languages are orthogonal; the languages which are described in this book are compared in a qualitative fashion in Fig. 6.2.

In the sections that follow, we will describe some example programming languages. We choose as our major division the method of expression. Some programming languages have been devised to suit particular application areas, for example commercial or scientific/engineering. We choose to divide the procedural languages according to their particular application area.

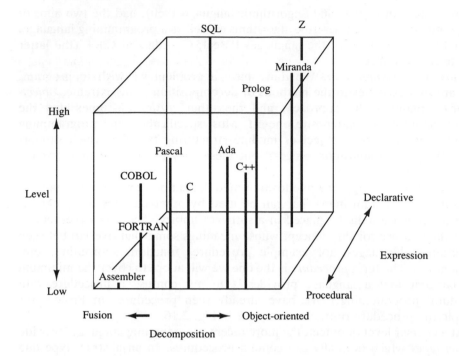

Figure 6.2 Languages qualitatively compared—level, method of expression and method of decomposition.

6.1 DECLARATIVE LANGUAGES

For many types of problem, where the sequencing of steps does not matter, the specification or programming can be expressed by describing *what* the problem is, rather than *how* to solve it. Languages with this method of expression are typically known as *declarative* languages.

In this section we describe a specification language, and then three programming languages. All four languages are well founded in branches of mathematics which are conducive to problem specification, and the programming languages are in branches of mathematics that provide general problem solving methods. For example, a study of logic covers not only specifying logical relationships, it also deals with proof processes.

For a programming language, as distinct from a purely specification language, clearly the *how* has still to be done, but this is done by the computer. The principle is as follows. If a problem can be specified in some formal framework, for example *logic*, and a calculus exists which, given the specification, can determine a solution (for example the proof procedures used by logicians), then it should be possible to devise a software system in which the calculus is embedded. This software system, given a problem expressed in the language of the formal framework, for example a problem that can be expressed in logic, can then solve the problem. Declarative programming systems have significant advantages in that:

1. The specification of the problem *is* the program.
2. There is no requirement to impart sequence to the statements that make up the program.
3. The actual solution chosen by the software system can be an *optimal* one in terms of the time taken by the computer. An example of this is given in the section on SQL below.
4. Some computer hardware systems have more than one processing unit (CPU). The implementation of a declarative language program by the computer's program development and execution systems can take advantage of multiple processing units by splitting up the processing so that it can be done in parallel. On the other hand, in a procedural language, the programmer may have to explicitly program the use of multiple processing units, though there do exist 'parallel' versions of procedural languages that provide some inbuilt support for multiple processing units. In other words, the ability to take advantage of processing done in parallel is implicit in declarative languages, whilst it is often explicit in procedural languages.
5. There are some features that obtain in procedural languages (to varying degrees) that are not present in declarative languages. The reason for this is that procedural languages are essentially 'friendly' ways of programming in machine language. This means that CPU and memory hardware characteristics must be managed by the programmer. In the case of declarative languages, these characteristics are managed on behalf of the programmer by the declarative programming system. The features of procedural languages that are *not* present, as far as the programmer is concerned, in declarative languages are as follows:

   - *Pointers*. A pointer is a value that is the address of a location in the computer's memory. (Pointers were introduced in the discussion on structured types in Section 2.3.4.)
   - *Explicit memory management* (the obtaining and relinquishing of areas of memory) over and above the implicit memory management facilities provided by the procedural language (normally implemented by means of a stack).

However declarative systems do have their disadvantages:

1. The domain of problems that can be specified is constrained by the representation method. For example one cannot express self-referencing, i.e. *recursive*, relations like has_ancestor (in Fig. 2.16) in a relational language like SQL.
2. The time taken and the amount of memory required by the system can be significantly more than a procedural program that has the same functionality. The reasons for this are that the programmer employing a procedural language can make decisions during the design of program, whilst in a declarative programming language system, such decisions are usually made during the execution of the program.

In this section we are interested in declarative languages that are 'close' to mathematics in that we can express our problems using a mathematically sound basis, and for the programming languages, the programs model the mathematical manipulations in a 'mechanical' fashion. By mathematics, it must be understood we do not mean just arithmetic! In this respect all the languages are high-level. The specification of (low-level) machine languages, and their programs, can be expressed mathematically, but not in a manner close to an established area of mathematics that can also be used for general problem solving in mathematics. On the other hand, each of the declarative languages described models a well understood approach to problem solving in mathematics. We describe four models of declarative language. The names of these correspond to the area of mathematics that the particular languages serve to express. The models and the particular languages that are used as examples are:

- *Formal specification languages*; for example **Z**, a specification-only language (not a programming language).
- *Relational programming languages*; for example the database programming language SQL.
- *Logic programming languages*; for example the logic programming language Prolog.
- *Functional programming languages*; for example the functional programming language Miranda.

6.1.1 Z—a formal specification language

Z is a language for specifying the function of a computer program; that is stating the relationship between the input data and the output data. The processing that occurs when the program is executed should conform to this specification. **Z** is a *formal* specification language because it is based on a formal system of mathematics, which is based on logic and set theory. **Z** has its own notation, and this was developed at Oxford University's Programming Research Group in the late 1970s and early 1980s by Jean-Raymond Abrial, Bernard Sufrin and Ib Sørensen. A good book on **Z** is Diller (1990).

    Z is a specification language; it is not a programming language. This does not mean that **Z** or other formal specification languages (that are not programming languages) are not useful. A program that does not conform to its specification is incorrect. It is essential therefore that we have sound methods to specify programs in the first place. Because **Z** is not a programming language, there is the requirement to translate a **Z** specification to a program, in a programming language. Some of the programming examples used in this book are (hand) translations of the example **Z** specification which follows.

    For an example **Z** specification, the specification of the average of a collection of numbers is now developed. The average of a collection of numbers is the sum of the numbers divided by the number of numbers. For example the average of 3, 2, 6, 0, 1, 2 using normal mathematical notation, is:

$$\frac{3 + 2 + 6 + 0 + 1 + 2}{6}$$

```
  ┌─ Average ──────────────────────────
  │  numbers? : collectionN
  │  average! : R
  ├─────────────────
  │  numbers? ≠ {}
  │  average! = sum(numbers?)/kount(numbers?)
  │  average! ≥ 0
  └────────────────────────────────────
```

Figure 6.3 **Z** specification of the average of a collection of numbers.

A **Z** specification of the average of a collection of numbers is shown in the *schema box* in Fig. 6.3. Above the central (short) horizontal line appears a number of *declarations*. Below the central line appears a number of *predicates* all of which must be true (they are implicitly linked with the logical 'and' (conjunction) operator $\wedge$).

Declarations describe the types of identifiers such as *average!*; that is, of which set the identifier is a member. N is the type of all non-negative natural numbers (positive whole numbers), and R is the type of all real numbers. Thus *numbers?* is a *collection* of natural numbers and *average!* is a real number. Identifiers that are input have a final ?, and output a final !.

Predicates describe further constraints on the values in the data structures. Thus for example the collection of numbers must exist (not be the empty set {}), the average must be the sum of the numbers divided by the count of the numbers, and the average must be greater than or equal to zero.

Figure 6.3 is a mathematical definition, employing the **Z** notation, that specifies what is meant by the average of a collection of numbers. The specification neither states how the average is to be calculated, nor does it state in concrete data type terms how the collection of numbers is to be represented. Instead, it just states the names of the types of input data, the types of output data, and the functional relationships between input data and output data values. A program that is written to calculate the average of a collection of non-negative natural numbers, by processing as input data the collection and providing as output data the value of the average, must conform to this specification.

Figure 6.3 leaves several symbols undefined, for example *collection*, *sum*, {}, /, and *kount*. **Z** itself has a set of predefined symbols. These predefined symbols, for example {} and /, are themselves eventually defined at the level of basic mathematical logic and set theory. *collection*, *sum* and *kount* are not predefined **Z** symbols; **Z** specifications of these symbols are presented shortly. In Fig. 6.3 *kount* is used (rather than *count*) as *count* is actually a predefined function in **Z** and the functionality of *count* is not what we want in this specification.

Figure 6.3 is itself independent of the specifications of *collection*, *sum* and *kount*. This illustrates the concept of *abstraction*. At the top-level specification, one is not concerned with how data is represented (for example a *collection*) or how values, such as *sum* and *kount* are to be computed. The **Z** specification is an abstract type specification. Thus the **Z** specification is general purpose; we can use it in a 'reusable' fashion. Indeed, we will show more than one set of specifications for *collection*, *sum* and *kount*.

Suppose the collection of numbers for which an average is required is:

3,2,6,0,1,2

Note that 2 occurs more than once. Representing the collection of numbers as a mathematical set of numbers:

{3,2,6,0,1}

is not possible as the members of a set are unique. Thus we must employ some other method.

To illustrate the concept of decomposition from the abstract to the concrete, we are going to use two distinct methods to represent a collection. Later in this chapter we will give implementations in various programming languages of one or other of the concrete techniques. In the case of the 'object-oriented' programming language C++ the examples illustrate both techniques. There are other techniques that might be devised to represent a collection—a *stack* is used in the Ada programming language example.

The first method used is to represent the collection as a set sequence; see the **Z** specification in Fig. 6.4 in which seq is a predefined **Z** symbol. A *sequence* in mathematical set theory has similarity to a sequence in structured data design and structured programming, but it has a particular mathematical formulation. For this reason the term 'set sequence' will be used for a mathematical sequence in this book. A set sequence is a set of ordered pairs in which the first component is the position of the data value and the second component is the value. Because the first value in each pair is unique (the position of the data value in the sequence), using a set sequence enables us to have collections of numbers in which a given value occurs more than once (such as 2). So, expressed as a set sequence, the collection of numbers is the set:

$\{1 \mapsto 3,2 \mapsto 2,3 \mapsto 6,4 \mapsto 0,5 \mapsto 1,6 \mapsto 2\}$

which is clearer than writing the set as:

{(1,3),(2,2),(3,6),(4,0),(5,1),(6,2)}

Figure 6.4 can be paraphrased as follows:

• *collection*

In the specifications, where *collection* appears, replace it with seq.

• *sum*

Above the horizontal line: *sum* is a function with domain a set sequence of natural numbers and range a natural number.

$collection == seq$

$$sum : seq\ N \rightarrow N$$

$\forall i, j : N;\ rest : seq\ N \bullet$
$\qquad sum\{\} = 0 \wedge$
$\qquad sum(\{i \mapsto j\} \cup rest) = j + sum\ rest$

$kount : seq\ N \rightarrow N$

$kount = \#collection$

Figure 6.4 **Z** specification of collection as a set sequence, and of the sum of a set sequence of natural numbers.

> *Below the horizontal line*: for any i and j that are natural numbers: *rest* is a set sequence of natural numbers; it is true that the sum of the empty set sequence is zero; and the sum of any member of the set sequence united with the rest of the set sequence is the member's value component added to the sum of the rest of the set sequence.

- *kount*

  > *Above the horizontal line*: *kount* is a function with domain a set sequence of natural numbers and range a natural number.
  > *Below the horizontal line*: *kount* is the cardinality (number of members) in the set *collection*.

The specification of *average* in Fig. 6.3 requires that the collection of numbers is not an empty collection; this is ensured by the predicate:

$$numbers? \neq \{\}$$

However, in Fig. 6.4 both the functions *sum* and *kount* will handle empty sequences. In the uses of *sum* and *kount* in *average* neither of these uses can occur, because of the above predicate. There is a trade-off between generality (for example the specifications *sum* and/or *kount* might appear in a software library) and specificity.

The second representation of the collection is illustrated by a *bag*; see the **Z** specification in Fig. 6.5. The example collection of numbers:

$$3,2,6,0,1,2$$

is expressed in **Z** notation as the bag:

$$[\![3,2,6,0,1,2]\!]$$

collection == bag

---

sum : bag $N \to N$

$\forall i, j : N;\ L:$ bag $N\ \bullet$
$\quad sum[\![]\!] = 0\ \land$
$\quad sum(\{i \mapsto j\} \cup L) = i * j + sum\ L$

$kount$: bag $N \to N$

$\forall i, j : N;\ L :$ bag $N\ \bullet$
$\quad kount[\![]\!] = 0\ \land$

$\quad kount(\{i \mapsto j\} \cup L) = j + sum\ L$

Figure 6.5 **Z** specification of collection as a bag, and of the sum of a bag of numbers.

A bag is a set of ordered pairs in which the first component is a value and the second the number of times it occurs. Because the first value in each pair is unique (the value of one or more instances of data), using a bag enables us to have collections of numbers in which a given value occurs more than once. So the bag is in fact the set:

$$\{3 \mapsto 1, 2 \mapsto 2, 6 \mapsto 1, 0 \mapsto 1, 1 \mapsto 1\}$$

which, again, is clearer than writing the set as:

$$\{(3,1),(2,2),(6,1),(0,1),(1,1)\}$$

Compare a bag with a set sequence. Notice that it is the first value in the pairs that is unique in both these mathematical structures. In fact both a set sequence and a bag are mathematical functions, which map the first value to the second for any pair in their respective sets.

6.1.2 SQL—a relational programming language

Structured Query Language (SQL) is used to solve queries against the relations in relational databases. SQL was introduced, with examples, in Chapter 2. Figure 6.6 illustrates the problem of finding the average of a collection of numbers by finding the average of the members' points in the table MEMBERSHIP (see Fig. 2.3). The query uses the aggregate function AVG.

We now turn to programming aspects of SQL. Being declarative, an SQL query specifies only what is required, not how to carry out the query. Both the SQL

```
SELECT AVG (POINTS)
  FROM MEMBERSHIP
```

Figure 6.6 Program in the high-level language SQL to calculate the average of a collection of numbers.

programmer and the SQL computer system can take advantage of the declarative aspect.

Firstly consider the SQL programmer. For example compare the query that appears in Fig. 2.12 and is reproduced here:

```
SELECT      ATTENDS.STUDENT, TEACHES.LECTURER,
            ATTENDS.COURSE
FROM        REGISTERS, ATTENDS, TEACHES
WHERE       ATTENDS.COURSE = TEACHES.COURSE
AND         REGISTERS.FACULTY = 'Arts'
AND         TEACHES.LECTURER = 'A.N. Other'
AND         REGISTERS.YEAR = 3;
```

with another query, say:

```
SELECT      TEACHES.LECTURER, ATTENDS.STUDENT,
            ATTENDS.COURSE
FROM        ATTENDS, TEACHES, REGISTERS
WHERE       REGISTERS.YEAR = 3
AND         ATTENDS.COURSE = TEACHES.COURSE
AND         ATTENDS.FACULTY = 'Arts'
AND         TEACHES.LECTURER = 'A.N. Other'; .
```

These two queries have exactly the same meaning. Notice that the order of the SQL items for SELECT, FROM and WHERE have no effect on the meaning. Thus the SQL programmer need not be concerned with ordering choices within a SELECT query.

But now consider the SQL database management system. If the SQL system executes the SELECT query as a sentence of procedures, one step after another, then very different elapsed processing times could occur for each of the above two queries. The reason is that the processing time is dependent on the actual numbers of tuples in the tables named in the FROM, and the values of attributes named in the WHERE and AND.

Advantage is sometimes taken by computer systems that implement declarative languages in that the software system can try to construct an optimal procedure to form the solution in terms of the projected time taken to produce a result. In the case of an SQL system, the system can maintain a count of the number of tuples in each table, and use these counts in determining a query strategy.

6.1.3 Prolog—a logic programming language

Prolog is a high level language that enables problems to be specified in Horn clause logic. It has already been introduced in Chapter 2 (see Figs 2.16 and 2.17). Horn clause logic is based on a branch of mathematical logic called predicate logic. Prolog typically has an associated programming and program execution system. The execution of Prolog programs is based on a branch of mathematical logic called predicate calculus. A Prolog system is a software system that enables the development and execution of Prolog programs.

Prolog is used for example in knowledge processing applications (cf. information processing) where the manipulation of symbols and the need to express knowledge in a transparent, declarative manner is required. The knowledge based application examples illustrated in Chapter 4 are all implemented in Prolog.

A Prolog program can be interpreted by the declarative method or the procedural method. The declarative method corresponds to treating the program as a set of logical expressions, Horn clauses, whilst the procedural method corresponds to executing the program as a sequence of procedure calls. That Prolog is executed in a procedural manner can lead to difficulties for the unwary programmer.

A declaratively correct Prolog program may not terminate when interpreted procedurally. We use an example drawn from Fig. 2.16. If the clause:

```
has_ancestor(Person,Ancestor) :-
    has_parent(Person,Parent),
    has_ancestor(Parent,Ancestor).
```

is reformulated as:

```
has_ancestor(Person,Ancestor) :-
    has_ancestor(Parent,Ancestor),
    has_parent(Person,Parent).
```

this second clause is logically identical to the first clause. However, as executed by a Prolog system, a query such as:

```
?- has_ancestor(fred,bill).
```

instead of failing (Prolog replying no) according to the closed-world assumption, will instead not terminate. Procedurally, having exhausted the facts has_parent/2 called by the first has_ancestor/2 clause in Fig. 2.16, the second has_ancestor/2 clause (above) is called. This calls has_ancestor(Parent, bill) and the cycle repeats itself. In practice, in such instances the Prolog system may terminate eventually but with an error condition.

Prolog is an example of a *symbolic* programming language, as distinct from a numerical one, although one can do numerical work in Prolog. Numerical programs in Prolog, however, are typically outside pure logic, and they employ non-logical features. As a result, such programs are generally not declarative.

An example of a numeric application in Prolog using non-logical arithmetic features is shown in Fig. 6.7. Compare Fig. 6.7 with the **Z** specifications in Figs 6.3 and 6.4. In Prolog one can model a mathematical sequence with a Prolog list data structure. Furthermore, the procedure average/2, like the schema *average* in Fig. 6.3, is abstract in respect of the collection. As far as average/2 is concerned, average/2 does not state how the collection of numbers is to be implemented; the collection could be implemented by methods other than a list.

Neither the procedure average/2 nor sum/2 is declarative. For example, average/2 requires both Sum and Count (by sum/2 and count/2) to have been

```
/*
average (+Numbers, -Average) :-
        Average is the average of the collection of natural numbers Numbers.
*/
average (Numbers, Average) :-
        not_empty (Numbers),              /* Numbers not the empty        *
        collection.
        sum (Numbers, Sum),
        count (Numbers, Count),
        Average is Sum/Count.


/*
not_empty (L) :-
        L is not the empty list [].
*/
not_empty ([_|_]).


/*
sum (+L, -Sum) :-
        Sum is the sum of the list of natural numbers L.
*/
sum ([], 0).
sum ([J|L], Sum) :-
        J >= 0,                           /* J is a natural number        *
        sum (L, Sum_L),
        Sum is J + Sum_L.


/*
count (L, Count) :-
        Count is the number of members in the list L.
*/
count ([], 0).
count ([_|L], Count) :-
        count (L, Count_L),
        Count is Count_L + 1.


        Example of program execution, ? -is the prompt:

?- average ([3, 2, 6, 0, 1, 2], Average).
        Average=2.33333
```

Figure 6.7 Program in the high-level language Prolog to calculate the average of a collection of numbers.

evaluated before Average (by is/2, a built-in). The programmer must therefore firstly be aware of the procedural method of interpreting Prolog, and then order the items in the program with care. Furthermore, the argument Numbers is input to, and the argument Average is output from, average/2 (hence the significance of the + and − in the comments, cf. ? and ! in **Z**). A declarative procedure is impervious to whether its argument values are input or output.

6.1.4 Miranda—a functional programming language

Miranda is a high-level programming language that enables programs to be specified as mathematical functions. The Miranda system is a software system that enables the development and execution of Miranda programs. The language and the system are by Turner (1986).

An example of a Miranda program and its execution is shown in Fig. 6.8. In a functional programming language we can imagine that a function call in the program text is replaced, temporarily, by the value returned by the function.

Compare Fig. 6.8 with the **Z** specifications in Figs 6.3 and 6.4. In Fig. 6.8, sum' is used, as Miranda itself provides a built-in function sum. Comments in Miranda are the rest of lines after and including a ||. In Miranda one can model a mathematical sequence with a Miranda list data structure. In particular note that the concrete representation used for the collection of numbers is the Miranda list. Furthermore, the function average, like the schema *Average* in Fig. 6.3, is abstract in respect of the collection.

Miranda Program

```
|| average applied to a collection of numbers returns their average

average numbers = sum numbers / count numbers, not_empty numbers

|| not_empty applied to a non empty list is true
not_empty list = (list ~= [])

|| sum applied to a list of natural numbers returns the sum of these
sum' [] = 0
sum' (j: list) = j + sum' list, j >= 0

|| count applied to a list is the number of members in the list
count [] = 0
count (i: list) = 1 + count list
```

Example of program execution, Miranda is the prompt:

```
Miranda average [3, 2, 6, 0, 1, 2]
2.333333
```

Figure 6.8 Program in the high-level language Miranda to calculate the average of a collection of numbers.

6.2 PROCEDURAL LANGUAGES

Traditionally, programming languages have been of the method of expression in which the program describes *how* a problem is to be solved, that is, the program has been procedural. In this respect, such 'how' or procedural languages mirror in principle how the computer's central processing unit executes machine language programs.

Historically, three approaches have been devised for procedural programming. Chronologically, these have been machine language, assembly language and the high-level language. In this section, we first discuss the concept of high-level procedural language, then describe some commonly used high-level procedural programming languages, and finish with a description of assembly and machine languages.

6.2.1 High-level procedural programming languages

In a high-level procedural language, life is made easier for the programmer by making it possible to represent algorithms directly, rather than having to translate them into assembly language (or, much more tedious, machine language). High-level procedural programming languages supply a rich syntax and facilities such as powerful data and procedure structuring capabilities.

In high-level procedural languages, algorithms are executed in the order of the steps, as they appear in the procedure, even though the algorithm may not require that particular sequence of steps. For example in the following Pascal program fragment, representing a part of a larger algorithm, it does not matter if the circumference is calculated before the area is calculated, or afterwards, or (if there is more than one hardware processing unit) at the same time (in parallel).

```
    .
    .
    circumference : = 2 * pi * radius;
    area : = pi * radius * radius;
    .
    .
    .
```

Procedural languages thus define the order of execution at the time the program is written.

The method of classification we adopt is *area of application*. The areas of application used here are somewhat coarse and counter examples might be given. For example commercial users of computers may use sophisticated statistical programs written in a scientific programming language.

6.2.2 Pascal—a programming language for teaching programming

Pascal was introduced in Chapter 5. The program example developed there (Fig. 5.17) is extended in Fig. 6.9, together with an example of its execution in Fig. 6.10,

Pascal Program

```pascal
program AverageExtended(input,output);
        { Finds the average of a collection of integer numbers. }
        { Illustrates type definitions; structured data - Pascal records, and
          arrays;  procedure and functions declaration and use. }
  const  maxnumbers = 20;
  type   collectionmaxnumbers = 1..maxnumbers; { declare array bounds as
         type }
         collection =
           record                                { declare collection as type }
             seq : array [collectionmaxnumbers] of integer;
                                                 { sequence of numbers }
               count: integer;                   { count of integers }
               maxnumbers : integer              { size of array }
             end;
  var    numbers : collection;                   { declare instance of
                                                   collection }

         average : real;                         { declare average }

procedure readcollection(var instance : collection);
{ procedure reads integer numbers into collection instance }
  var    number : integer; { declare number to hold each number in turn }
begin
  instance.count :=0; { initialise count }
    writeln('Enter numbers:');
  while not eof do { eof is 'end of file' - end of inputted numbers }
  begin
    instance.count := instance.count + 1;
    readln(number); { input a number on a line by itself }
    if instance.count <= instance.maxnumbers then
      instance.seq[instance.count] := number;
  end;
end {readcollection};


function sum(instance : collection): integer;
{ function returns the sum of the numbers in collection instance }
  var    accumulator, i: integer;
begin
  with instance do
  begin
    accumulator :=0; { initialise eventual value of sum }
    for i := 1 to count do { iterate through the array }
    begin
      accumulator :=seq[i] + accumulator;
    end;
    sum := accumulator;
  end
end; {sum}; { return value of sum }
```

Figure 6.9 Program in the programming language Pascal to find the average of a collection of numbers; extended to illustrate high-level language features.

```
begin
  numbers;maxnumbers := maxnumbers; { Store the size of the array in the numbers
                                      record }
    readcollection(numbers); { call procedure to read the collection of numbers }
    if numbers.count > 0 then
      if numbers.count <= maxnumbers then
        begin
          average := sum(numbers) / numbers.count; { compute average }
          write('Average=');
          writeln(average:5:3)                { output average }
        end
      else
        writeln('Too many numbers')
    else  writeln('No numbers')
end {AverageExtended}.
```

Figure 6.9 (continued)

The program execution:

```
averageextended
Enter numbers:
3
2
6
0
1
2
Average = 2.333
```

Figure 6.10 Example execution of the extended Pascal program.

to illustrate the programming concepts: type, structured data, procedure and function. These concepts are shared by other procedural programming languages such as Ada, C, and C++.

The reasons for these programming concepts are that they each variously contribute to:

- Reusability of program components.
- Preservation of the design structure in the program structure.
- Enriched syntax, providing detection and location of some types of programming error by syntax analysis, which occurs in any case at program translation time (to machine language).

We now analyse each of these concepts.

Type Pascal permits the definition of user defined types. Such a type must be in terms of already defined user types or built-in types. Figure 6.9 shows `collectionmaxnumbers` and `collection` as examples of user defined types, whilst `integer` and `real` are built-in types (see Fig. 2.2). The variable `numbers` (declared with the statement starting with `var`) is the symbolic name for the memory locations that can hold the collection of actual numbers and their count. We say that `numbers` is an *instance* of type `collection`.

Structured data—record and array Where we want to group data items together we can use named data structures. If the items are of different type we can use a record (see Sec. 2.3.7); `collection` is a record type:

```
collection =
    record                    { declare collection as type }
        seq : array [collectionmaxnumbers] of integer;
                                  { sequence of numbers }
        count : integer;              { count of integers }
        maxnumbers : integer            { size of array }
    end;
```

Such a record type is analogous to a sequence (in the sense of the trio sequence, selection and iteration).

   `numbers` is an instance of type `collection`. Within `numbers` there will be an instance of another sort of structure, an array (Sec. 2.3.6), here called `seq`. `seq` is so named because it can be used to model a mathematical set sequence (cf. `seq` in **Z**, Fig. 6.4). An array comprises one or more instances of the *same* type of data, each associated with a particular location in the array. In the example, those array locations starting at the beginning of the array will, on completion of input of the numbers, contain the values for which an average is to be computed (Fig. 6.11). The remaining array locations contain *undefined* data values, shown pictorially as '. . .'. One can access an array by *indexing* (also known as *subscripting*) it; that is by referring to the relevant location in the array by its ordinal position (for arrays numbered from one to the maximum number of numbers in this example). In the statement:

```
accumulator : = seq[i] + accumulator;
```

the `i`th location in the array `seq` is being accessed.

   An array is analogous to an iteration (in the sense of the trio sequence, selection and iteration). High-level languages such as Pascal usually also provide selection of data; in Pascal this is provided by the *variant record* facility.

   Usage of an array usually needs other data to manage the array. This is the reason for the need for `count` and `maxnumbers`, and why it makes sense to group them with the array `seq` in the record of type `collection`.

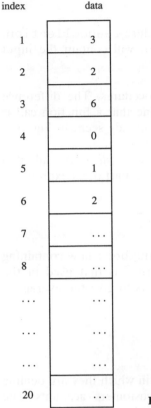

index	data
1	3
2	2
3	6
4	0
5	1
6	2
7	...
8	...
...	...
...	...
...	...
20	...

Figure 6.11 Example of an array containing inputted data values.

Arrays being effectively data iterations, procedural iterations are often used in programs that deal with arrays. The example contains two such procedural iterations for which high level languages usually provide statements. The program uses, as well as the Pascal while statement (seen before in Fig. 5.17), the for statement. The for statement causes the repetition of a sequence of program statements, providing a variable (often called the *control* variable) that steps through a range of values. As in the example, the control variable is often used as an array index (the integer i).

Procedures When a piece of program might be reused in the same or a different program, then the concept of a procedure is used. We have already seen their use in Prolog; for example has_parent/2, has_ancestor/2 and has_descendant/2 in Fig. 2.16. In this example the procedure readcollection reads the numbers into the collection instance from the external world, and also stores in the collection the count of numbers.

Procedures are executed when they are *called*; in the example this happens with the statement:

```
readcollection(numbers);
```

numbers is an argument (cf. Prolog) passed to the procedure readcollection. When readcollection *returns* from the call, numbers will contain the input data from the external world and the count.

Functions Functions are used for the same reason as procedures. The difference between a function and a procedure is that we can imagine that a function call is replaced by the value returned by the function. We have already seen, in Fig. 6.8, functions in the functional programming language Miranda.

Functions, like procedures, are executed when they are *called*. A call of a procedure stands on its own, but a function call occurs as or as part of an expression. When the statement:

```
average := sum(numbers) / numbers.count;
```

is executed, the function sum is called with the argument numbers now containing the input data from the external world. The value returned is that used in the expression—here to be divided by the count of the numbers to give the average.

6.2.3 COBOL—a commercial programming language

Commercial users of computers typically have applications in which they are dealing with large numbers of repeated data items, for example customers' accounts. The data items are both alphabetic (e.g. names), numeric (e.g. balances) and mixed— alphanumeric (e.g. addresses). There is the requirement to structure data, for example a customer account might be a structure containing the customer name, address, telephone number and balance. Calculations are required but these tend to be fairly simple; for example addition to perform totalling and subtraction to calculate balances. Other facilities required are ways to sort data—such as into alphabetic order (for example customer names in cities) or numerical order (for example ranking of sales offices' performance)—and to be able to locate a specific data item (typically known as a record)—such as a particular customer's account.

The most common commercial programming language used is Common Business Oriented Language (COBOL) which was devised by a committee in the USA in 1960, chaired by Rear Admiral Grace Murray Hopper of the US Navy.

An example COBOL program is given in Fig. 6.12 and an example of an execution of the program is shown in Fig. 6.13. The program finds the average of a collection of numbers. COBOL comment lines are those apparently starting with an *; in fact the * is in the seventh position from the leftmost edge of the program source text. COBOL source text has fixed layout rules that must be adhered to; it was designed in the era when punched cards (paper cards with holes punched in significant positions) were used as a medium for both input and output data. The comments correspond to text in Fig. 5.15. Data iterations in COBOL are typically implemented by a sequence of records in a file that is external to the program. In

```
      IDENTIFICATION DIVISION.
      PROGRAM-ID. AVERAGE.
      AUTHOR. A-N-OTHER.
      ENVIRONMENT DIVISION.
      INPUT-OUTPUT SECTION.
      FILE-CONTROL.
          SELECT NUMBERS-FILE ASSIGN TO DISK.
          SELECT RESULT-FILE ASSIGN TO PRINTER.
    DATA DIVISION.
    FILE SECTION.
    FD   NUMBERS-FILE VALUE OF ID IS "numbers.dat".
    01   NUMBER-ITEM PICTURE 9.
    FD   RESULT-FILE VALUE OF ID IS "result.dat".
    01   RESULT-LINE PICTURE X(15).
    WORKING-STORAGE SECTION.
    77   SUM-NUMBERS           PICTURE 99.
    77   COUNT-NUMBERS         PICTURE 9.
    77   AVERAGE NUMBER        PICTURE 9V999.
    01   AVERAGE-LINE.
         02  FILLER VALUE 'Average = ' PICTURE X(10).
         02  AVERAGE-OUT PICTURE 9.999.
    01   END-OF-NUMBERS-FILE-STATUS PICTURE X.
    88   END-OF-NUMBERS-FILE VALUE IS "T".
    PROCEDURE DIVISION.
    MAIN.
*  Initialize
      MOVE ZERO TO SUM-NUMBERS.
      MOVE ZERO TO COUNT-NUMBERS.
      OPEN INPUT NUMBERS-FILE.
      MOVE "F" TO END-OF-NUMBERS-FILE-STATUS.
      OPEN OUTPUT RESULT-FILE.
*  Compute sum
      PERFORM COMPUTE-SUM
         UNTIL END-OF-NUMBERS-FILE.
*  count > zero?
      IF COUNT-NUMBERS GREATER THAN ZERO
*  Compute average.
         DIVIDE SUM-NUMBERS BY COUNT-NUMBERS GIVING AVERAGE-NUMBER
*  Output average.
         MOVE AVERAGE-NUMBER TO AVERAGE-OUT
         WRITE RESULT-LINE FROM AVERAGE-LINE
      ELSE
         DISPLAY "No numbers".
*  Terminate
      CLOSE NUMBERS-FILE.
      CLOSE RESULT-FILE.
      STOP RUN.
    COMPUTER-SUM.
*  Input number
      READ NUMBERS-FILE
         AT END MOVE "T" TO END-OF-NUMBERS-FILE-STATUS.
      IF NOT END-OF-NUMBERS-FILE
*  Add number to sum
         ADD NUMBER-ITEM TO SUM-NUMBERS
*  Increment count
         ADD 1 TO COUNT-NUMBERS.
```

Figure 6.12 Program in the high-level language COBOL to calculate the average of a collection of numbers.

Input file numbers.dat

```
3
2
6
0
1
2
```

Output file result.dat

Average = 2.333

Figure 6.13 Example execution of the COBOL program.

this example this file is named numbers.dat. The file corresponds to the iteration numbers in the algorithm shown in Fig. 5.15. The content of file numbers.dat is shown in Fig. 6.13.

6.2.4 FORTRAN—a scientific programming language

Scientific users want to be able to do mathematical calculations but typically these must be repeated over large quantities of data—for example in stress analysis where a large structure is broken down into smaller parts amenable to individual calculations, which are composed to produce the overall stresses.

The most common scientific programming language used is FORTRAN—derived from formula translator—which was devised by John Backus of the IBM Corporation in 1954. A sample program is given in Fig. 6.14. Comments in FORTRAN are lines that start with a C. FORTRAN source text has fixed layout rules; see the discussion on this matter for COBOL. The comments correspond to text in Fig. 5.15. FORTRAN was not originally a block-structured language, but the version used here, FORTRAN 77, has some block structure features in respect of the procedural statements; for example if . . . then . . . else . . . endif.

6.2.5 Ada—a real-time programming language

Real-time programming languages must provide the programmer with facilities to control *processes* in *real-time*. Events may occur at arbitrary times and these must be serviced by the program. For example a complex chemical plant may involve a large number of sensors and control valves. The computer application that manages such a chemical plant must be able to respond to the many sensors in order to control the plant by means of the control valves. Events whose times cannot be predicted, for example a sensor may detect an alarm condition, must be responded to by the real-time system within a predictable period of time. Thus different programs or parts of a program corresponding to the various processes may have

FORTRAN Program

```
c finds the average of a collection of integer numbers.
      integer sum, count
c initialize
      datasum/0/, count/0/, limit/20/
      write(6,100)
  100 format('Enter numbers: ')
c compute sum
      do 10 count = 0, limit
c input next number; if none, continue with statement 20
          read(5,110,end = 20) number
  110     format(i5)
          sum = sum + number
c last statement of iteration; 'do' statement increments count
10        continue
      write(6,120)
  120 format('Too many numbers')
      stop
c count > zero?
20        continue
      if (count .gt. 0) then
          average = float(sum) / float(count)
c output the average
          write(6,130) average
  130     format('Average = ',f5.3)
      else
          write(6,140)
  140     format('No numbers')
      endif
      stop
      end
```

The program execution:

```
average
Enter numbers:
3
2
6
0
1
2
Average = 2.333
average
Enter numbers:
No Numbers
```

Figure 6.14 Program in the high-level language FORTRAN to calculate the average of a collection of numbers.

to be processed apparently concurrently, but with a higher priority process temporarily pre-empting the lower priority processes.

The programming language Ada is a real-time programming language. Its design, implementation and mandatory use has been directed by the US Department of Defense. The Ada design team, led by Jean D. Ichbiah of the CII Honeywell Bull Company, France, in the latter 1970s, took ideas from the high-level language Pascal which we have already seen. Ada is named after Ada, Countess Lovelace, Lord Byron's daughter. She worked with Charles Babbage, the nineteenth century computer pioneer, and has been accredited as the world's first computer programmer. The reference text for the language is Ada Joint Program Office (1983).

To serve the needs of real time programming, Ada provides *tasking* in which one can arrange that the execution of the program is split into separate *tasks*. A task thus corresponds to a process.

To guard against parts of the program, which when executed, access and perhaps *corrupt* data private to other parts of the program, Ada provides the concept of *packaging* to assist in structuring the program and providing *encapsulation*. Packaging is particularly important for safety critical applications.

Real time systems must be robust; they should handle *exceptions*. An example of an exception is if a 'watch-dog timer' runs out. Watch-dog timers are used in real time systems to ensure that the system is continuing to function and has not either failed or become overloaded with work, meaning it cannot respond to events in time. The system must explicitly reset the watch-dog timer before the latter runs out. The analogy is resetting the alarm clock before it rings to some future time—usually a fixed time interval from the current time. Ada provides an *exception handling* facility. This does not mean that exception conditions can be ignored by the programmer! On the contrary, they must be recognized and programmed; Ada makes their recognition and handling easier to program.

An example Ada program to calculate the average of a collection of numbers which uses packages and exceptions is given in Figs 6.15 and 6.16, and an example of executions with different sets of input data appears in Fig. 6.17. The content of Fig. 6.16 is taken from the reference manual for the Ada programming language. Comments in Ada are the rest of a line after and including --.

A stack is a data structure type, introduced in Chapter 2, which is frequently used in computing to store and retrieve data on a 'first-in' 'last-out' basis. PUSH is the operation on a stack that 'pushes' a data item on to the top of the stack, whilst POP is the operation that 'pops' the topmost item off the stack. The package allows a programmer to operate on an instance of STACK *only* by means of PUSH and POP (as used in Fig. 6.15 by for example COLLECTION.PUSH(NUMBER)). The programmer using an instance of the package STACK (COLLECTION in Fig. 6.15) cannot access data in the STACK instance's body (Fig. 6.16), for example SPACE in which data items are stored and INDEX which points to the top of the stack.

Three exception condition *handlers* are illustrated in Fig. 6.15. First, the exception END_ERROR (an exception name provided by, and raised by the Ada supplied TEXT_IO package) is used to handle the end of the numbers being input. Second, if there are more numbers than will fit in the stack instance COLLECTION, the exception OVERFLOW is raised (see Fig. 6.16), and the program itself is exited

Ada Main Procedure

```ada
with STACK; with TEXT_IO; use TEXT_IO;
procedure AVERAGE is

   -- Finds the average of a colleciton of integer numbers
   MAXNUMBERS              : constant : = 20;
   package COLLECTION      is new STACK (SIZE => MAXNUMBERS, ITEM =>
                           INTEGER); -- declare stack
   package NUMBER_IO       is new INTEGER_IO (INTEGER);
   package AVERAGE_IO      is new FLOAT_IO (FLOAT);
   SUM, COUNT, NUMBER      : INTEGER;
   AVERAGE                 : FLOAT;
begin
   SUM : = 0;                              -- initialize sum of numbers
   COUNT : = 0;                            -- initialize count of numbers
   PUT_LINE ("Enter numbers: ");
   INPUT:
   loop
     begin
       NUMBER_IO. GET (NUMBER);            --input number
       COLLECTION. PUSH (NUMBER);          --push number on stack
     exception                            --exception handlers:
       when END_ERROR => exit;            --     when no more numbers,
                                          --          exit input loop
       when COLLECTION. OVERFLOW =>       --     when there are too many
                                          --          numbers
         PUT_LINE ("Too many numbers");
         return;                          --     exit program
     end;
   end loop INPUT;                        --no more numbers to input

   COMPUTE:
   loop                                   --compute sum and count
     begin
       COLLECTION. POP (NUMBER);
       SUM : = NUMBER + SUM;
       COUNT : = COUNT + 1;
     exception                            --exception handler:
       when COLLECTION, UNDERFLOW => exit;  --     no more numbers in stack
     end
   end loop COMPUTE;

   IF COUNT > 0 THEN                      --count > zero?
     AVERAGE : = FLOAT (SUM) / FLOAT (COUNT);  --yes: compute average
     PUT ('Average = ");
     AVERAGE_IO. PUT (AVERAGE);
     NEW_LINE;
   ELSE
     PUT_LINE ("No numbers");             --no:
   END IF;
end AVERAGE;
```

Figure 6.15 Program (main procedure part) in the high-level programming language Ada to find the average of a collection of numbers.

Ada Package

```
generic
   SIZE : POSITIVE;
   type ITEM is private;
package STACK is
   procedure PUSH(E : in ITEM);
   procedure POP (E : out ITEM);
   OVERFLOW, UNDERFLOW : exception;
end STACK;

package body STACK is

   type TABLE is array (POSITIVE range <>) of ITEM;
   SPACE : TABLE(1 .. SIZE);
   INDEX : NATURAL : = 0;

   procedure PUSH(E : in ITEM) is
   begin
      if INDEX >= SIZE then
         raise OVERFLOW;
      end if;
      INDEX : = INDEX + 1;
      SPACE(INDEX) : = E;
   end PUSH;

   procedure POP(E : out ITEM) is
   begin
      if INDEX = 0 then
         raise UNDERFLOW;
      end if;
      E : = SPACE(INDEX);
      INDEX : = INDEX − 1;
   end pop;

end STACK;
```

Figure 6.16 Generic package STACK in Ada. The content of this figure is taken from the reference manual for the Ada programming language.

by the return statement (for an example execution see Fig. 6.17). Finally, unlike the Pascal programs in Figs 5.17 and 6.9 where the count of numbers is computed during the input of the numbers, in this Ada example the count is computed (Fig. 6.15) during the popping of numbers from the stack. In Fig. 6.16, the exception UNDERFLOW is raised if POP is applied to an empty stack. In Fig. 6.15, there is an exception handler for UNDERFLOW:

```
exception
   when COLLECTION.UNDERFLOW => exit;
```

The program execution:

```
average
Enter numbers:
3 2 6 0 1 2
Average = 2.33333E+00

average
Enter numbers:
No numbers

average
Enter numbers:
1 2 3 4 5 6 7 8 9 10 11 12 13 14 15 16 17 18 19 20 21
Too many numbers
```

Figure 6.17 Example executions of the Ada program average.

C Program

```
#include <stdio.h>
main() /* Finds the average of a collection of integer numbers.        */
{
  int sum = 0, count = 0, number;      /* initialize sum and count      */
  float average;                       /* average is floating point     */
  printf ("Enter numbers:\n");
  while (scanf ("%d", &number) != EOF) {  /* compute sum, input number   |*/
    sum += number;                     /* add number to sum             */
    ++ count;                          /* increment count               */
  };
  if (count > 0) {                     /* count > 0?                     */
    average = (float) sum / (float) count;  /* yes: compute average      */
    printf ("Average = %5.3f\n", average);  /*      output average       */
  }
    else printf ("No numbers\n");      /*no:                             */
}
```

The program execution:

```
average
Enter numbers:
3
2
6
0
1
2
Average = 2.333
average
Enter numbers:
No numbers
```

Figure 6.18 Program in the high-level language C to calculate the average of a collection of numbers.

Figure 6.16 illustrates an example of a *generic* package; the type of the data items that are to be stacked is *not* specified in the definition of the package but when the package is instantiated (as in Fig. 6.15 where the type of the ITEMs in the stack instance COLLECTION is declared to be integer). The generic package STACK (Fig. 6.16) in its own right thus represents an abstract type definition.

6.2.6 C—a systems-programming language

Programming languages are needed in which the various software tools can be written. SQL and word-processors are examples of programs which themselves have to be written in a programming language. Programming languages are also needed to write the programs that make up the operating system of a computer, the set of programs (described in Chapter 11) present in computers that enable the other programs to be executed on the computer.

The language C is an example of a systems-programming oriented high-level procedural language. C was devised in 1970 at Bell Laboratories in the USA, see Kernighan and Ritchie (1978). The UNIX operating system is written in C. Many of the ideas in C stem from the language BCPL devised by Martin Richards of Cambridge University, England, in the early 1960s. An example C program is given in Fig. 6.18. Comments in C are between the 'brackets' /* and */.

6.2.7 C++—an object-oriented programming language

In an object-oriented language, we are able to keep our partially decomposed problems at stages that we think are going to be generally useful. At the same time we can keep 'lower level' problem solutions, which again are likely to be generally useful. Our stages amount to the specifications of interfaces (cf. *object description* described in Chapter 7). Programming languages that make it easy to develop reusable components that can be put together and further developed are called

1. Explicit structure
   The design structure of a program in an OO language is explicit; it is a faithful rendering of the design.

2. Partial definition
   In this case, when we define an object, we do not have to complete the definition. Thus the design also reflects the stages in the problem decomposition.

3. Inheritance of object characteristics
   In an OO language, when we develop a design, we may either want to *inherit* a type defining an object, or define our own more specialized version. (The example programs do not illustrate inheritance.)

4. Information hiding
   When we develop a software component, as an object, we wish to hide the internal data structures and program. In such an 'opaque box' design, all that needs to be available is the interface.

Figure 6.19 Object-oriented programming language facilities.

C++ Program

```
#include <stream.h>

#include "collection.h"

main()    {// Finds the average of a collection of numbers
    collection numbers;
    float average;
    if (numbers.not_empty()) {
       average = float(numbers.sum())/float(numbers.count());
       cout << "Average = " << average << "\n";
    }
    else cout << "Numbers empty\n";
}
```

Figure 6.20 Program (main part) in the high-level language C++ to calculate the average of a collection of numbers.

object-oriented (OO). OO languages provide four facilities: explicit design structure, partial definition, inheritance of object characteristics, and information hiding. These are elaborated on in Fig. 6.19.

In this chapter, previous programming languages have exhibited, in varying degrees, object oriented programming language facilities; for example the package

```
//seqarray.c

// A collection implemented as a set sequence using an array of
//integer numbers.

// The value of the first component in a set sequence ordered pair
// - the pair's position, is the position of the location in the
//array.

// The value of the second component in a set sequence ordered pair
// - the object's value, is the value in that location in the array.

const error = -1;
const max_numbers = 20;

class collection {
  private:
    int seq[max_numbers];                  // sequence as array of integer numbers
    int count_numbers;
  public:
    collection();
    ~collection() {};
    int not_empty();
    int sum();
    int count();
};
```

Figure 6.21 Set sequence implemented in C++ using an *array*—class definition.

```
// seqarray.c

// memberfunctions

#include <stream.h>

#include "seqarray.h"

collection::collection() {            // Create and input collection
    int number;
    count_numbers = 0;
    cout << "Enter numbers:\n";
    while (cin>>number) {             // Input a number data item
        if (number < 0) {
            cout << "Number " << number << " is not a natural number\n";
            exit(error);
        }
        else
            if (count_numbers == max_numbers) {
                cout << "Count of numbers greater than maximum numbers: "
                    << max_numbers << "\n";
                exit (error);
            }
            else {
                seq[count_numbers] = number;//object's value
                count_numbers++;              // increment the count of numbers
            }
    }
}

int collection::not_empty() {
    return count_numbers > 0;
}

int collection::sum() {               // Sum the objects' values
    int sum_numbers = 0;
    for (int i=0; i<count_numbers; i++)
        sum_numbers += seq[i];        //Accumulate sum
    return sum_numbers;
}

int collection::count() {             // Count the number of objects
    return count_numbers;
}
```

Figure 6.22 Set sequence implemented in C++ using an *array*—member functions.

facility in Ada. To illustrate an object oriented programming language in some
detail, we here use C++. C++ was devised by Stroustrup (1991). The C++
programs illustrate concepts of object design (see Fig. 7.4) and of abstract type.

We use as an example the finding of the average of a collection of numbers.
The programs are based on the **Z** specifications introduced earlier in the chapter.
The main C++ program, illustrated in Fig. 6.20, corresponds to the top-level **Z**

specification in Fig. 6.3. Comments in C++ are the rest of lines after and including a //.

For the **Z** specification set sequence representation in Fig. 6.4 we show two different concrete representations. The first representation uses a C++ *array* and is shown in Figs 6.21 and 6.22. The second representation uses a *list*, as shown in Figs 6.23 and 6.24. For the **Z** bag representation, in Fig. 6.5, we show in Figs 6.25 and 6.26 one concrete representation that uses an *array* of C++ *record* pairs, each pair corresponding to a member of the bag. C++ records are defined using struct. Figure 6.27 shows an example execution for each of the three C++ implementations.

The C++ programs illustrate the concepts of object design (see Fig. 7.4) and of abstract type. Each pair of figures, 6.21 and 6.22, 6.23 and 6.24, 6.25 and 6.26 illustrates C++ class definitions and the classes member functions respectively. The former correspond to the declarations in a **Z** schema box and the latter, the

```
// seqlist.h

// A collection implemented as a set sequence using a list of
// integer numbers.

// The value of the first component in a set sequence ordered
// member pair – the pair's position, is the position of the location
// in the list.

// The value of the second component in a set sequence ordered
// member pair – the object's value, is the value in that location in
// the list.

const error = -1;
const empty = 0;

struct member;

typedef member* member_pointer;       // Define a name for a pointer type

struct member {                        // Structure of each member of sequence
   member_pointer previous;            // Pointer to previous member of sequence
   int object;                         // The object's value
   member () {previous = empty;};      // Initialize previous pointer to empty
};

class collection {
 private:
   member_pointer seq;                 // sequence as list of integer numbers
 public:
   collection();
   ~collection();
   int not_empty();
   int sum();
   int count();
};
```

Figure 6.23 Set sequence implemented in C++ using a *list*—class definition.

```
// seqlist.c

// member functions

#include <stream.h>

#include "seqlist.h"

collection::collection() {                    // Create and input collection
   int number;
   seq = empty;                               // Initialize sequence to be empty
   cout << "Enter numbers:\n";
   while (cin>>number) {                       //  Input a number data item
      if (number < 0) {
         cout << "Number " << number << " is not a natural number\n";
         exit(error);
      }
      else {
         member_pointer new_member = new member; //  Get memory for new member
         new_member -> previous = seq;     //  points to previous member
         new_member -> object = number;    //  object's value
         seq = new_member;
      }
   }
}

collection::~collection() {                   //Finish with collection
   while (seq != empty) {
      member_pointer current = seq;
      seq = current -> previous;
      delete current;                         // Return member's memory
   }
}

int collection::not_empty() {
   return seq != empty;
}

int collection::sum() {                       // Sum the objects' values
   int sum_numbers = 0;
   member_pointer current = seq;
   while (current != empty) {
      sum_numbers += current -> object; //Accumulate sum
      current = current -> previous;
   }
   return sum_numbers;
}

int collection::count() {                     // Count the number of objects
   int count_numbers = 0;
   member_pointer current = seq;
   while (current != empty) {
      count_numbers++;                        //Accumulate count
      current = current -> previous;
   }
   return count_numbers;
}
```

Figure 6.24 Set sequence implemented in C++ using a *list*—member functions.

```
// bagarray.h

// A collection implemented as a bag using an array of structures
// representing ordered pairs.

// The value of the first component in a bag ordered pair – the
// objects' value, is the object value in the structure at that
// location in the array.

// The value of the second component in a bag ordered pair – the
// count of occurrences of identical objects, is the object count
// in the structure at that location in the array.

const error = -1;
const max_members = 20;

struct member {              // Structure of each member pair of bag
    int object;              // The objects' value
    int count;               // The count of occurrences
};

class collection {
    private:
        member seq[max_members];// bag as array of pairs
        int count_members;
    public:
        collection();
        ~collection() {};
        int not_empty();
        int sum();
        int count();
};
```

Figure 6.25 Bag implemented in C++ using an *array* of *structured* pairs—class definition.

member functions, to the predicates in a **Z** schema box. Each pair of figures contains a programmed implementation of an object design. It is of interest to compare these C++ class definitions with the content of an object design as described in Fig. 7.4.

6.2.8 Assembly and machine languages

An *assembly* programming language allows the programmer to use symbolic names in order to specify machine language instructions and machine language data representations. Machine language programming requires the programmer to specify numerically the instructions to be executed by the computer's central processing unit (CPU).

Assembly language There is a different assembly language for every machine language. The assembly language to machine language translation program is called an *assembler*.

```
// bagarray.c

// memberfunctions

#include <stream.h>

#include "bagarray.h"

collection::collection() { // Create and input collection
    int number;
    count_members = 0;
    cout << "Enter each number followed by the count of its occurrences:\n".
    while (cin >> number) {
        if (number < 0) {
            cout << "Number " << number << " is not a natural number\n";
            exit(error);
        }
        else
            if (count_members == max_members) {
                cout << "Count of members greater than maximum number of members: "
                    << max_members << "\n";
                exit(error).
            }
            else {
                seq[count_members].object = number;  // object's value
                cin >> seq[count_members].count;     // countofoccurrences
                count_members++;
            }
    }
}

int collection::not_empty() {
    return count_members > 0;
}

int collection::sum() {        // Sumtheobjects'values
    int sum_numbers = 0;
    for (int i=0; i<count_members; i++)
        sum_numbers += seq[i].object * seq[i].count;      // Accumulate sum
    return sum_numbers;
}

int collection::count() {      // Count the number of objects
    int count_numbers = 0;
    for (int i=0; i<count_members; i++)
        count_numbers += seq[i].count;
    return count_numbers;
}
```

Figure 6.26 Bag implemented in C++ using an *array* of *structured* pairs—member functions.

Set sequence implemented in C++ using an array

```
seqarray
Enter numbers:
3
2
6
0
1
2
Average = 2.33333
```

Set sequence implemented in C++ using a list

```
seqlist
Enter numbers:
3
2
6
0
1
2
Average = 2.33333
```

Bag implemented in C++ using an array of structured pairs

```
bagarray
Enter each number followed by the count of its occurrences:
3 1
2 2
6 1
0 1
1 1
Average = 2.33333
```

Figure 6.27 The three C++ implementations—example runs.

Figure 6.1 presented examples of the same programming problem expressed in the high-level programming language Pascal, an assembly and machine language (these two latter languages being hypothetical). Figure 6.28 illustrates the assembly language program in more detail. The function of the program is to add two numbers, already present in the computer's memory, together and store the result.

The program comprises three *assembler instructions* followed by three *machine instructions*. The assembler instructions set aside three memory locations to hold data items of built-in type integer, and assign each a label, x, y and z. The machine instructions cause memory locations to be set aside and to have placed in each the binary representation of the specified instruction. Load, add and store are symbolic (and mnemonic) operation codes.

The function of the assembler is to translate an assembly language program, such as in Fig. 6.28, to its machine language representation. This representation can

label	op code	operand
x	integer	
y	integer	
z	integer	
	.	
	.	
	load	x
	add	y
	store	z

Figure 6.28 Example Assembly language program for a very simple hypothetical computer.

then be placed in locations in the computer's memory to be executed by the CPU immediately, or at some time in the future.

Assembly language source text may have fixed layout rules that must be adhered to. The boxing and labelling in Fig. 6.28 is for exposition purposes to indicate such a layout. Machine instructions require labelling (like the assembler data instructions in Fig. 6.28) if they are referenced (for example in a selection).

Machine language Figure 6.29 repeats the illustration of the machine language program in Fig. 6.1 for adding two numbers together that are already in the computer's memory, and storing the result in the computer's memory. The program is shown in binary form, as it appears in the hypothetical computer's memory. The machine language program in Fig. 6.29 is the translation of the assembly language program in Fig. 6.28.

Each machine language instruction is obeyed by the CPU when it executes the program. The CPU executes the instructions in the order they appear in memory. The first machine instruction specifies that the numerical value at the memory location whose symbolic name is x is to be loaded into the 'accumulator' register of the CPU. The second instruction specifies that the numerical value at the memory location whose assembly language symbolic name is y is to be added to the contents

address	contents
. . 0 0 1 0	. . . .
. . 0 0 1 1	. . . .
. . 0 1 0 0	. . . .
. . . . . .	. . . .
. . . . . .	. . . .
. . . . . .	. . . .
. . 1 0 0 1	0 0 0 1 . . 0 0 1 0
. . 1 0 1 0	0 1 0 0 . . 0 0 1 1
. . 1 0 1 1	0 0 1 0 . . 0 1 0 0

Figure 6.29 Program fragment in a hypothetical machine language.

of the accumulator. The final instruction specifies that the contents of the accumulator are to be stored in the memory location with symbolic address z.

Programmers rarely program directly in machine languages. Even if a new CPU design requires a new machine language, the first programmers will typically devise other means. For example they might use or modify an existing assembler on an existing computer.

SEVEN
SOFTWARE ENGINEERING

Software Engineering is the discipline of producing computer-based solutions where there is a software content using methods based on those used in engineering. Software is an artifact just as is a bridge, a motor car or a television set. The objective then of software engineering is to produce *reliable* software that meets its *specification*, on time, and to a given cost. In this chapter software engineering is described and the concept of the *software life-cycle* is explained. A good book on software engineering is Pressman (1987).

Software engineers are people who produce computer systems. However, just as conventionally engineered artifacts such as bridges and houses are composed of standardized components (such as bricks and doors), the same is true of software. Software engineers may be involved in producing explicitly 'reusable' components, just as much as assembling these and constructing new components for a particular application. Software may require maintenance if faults are found. Because software is expensive to produce and maintain (it is labour intensive), approaches are taken to both 'reuse' software components and to reduce the labour intensive nature of programming. The *object-oriented* approach to software development serves the reusable approach, in which the components are called *objects*. Programmable application packages, often called *application generators*, are another approach to reduce the cost of programming, and to increase the availability and utility of software.

Software engineers, like their counterparts in other engineering disciplines, employ tools. *Software tools* are programs that are used in the production of software. For example, a compiler is a software tool that enables a program in a programming language (such as Pascal) to be translated to the *native language* of the computer, machine language. Software tools can be involved in the control of the production of software, for example in integrating the various objects making up a software-based system, or to assist in the management of a software project. Software tools are artifacts in their own right, and thus they too are computer-based solutions. Thus a computer-based solution may not only be an application. It may be a library of reusable objects, or it may be a software tool, to be used to produce other software items.

7.1 THE SOFTWARE LIFE-CYCLE

1. Requirements Study
2. Feasibility Study
3. Systems Analysis
4. Specification
5. Design
6. Programming
7. Integration
8. Delivery
9. Maintenance
10. Upgrading

Figure 7.1   The software project life-cycle steps.

The process of producing computer-based solutions is split up into a sequence of steps, as listed in Fig. 7.1. Each of the steps names a process. Each process has input(s) and output(s) that act as links with the previous and next process. For example the output of a feasibility study will typically be a document while the input to programming will be precise specifications of the programs to be written, again probably in the form of documents.

All the life-cycle steps generate documents. In some cases these are to be input to the subsequent step, for example the design step has as output program specifications. In other cases they are produced for particular people; for example user manuals and the instructions for installing the application on a user's computer. Both categories of document are used by maintenance personnel, and also by quality assurance personnel.

The steps and their input(s) and output(s) are now described in detail.

7.1.1 Requirements study

The first step in the software life-cycle is to find out *what* it is that the *client* wishes the computer to do. Requirements may be expressed in a high-level manner in which a problem is described in various ways. In a commercial environment the requirements study is done after a business study has identified the problem, for example 'to maintain competitiveness it is necessary to reduce stock levels to reduce money tied up and this presupposes investment in, and installation of, a computer-based stock management system'. Requirements may be expressed in which there is no mention of a computer system or systems. Requirements may also mention *constraints*, for example a requirement to be compatible with a communications standard for electronic transfer of data. In a stock management system this might mean the ability for the system to order stock from suppliers using inter-computer communication.

7.1.2 Feasibility study

The next step in the software life-cycle, the feasibility study, involves examining possible solutions and examining the feasibility of each. There may be a comparative cost analysis, or a social benefit analysis. Chapter 13 includes material to assist in conducting a feasibility study. One outcome of a feasibility study may be:

- Do nothing. Carry on with the present system, be it manual or computer based.

7.1.3 Systems analysis

The next step in the software life-cycle, assuming the feasibility study has recommended a computer-based solution, is the analysis of the system. Systems Analysts (humans) *analyse* an existing manual/mechanical system or an existing computer system that the feasibility study has deemed is to be replaced. They determine the various processes and the inputs and outputs and they identify the various classes of users, both in the existing system and the proposed system. For a new system, or where the existing system is to be extended, the systems analyst must *synthesize* (rather than analyse) these items.

Systems analysts use tabular and diagrammatic aids in their work. With these aids they can organize the analysis of the eventual system's users, processes, inputs and outputs into a manageable form that can be discussed and validated against the requirements. These aids may be supported by software tools which can also assist in the verification of the analysis. A verification tool would typically check on the consistency of the analysis; for example an output without a corresponding input, or an isolated process.

7.1.4 Specification

The next step in the software life-cycle is the specification of the system. The specification is in two parts; the *functional specification* and the *non-functional specification*.

The functional specification defines *precisely* what the processes do, and the *precise* content of their inputs and outputs. It is derived directly from the systems analysis. For example the functional specification of a program to sort an array of numbers into ascending numerical order essentially states that adjacent numbers in the output must be in order. Thus the functional specification states *what* is wanted; it does not say *how* it is to be achieved. The functional specification can be expressed informally, or formally using a specification language such as **Z**.

There are instances when the functional specification can be used as a program and executed—an *executable specification*. Examples are programs written in declarative high-level programming languages. They can be run 'immediately', if only to validate the functional specification against the requirements. We will have more to say on this matter below when discussing prototyping (see Sec. 7.2.3).

The non-functional specification is concerned with 'everything else'. It is sometimes split into two parts, project dependent and project independent. Examples of non-functional specification items are the speed of the various functions, the maximum time it takes to save the system's files for backup purposes, the number of screens and keyboards, any special input/output devices (and their characteristics), and so on. The non-functional specification may specify any *standards* to be adopted, for example the *format* of disks so other computer systems can read these, or the high-level language to be used which can influence for example the maintainability of the system, or the communications standards to be used to ensure that files can be transferred between computers. The non-functional specification also states how the overall system is to be *validated*, that is, 'does the system work correctly according to the requirements?'.

The functional specification states *what* the problem is. Unless a declarative approach to programming is to be used, or an application package is available (for example see *application generators*, below), we now have to solve the problem by finding a solution; that is, derive the *how*. A question that should be asked is 'has the problem in whole or part been solved before?'. If it has, 'could we use or amend a previous solution?'. In this context an application package might be attractive. If a package is feasible this can result in savings both in cost, time and the recurring cost of maintenance of one's own specific software solution. Use of a package can reduce or eliminate the design and programming steps in the project's life-cycle. Packages are discussed below in Sec. 7.3.

7.1.5 Design

The functional specification defines the processes and their inputs and outputs, that is, *what* the system is to do.

Design proceeds using the technique of *functional decomposition*. This is the same as the method that is used for refining the specification, producing data structures, and developing algorithms. Fundamentally, functional decomposition involves taking the *opaque box* specification (to start with the whole system is a single opaque 'box' and 'opening it up' to reveal a *transparent box* which has constituent opaque boxes with their respective inputs and outputs. We use the term 'opaque box' to indicate that at a given stage in the decomposition, we are only concerned with the definition of the inputs, the ouputs, and *what* the box does; we are not interested at this stage as to *how* it works. This process continues until we have opaque boxes whose functions are sufficiently simple that they can be easily programmed. Thus one develops a design to the stage where it can be used as input to the next life-cycle step, programming.

Functional decomposition—a data flow example We have in effect already seen examples of functional decomposition, to derive the contents of Fig. 5.15 and the **Z** and C++ examples in Chapter 6. To illustrate functional decomposition applied to data flow we use the database transaction example from Chapter 2.

Suppose the data flow diagram illustrated there (Fig. 2.13) and repeated here as Fig. 7.2, requires further decomposition before transaction definitions can be derived. This is because the application is to be more complex than that derived in Chapter 2. As before, the student selects a course from a published list and goes to the faculty office. The administrator accesses the course enrolment application on the computer terminal. If the student can be accommodated on a given course

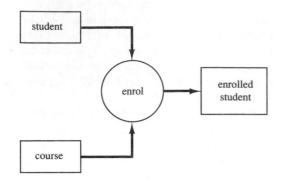

Figure 7.2 Data flow diagram—course enrolment application—top-level.

(a course may have an upper limit on the number of students who can attend), in this system they are presented with a ticket to be given to the lecturer at the first attendance. The lecturer signs and returns the ticket to the faculty office, whence the administrator accesses the enrolment application a second time, but this time to complete the student's enrolment on the course.

Using functional decomposition, the `enrol` process, an 'opaque box', is decomposed into constituent processes, `accommodate` and `complete`. The inputs and outputs to the constituent processes as a whole remain unchanged, but between the constituent processes other data flows occur. The result is shown in Fig. 7.3. In this second level diagram, the enrol process as a whole, now a 'transparent box', is shown for exposition purposes, whilst the constituent processes are the newly revealed 'opaque boxes'. Some of the revealed inputs and outputs can be tables; for example REGISTERS and ATTENDS.

Information needs to be recorded for each student who has elected to take a course. The record is cleared when the lecturer returns the signed ticket. To provide this could be the subject of further decomposition of the `accommodate` and `complete` processes, and further database design. One might for example have another table ENROLLING; another technique would involve an extra attribute to the table ATTENDS, named ENROLLING and of boolean type (cf. the attribute SUBSCRIPTION in Fig. 2.3).

On completion of the design step, in the case of an application or software tool, the output of the step typically consists of a full and detailed description. This will comprise definitions of the data structures down to the concrete types of individual data items, and the program specifications; for example SQL commands, transaction definitions or the algorithms to be employed.

Object-oriented design In the case of reusable objects (for example objects to allow menu systems to be easily built), the intention may be that a subsequent user will

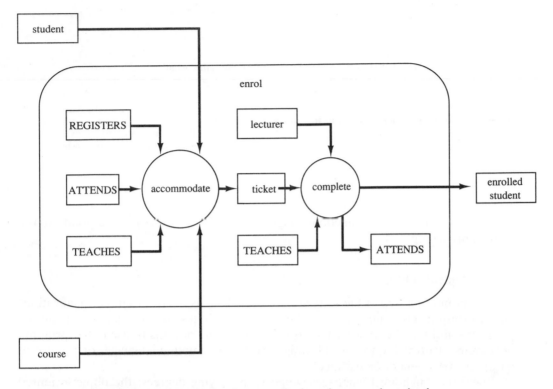

Figure 7.3 Data flow diagram—course enrolment application—decomposed one level.

provide more specific data representations and algorithms. In effect the design is partially completed, and can be further 'customized' by a subsequent designer or programmer. There will typically be such a design description for each transparent box—an object design. The content of an object design is shown in Fig. 7.4. It is evident that an object design is itself an instance of a type 'object', and furthermore that software tools can use this structure. Thus we might have a library of objects, and we might have software tools to check in some manner an individual object, or the consistency of a collection of objects. A good book on object-oriented design is Meyer (1988).

The external or public part of an object design defines the *interface* between the object and others in the system. Agreement is essential between the designers of objects which must interface with each other.

In Chapter 6 we introduced the **Z** specification language, and the object-oriented language C++. Both these languages enable an object-oriented design approach. C++ has particular facilities which are useful, in that one preserves the design structure. The C++ class concept corresponds to the object design. You may wish to compare the C++ class declarations in Figs 6.21, 6.23, and 6.25 with Fig.

1. External or public part
   - Object name, date and version identification.
   - Input data specification.
   - Output data specification.
   - Functional relationship between the input and output—the 'what'.
   - How the object is to be tested.
   - Non-functional specification items.
2. Internal or private part
   - Specification of data internal to the object.
   - Algorithms (where required) that relate the input data to the output data—the 'how'.
     Within an algorithm there may be references to other instances of objects in the system.

Figure 7.4   Object design.

7.4. The C++ member functions (Figs 6.22, 6.24 and 6.26) correspond to the algorithms in Fig. 7.4.

7.1.6 Programming

The programming step of the software life-cycle has, as input, program specifications and, as output, programs that have been thoroughly tested. Programmers *write* the programs and test them, according to the *design*. The norm is to use either program development involving the use of a high-level programming language, or the use of an application generator package.

Particular high-level languages support, in varying degrees, the object-oriented approach to software design and programming. A programmer will typically both write new programs, and refer to and include existing reusable type definitions and procedures from libraries. Thus the experienced programmer needs to know both programming and how to make best use of libraries and their contents. Knowing just the language is usually insufficient. Use of the program development process in terms of the software tools and facilities the programmer uses, and how these work, is discussed further in Chapter 8.

Commercial applications in particular are often users of *application generators* as an alternative to programming using programming languages. Application generators are discussed later in Sec. 7.3.

7.1.7 Integration

The various programs that make up the complete system, together with any special hardware, must be *integrated* into a whole system.

Successful integration requires a rigid adherence by all the objects that make up the system to the various interfaces between them. Thus just as doors must match door frames, the various programs that 'call' other programs must have mutually consistent interfaces. Integration will fail, for example, if a sorting program that is programmed to sort a collection of numbers is presented with a collection of character data items. Programming language systems can provide checks of such type ill-usage.

7.1.8 Delivery

Delivery is the step in the software life-cycle in which all the parts of the system are made available to the client. Prior to delivery, the client may require the system to be *commissioned* before it is handed over. A delivered system is usually more than just the software. Typically the following items are found in a delivered system:

1. *The 'software'*. This comprises programs and any control files and the method of *installing* these on the computer. The programs are usually in the *object code* form (machine language instructions as produced by a high-level language compiler) rather than in the high-level language source form. Installation can be complex, and may require a program itself.
2. *Documentation*. This comprises both user manuals and maintenance manuals. Increasingly *on-line documentation* is provided—manuals that the user can display directly on a screen.
3. *Hardware*. As well as the normally available hardware, which may or may not be supplied, there may be special hardware, for example speech recognition input devices.
4. *Training*. Depending on the nature of the computer based solution, training courses for the users may have to be devised and given. The users include not only those people using keyboards and screens, the direct users, but also the other personnel whose work might be affected by the computer system.

7.1.9 Maintenance

Maintenance is concerned with faults in a system and how to manage and rectify these. Errors may enter the system at any of the previous steps in the life-cycle but may not manifest themselves as faults until the delivered system is in use. Maintenance is a step in the software life-cycle which in effect lasts as long as there is either a need, or a contractual agreement is binding. Maintenance involves detection, notification (to other users as well as the suppliers) and rectification of errors. Rectification of a given fault might be by means of a *work-around*. Alternatively a change to an existing part of the system may be required.

Maintenance of the system requires that the documentation associated with each of the life-cycle steps is available. This documentation includes the program source files. Using these, the necessary modifications and additions are made to the software to produce a revised integrated system available for delivery.

7.1.10 Upgrading

Upgrading a system can arise due to a change in requirements or the change to a new environment. For example:

1. *Change in requirements*. A payroll system may require modification due to a change in the tax laws.
2. *Change in environment*. The system is to be *ported* to computer hardware which is different in some manner to the existing computer; for example the CPU uses a different machine language.

7.2 WHY SOFTWARE *ENGINEERING*?

Engineering is concerned with producing artifacts that are correct in respect of their requirements and specifications, that work reliably, to a stated cost, to a stated level of quality, and where delivery is complete by a stated time. Software engineering is concerned with using engineering methods in the production of software in order to achieve these aims.

Engineering requires and relies on the usage of *standards*. Standards enable artifacts to be put together but the artifacts can be produced quite independently of one another. Standards assist the client in the validation of the artifact. We have already seen the use of standards in computing; for example standard high-level languages (e.g. Ada) and database query languages (e.g. SQL). Other standards abound; for example standard file formats on disk for easy data exchange and standard library procedures for the operating system services. Standards define the formats and contents of the various documents, for example the specification, or a particular program source. Programming standards will require general levels of good practice (e.g. the style and type of comments, and the layout of the program source text), and project specific standards such as the naming conventions for programs and data mnemonics are normal practice.

Provided that sound engineering practices are adhered to, it should be possible to have different organizations produce each step or parts of a step in the software life-cycle. To accomplish this requires agreement on the specification of the *interfaces* between the objects making up the system. We do not expect to find round-pinned power plugs on electrical equipment used in the United Kingdom where square-pinned sockets are used. It is not infrequent in the commercial world therefore for the specification of the system to be a contractual document—the specification in this respect being akin to an engineering drawing, as an engineering drawing fully specifies the artifact to be produced.

7.2.1 Quality assurance

Quality assurance is concerned with producing a *valid* system; that is, one that meets the requirements.

Traditionally, quality assurance has been applied after the integration step has produced an integrated system. The whole computer system is checked to find if it conforms to the specification. Only when the system has 'passed' the (extra) quality assurance step, after integration and before delivery, is it ready for delivery. However the individual steps in the life-cycle do have their own checks to ensure that the step or items within the step have been carried out correctly—that the step or item can be *verified*. Furthermore some steps will specify checks that subsequent steps must comply with; for example a design of an object will include the specification of tests that the ensuing program must comply with.

It is increasingly the case that the practice of quality assurance is applied throughout the software life-cycle. This practice is particularly important where applications involving safety and/or security are being produced.

7.2.2 Proving the correctness of software

There is a demand that software should be proved to be correct. The impetus for this interest comes from applications where *safety* and/or *security* are of paramount importance. We must clearly distinguish between the *validation* and *verification* of software.

Validation is concerned with proving that the software meets the requirements. Prototyping and functional specifications that are executable are attractive for this endeavour as they can be used *early* in the software life-cycle to ensure that 'what is going to be produced is what is actually wanted'.

Verification is concerned with proving that each step in the software life-cycle to the point of the executing program in the delivered system has been correctly produced from the previous step. For example the binary machine language program from the high-level language program, or the design from the functional specification. Verification has been rarely done in a formal manner as it has been so difficult to do; the very proofs can have bugs in them.

Mathematical techniques have recently been developed to the stage of practicability to assist in producing the verification proofs and are beginning to be used, certainly in safety critical applications. Such techniques rely on the use of *formal methods*. *Formal languages* such as **Z** are used for specifying the functional specification. It is then possible to reason about the specification in a sound manner. So, the idea is that instead of trying to prove a program is correct, we start with the specification in a mathematically sound form, and transform the specification to the eventual program by means of transformations that have themselves been proved to be correct.

7.2.3 Prototyping

Prototypes in software engineering are different from the traditional engineering prototype concept where one produces one or more examples of the completed artifact. Rather, software prototypes are typically produced to assist the *validation* process. They may not have the full functionality of the eventual system. In this respect they are more akin to the traditional engineering concept of the *mockup*. An example might be a prototype of the users' interfaces to the system. Other prototypes might be involved with a non-functional aspect of the system. An example is performance validation—will the eventual system's speed be sufficient?

7.3 SOFTWARE TOOLS AND PACKAGES

A software tool is a program that assists in one or more steps in the software life-cycle. Many of the programming languages and application packages that have been described are clearly of immediate use in the life-cycle. For example word-processors assist document preparation and editing.

In some instances the software tool can be used embedded in the software solution itself, i.e. in the delivered system. Examples are *packages* and *application generators* (discussed below). A package is previously written software that may be programmable to some extent and which is written to solve specific application problems. Packages that are in general use include word-processors, and database management systems. An example of a more specific package is that of a payroll package.

The various aspects that need to be considered in coming to a decision in respect of whether to use reusable software such as a package are discussed in Chapter 14.

7.3.1 Configuration management

Configuration management is an example of a common engineering practice that has been introduced, together with associated software tools, into software engineering. *Configuration management* is concerned with keeping the various objects that make up both the project's internal objects and the eventual deliverable objects in a consistent and up-to-date whole—a *configuration*. For example the objects include programs, data files, and documents produced during a project—often by different people and perhaps by different organizations. This is of importance as programs are usually interdependent—a change in one might have side-effects on others. This is especially the case where the design of an object's interface is amended.

We take as an example the objects that make up a specification and the consequential program to calculate the average of a collection of numbers. The specification is expressed in **Z** and the program in C++. Figure 6.3 shows the top-level **Z** specification, and Fig. 6.20 the corresponding main C++ program. The method chosen to represent the collection of numbers is as a set sequence, the **Z** specification of which is shown in Fig. 6.4. The concrete representation of the set sequence chosen is that using a C++ array, the class declaration of this being shown in Fig. 6.21 and the member functions in Fig. 6.22.

The objects making up the configuration for the specification and the program are listed in Fig. 7.5. Each object has a unique name, such as the name of its file in the filing system of the computer being used to produce the software.

The structure of a configuration can be represented by a *dependency graph*. The full dependency graph of an application represents the dependencies between the objects within the configuration of the application over its life-cycle. An object is *dependent* upon another object if either it is a *derived* object or a *component dependent* object.

- *Derived object*. The dependent object is directly *derived* from a previously existing object during the software life-cycle. For example functional decomposition results in a derived (and thus dependent) object formed by decomposing a more abstract object.
- *Component dependent object*. The dependent object requires another object as a *component* part. The main program in Fig. 6.20 for example makes reference to the function c o u t to output data values to the computer's screen. Part of

Name	Explanation	Fig.
average.z	**Z** top-level specification	6.3
<stream.h>	Standard C++ input/output source program library	—
collection.h	C++ file to select representation—contains #include "seqarray.c"	—
average.c	C++ main program	6.20
sequence.z	**Z** specification of collection of numbers as a set sequence	6.4
seqarray.h	C++ class declaration of set sequence using an array	6.21
seqarray.c	C++ member functions of set sequence using an array	6.22
libC.a	C++ library of object programs	—
average	machine language program	—

Figure 7.5 Objects making up the configuration for an application to find the average of a collection of numbers.

cout is present in <stream.h>, the C++ input/output source program library, and the rest is present in libC.a, the C++ library of object programs. (In fact cout calls an *operating system service* which performs the low level output of the data, as explained in Chapter 10.) Libraries and their usage are explained in Chapter 8.

The dependency graph for the objects making up the configuration listed in Fig. 7.5 is illustrated in Fig. 7.6. Where there exists a program that has as inputs dependent objects to make an object, this is shown in [ ] brackets. Such programs translate the objects immediately to their left to the object on their right. CC is the

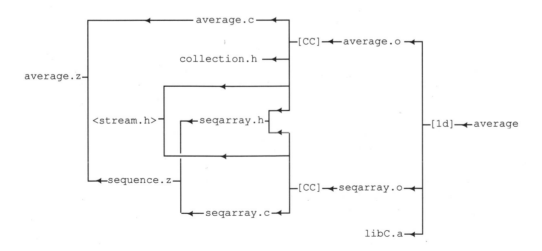

Figure 7.6 Configuration management dependency graph example.

C++ compiler. Thus average.o is the object program version of the source program average.c (see Fig. 7.5). CC takes as input average.c, collection.h, <stream.h> and seqarray.h to output average.o. ld is the linker which has as input the object program average.o and the library libC.a and output the machine language program average that can be executed by the computer's CPU.

Each object (see Fig. 7.5) in the filing system of the computer being used to build the application has a record of the last date and time that it, the object, was changed. This 'date-stamping' is a facility provided by the computer's filing system. Using the application's configuration dependency graph it is possible to check that a given object is up-to-date with respect to what it is dependent on. If an object is changed (perhaps there is a change in specification or an error has been rectified), it is possible to find all the other objects that are dependent on the changed object and thus have to be checked or remade (for example in the case of source programs, retranslated to object programs).

Configuration management tools An example of a pair of complementary software tools used in configuration management is the 'make' program and the Source Code Control System, used with the UNIX operating system:

- *Make*. The make program is used to generate and regenerate groups of objects that are produced during the software life-cycle where programs (such as those in [ ] brackets in Fig. 7.6) exist to do the generation. 'make' provides built-in facilities for objects expressed in the standard UNIX programming languages, such as C. It can be extended to other objects, for example text files for documentation.

   'make' uses a file called 'makefile' which contains a representation of a configuration's dependency graph and the rules by which a dependent *file* can be produced from the files it depends on in the event that the dependent file either does not exist or a change to a file or files means that a dependent file has to be remade. A rule is typically the use of a software tool which processes as input the files a dependent file depends on to produce as output the dependent file.

   In the configuration of the program to find the average of a collection of numbers, whose dependency graph is illustrated in Fig. 7.6, the makefile would have a rule specifying that the C++ compiler is to be used to produce the object programs (C++ is not recognized as a built-in language by 'make'). This rule would be invoked by 'make' if the date-stamp on any of the files that average.o, say, is dependent on, is more recent than the date-stamp on average.o itself. 'make' applies the date-stamp check recursively. Thus, if 'make' were used to manage that part of the configuration in Fig. 7.6 for which programs are used to do the translations, the date-stamp checks would be done from right to left, and then any application of rules would be from left to right.

- *Source code control system*. When one or more people are developing an application comprising perhaps several source objects, a significant project management activity is that of version control. A particular configuration does not comprise the objects *per se*, as a given object is subject to change. For example a design error is discovered, thus necessitating a change to one or more objects. Thus in a configuration each object has a specific and identifiable version.

The source code control system (SCCS) is a database in which one stores objects, typically source program files. Whenever one wishes to edit an object, one gets (usually) the latest version from the SCCS database, makes the necessary changes to produce a new (next) version, and then places that next version back in the SCCS database. SCCS can recreate any of the previous versions if one so wishes. Thus one has a complete history of the versions for the given source program file.

The make program will get the latest version of dependent objects from the SCCS database.

7.3.2 Application generators

Application generators are packages which incorporate databases and typically declarative programming, often with an interactive interface for the programmer to use. Such packages are sometimes called 'fourth generation languages', or 'fourth generation systems'. Thus application generators permit the generation of programs but they may be restricted in their applicability; for example in the screen layouts possible. The interface used by the 'programmer' to the package is deliberately oriented to ease of understanding. Application generators however are general in nature; they are applicable across various users and industries; in this respect they are *horizontal* in terms of who and what organization might use them. The terms 'horizontal' and 'vertical' are described in more detail in Chapter 13.

Because one can rapidly produce user interfaces with application generators, they are often used for prototyping systems in order to assist in validating the client's requirements.

7.3.3 Computer-aided software engineering

For some time engineers who design physical artifacts, for example architects, highway design engineers, electronic product designers and automotive designers, have been using computer aided design (CAD). It has also been the case that, independent of the actual engineering discipline (mechanical, civil, electrical, etc.), engineers have been using computer-assisted *project management* techniques such as configuration management (explained above for configurations of software objects), and general purpose software tools that can assist in the planning of a project, for example critical path analysis.

Computer aided software engineering (*CASE*) is the analogue of CAD, but applied to the software life-cycle, with the various tools, including project management tools, integrated together.

FOUR

HOW COMPUTERS WORK

EIGHT

PROGRAM DEVELOPMENT AND EXECUTION

In this chapter we examine in more detail the processes and tools involved in developing and executing a program. Our starting point is the programming step of the software life-cycle in which a programming language, as distinct from an application generator package, is to be used. The source text of one or more programs will make up an application. Thus all the specification and design work has been completed, and the programmer has to 'code' a program in a high-level language representation using the relevant program specification. The source text of the program (what the programmer writes) may not yet be filed in the computer.

Before describing the processes and tools that the programmer uses to produce the eventual application, we need to examine program execution in more detail.

8.1 PROGRAM EXECUTION

Programs deal with concrete data such as alphabetic characters and numbers. The numbers may be directly related to numbers *per se* in the real world such as the price of a motor car spare part, or they may represent some physical quantity—for example the rate of flow of gas in a gas pipe or the colour and intensity of a particular point on a picture. We will be looking at how data items such as alphabetic characters and gas flows are *physically* represented in the computer in Chapter 9.

As far as the computer is concerned, a program states *how* the computer is to process the given input data at the time the program is used. In fact a computer program represents indirectly or directly a series of *instructions* and the description of how the data is to be organized. When a computer processes data as directed by the program, we say that the computer *executes* the program.

In the examples given so far in this book, we have expressed the data processing to be done by the computer by means of programs represented in more than one programming language. It is not unusual for a computer to be capable of executing programs expressed in more than one language.

Programs written in programming languages like Prolog and Pascal are not in fact directly executed by the computer's hardware, but are first translated (by another program!) to a functionally equivalent program. This equivalent program is in the computer's native language called *machine language*. The translated program can be directly executed by the computer's hardware. Languages like Prolog and Pascal are called *high-level* languages, as opposed to *low-level* languages such as machine language. High-level languages are so called because programs written in such languages are much closer to the way we naturally express problems and solutions than the functionally equivalent program written in machine language. Rather, machine languages reflect the way computers are designed as will be explained in Chapter 9. Thus a computer program represented in a high-level language is an *indirect* representation of the low-level *instructions* that the computer executes.

8.2 THE PROGRAM DEVELOPMENT PROCESS

How is the source program text placed in a computer file? How are programs organized and *loaded* (placed) into the computer's memory? Can pieces of program be reused in other programs; i.e. can we have libraries of reusable program objects (in a non-object-oriented language, these are typically called types and procedures)? Program development consists of a set of software tools and working practices. These support the software engineering approach. The sequence of processes involved in program development, together with their inputs and outputs, are shown in Fig. 8.1. A brief description of each process is as follows:

1. *Text editor.* A text editor is an application program used to input the program source text 'code' and output the program to a 'source code' file. It is also used to edit a source program file; for example if the program contains error. The user of a text editor uses a keyboard as the input device to the text editor, and a screen as one of the output devices, so that the current state of the source program can be displayed. The other output device usually includes a hardware device such as a disk drive and a disk on which the file can be saved. A text editor thus provides similar facilities to a word-processor; indeed, a word-processor is sometimes used for this task. Often the text editor recognizes the syntax of the particular high-level language. Various degrees of syntax direction may be provided in the user interface (Sec. 3.2.1). Thus the text editor provides facilities like automatic indentation, and warnings concerning absence of closing brackets; e.g. no corresponding) or] for a (or [.

     The text editor is also used to input and edit data files, and in particular when a program is being tested, *test data* files.

2. *Compilers and interpreters.* A compiler is a program that translates a program in source language form to the functionally equivalent object language form—i.e. a form of machine language. This object language form of the program is often called *object code*. The source program is present in a file, and the object program output by the compiler is placed in another file. Each programming

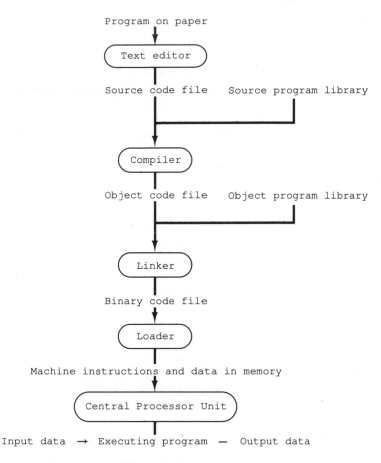

Figure 8.1 Program development and execution.

language will have an associated compiler. If the program is written in assembly language as distinct from a high-level language, the program that translates the assembly language program to the equivalent object language form is called an *assembler*.

Rather than translate a source language program, an *interpreter* executes it directly.

As an analogy, a compiler corresponds to the human translator of a book from one natural language to another, whilst an interpreter corresponds to a human interpreter giving a simultaneous translation of someone talking.

3. *Libraries*. Software libraries contain existing program components. A library is usually a computer file. There are two forms of library, *source libraries* and *object libraries*.

Source program libraries usually contain the type definitions. Because several programs and procedures within an application will be processing data structures of the same type, the type definitions are typically present just once, in the source library, rather than having a copy in each program. Object program libraries contain the translated (object code) form of procedures that have been deemed to be sufficiently useful to be reusable.

4. *Linker*. A linker is a program which takes as input a set of procedures in object language form, including the user's 'main' program or procedure, and neccesary procedures that the linker extracts from object program libraries. With these object procedures, the linker produces as output a single machine language program, placed in a file, which can be subsequently executed by the computer's central processing unit (CPU). Such executable programs are commonly called *binary* programs. The executable program comprises all the application within a single unit (but normally with the exception of input/output and other 'system' programs supplied by the operating system). Such programs are sometimes termed *stand-alone*.

5. *Loader*. This program takes as input a file containing a binary program, and loads, that is, places a copy of the binary program in particular locations in the computer's memory. Thus the 'output' of the loader is to an area of the computer's memory. The binary program may then be executed by the CPU.

6. *Miscellaneous items*. Other development software tools and facilities are needed to develop programs. An example is a *debugger*. When a program does not meet its specification there may be an error in the program; such an error is called a *bug*. A debugger is a program that allows the programmer to 'step' through a program a statement at a time examining the values of data items in the program and thereby provide the programmer with assistance in locating the bug.

8.3 COMPILERS AND INTERPRETERS

A program written in a high-level language cannot be directly executed by a computer. This is because any given high-level language and a computer's own machine language, as defined by its *instruction set*, differ very greatly. To enable programs written in high-level languages to be executed on a computer, two techniques are available: using a compiler or an interpreter.

8.3.1 Compilers

A compiler is a program that takes as input a *source* program written in a high-level language and produces as output the functionally equivalent *object* program, in the machine language representation for that type of central processing unit. By 'functionally equivalent' we mean that the functional specification of the program in its high-level form and its machine language form are *identical*. When subsequently linked with any other required procedures (also in machine language form) and loaded into the computer's memory, the translated program can be directly executed by the computer's CPU. Figure 8.2 illustrates the compilation process.

A programming language, just as in a natural language grammar, has a *lexical* definition, a *syntax* and *semantics*.

Source program → Compiler → Object program

Figure 8.2 The compilation process.

The lexical definition is concerned with the tokens—such as variable names and punctuation symbols. Thus tokens are the analogues of words and their associated parts of speech—nouns, verbs and so on, and punctuation symbols, as used in natural language.

Syntax is concerned with the grammatical structure of a program, just as grammar in natural languages is associated with how sentences are constructed from parts of speech. Programming languages have precisely defined *grammars*.

Semantics is concerned with how a program functions when it is *executed*.

Programming languages must be absolutely precise and unambiguous in their lexical definition, syntax and semantics.

Different programming languages will have different lexical definitions, syntax, and semantics. For example, the representation of a variable in Prolog starts with an upper case letter, but this is not a requirement in Pascal.

Compilers are structured into a sequence of three processes that reflect the three definitions associated with languages. Figure 8.3, which illustrates these processes and their inputs and outputs, is an expansion of the compilation process shown in Fig. 8.2. A brief description of each process follows:

1. *Lexical analyser*. The lexical analyser takes as input the sequence of characters in the high-level language source program and forms these into *tokens*. Figure 8.4 shows examples of Horn clause lexical tokens (taken from Fig. 2.16).
2. *Parser*. The compiler includes a *grammar* for the particular high-level language. The parser or *syntax analyser* uses the grammar to *parse* the sequence of lexical tokens and produces as output a parse (or syntax) tree representation of the program in terms of its syntactic units. Figure 8.5 shows a grammar for the Horn clauses of a small Prolog-based language.

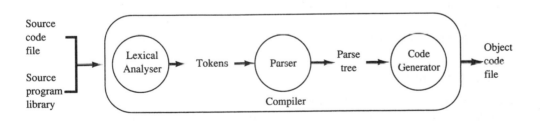

Figure 8.3 Steps within the compilation process.

Token	Examples
`atom`	`elizabeth george :-`
`variable`	`Person Parent Descendant`
`punctuation_char`	`( ) ,`
`comment`	`/* Clauses relating specific individuals: */`

Figure 8.4 Examples of lexical tokens.

The parsing process corresponds to the parsing of natural language sentences where we produce a parse tree diagram showing the structure of the sentence in terms of constructions such as subject, predicate, verb phrase, and parts of speech. Figure 8.6 shows the parse tree for the following Horn clause (from Fig. 2.16):

```
has_ancestor(Person,Parent) :-
     has_parent(Person,Parent).
```

both in diagrammatic form and as it would be represented as a Prolog data structure (as a Prolog `term`).

Because there is the need to allow an unlimited number of programs to be devised, as in natural language grammars, recursive grammar rules are used. It is interesting to compare the grammar in Fig. 8.5 with the natural language grammar in Fig. 4.2. In the case of the small Prolog grammar, there is more than one example of recursion. *Direct* recursion (for example the grammar rules headed `goals`) is used. *Indirect* recursion is also used (for example the grammar rules headed by `term` with those headed by `arguments`).

3. *Code generator.* In this last stage, *code generation*, the parse tree is translated into the machine language of the computer which will execute the program. If a compiler is to be used to compile a high-level language program for a different CPU, then this last stage is the one that is replaced.

Compilers are just computer programs, so they also need to be written in a programming language. In the past they were written in assembly language, but nowadays it is normal for them to be written in a high-level language. Many high-level languages have their compilers written in their own language!

8.3.2 Interpreters

An interpreter is a program that directly interprets another program. In contrast, a compiler translates a program to a machine language program. This machine language program is then interpreted, as many times as is desired, by the computer's central processing unit. An interpreter compresses the two processes, compilation followed by execution of the machine language program, into a single process.

```
/*          Definite Clause Grammar for a Small Prolog.              */

sentence →
          sentence_read_in, ".".

sentence_read_in →
          clause_.
sentence_read_in →
          directive.

clause_ →
          non_unit_clause.
clause_ →
          unit_clause;

non_unit_clause →
          head, ":-", goals.

unit_clause →
          head.

head →
          term.                      /* term must be a nonvariable.          */

directive →
          ":-", goals.

goals →
          goal.
goals →
          goal, ",", goals.

goal →
          term.                      /* term must be a nonvariable.          */

term →
          functor_, "(", arguments, ")".
term →
          atom.
term →
          variable.

functor_ →
          atom.

arguments →
          term.
arguments →
          term, ",", arguments.

atom →
          name.
```

Figure 8.5 Definite clause grammar for a small Prolog-based language.

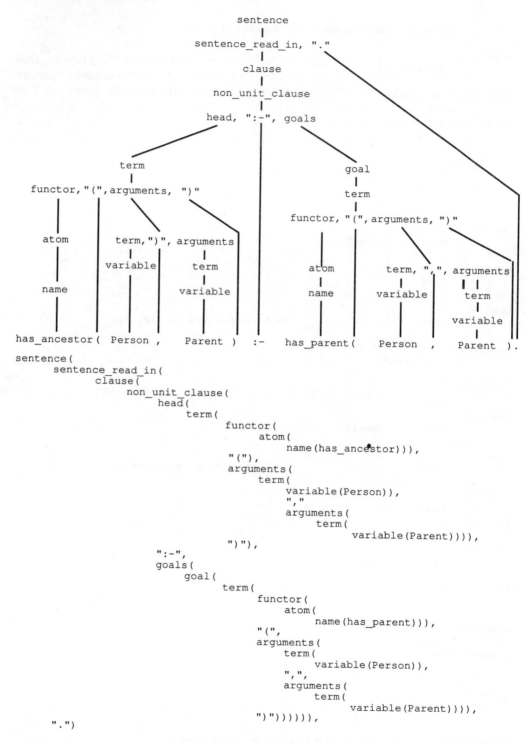

```
sentence(
    sentence_read_in(
        clause(
            non_unit_clause(
                head(
                    term(
                        functor(
                            atom(
                                name(has_ancestor))),
                        "(",
                        arguments(
                            term(
                                variable(Person)),
                            ",",
                            arguments(
                                term(
                                    variable(Parent)))),
                        ")"),
                ":-",
                goals(
                    goal(
                        term(
                            functor(
                                atom(
                                    name(has_parent))),
                            "(",
                            arguments(
                                term(
                                    variable(Person)),
                                ",",
                                arguments(
                                    term(
                                        variable(Parent)))),
                            ")")))))),
    ".")
```

Figure 8.6 Example parse tree in diagrammatic form and as a Prolog term.

An interpreter takes as input a program written in a particular language. The interpreter executes the program, statement by statement. Because interpreters work at a 'statement at a time', i.e. typically the current line of text in the program that they are executing, they execute the high-level language program considerably more slowly than the equivalent compiled machine language version of the program. This is because they must effectively partially translate each statement they execute; a given statement may thus be partially translated several times in the progress of a program's execution, unlike a compiler that fully translates each statement just once.

The source program is analysed, as in a compiler, using a lexical analyser followed by a parser. However, the parser, instead of constructing a parse tree, calls a procedure appropriate for the particular syntactic structure in hand. This called procedure carries out the execution using the actual values of any data items.

8.3.3 Compilation and interpretation compared

Because compilers produce machine language programs, time is expended in the compilation process which is done once, but the machine language object program can be executed as many times as one wants—at the raw speed of the CPU. However, if there is a problem with the resultant machine language program, finding out the error that caused it in the source program is difficult; for example the source program may not be available and there is usually no information kept in the machine language program that refers back to statements and symbolic variable names in the source program.

Because interpreters lexically analyse and parse each statement that they are to execute and then the execution is done by software (a program) rather than the CPU, interpreters characteristically execute their programs very much more slowly than the CPU interprets the machine language version of the program produced by a compiler. Developing a program using an interpreter is usually easier as it can often be operated in a debugging mode allowing, for example, the source language program to be stepped through one statement at a time.

It is increasingly the case that compilers are available that provide facilities to assist in relating the behaviour of the machine language object program with the source program.

8.4. ATTRIBUTES OF HIGH-LEVEL LANGUAGES

In this section, attributes of high- and low-level languages are compared and contrasted.

8.4.1 Advantages

1. *Ease of programming*. A particular high-level language is designed to be close to its domain of applicability or discipline; that is, it is suitable for expressing the solution to problems in the particular subject area for which the high-level language is designed. Thus programs are rendered:

- easy to write;
- easy for someone else to understand—for example when checking the program or maintaining the program.

   Both assembly language and machine language programming are difficult in that the programmer must translate problems to a language that is probably very different to that which would more naturally be used. In comparison with high-level languages, low-level languages provide no discourse that mimics even natural discourse. Rather the discourse is the set of machine language instructions of the computer's CPU and the representation of the hardware recognized built-in data types. (Refer to Fig. 6.1.) For machine language programs represented in binary, the discourse is in binary—in the very great majority of cases this is far from the manner in which a human would express the solution to a problem. In the case of assembly language, symbolic names with a mnemonic significance are usually used for machine language instructions, but the programmer must still translate the solution into the formats required for instructions and data, and the way the instruction set works; again these are nearly always far removed from the human's expression of the solution.

2. *Succinctness*. Machine instructions are typically very primitive; a given machine instruction carries out only a single and simple operation. As shown in Fig. 6.1, a given high-level language statement typically translates to several machine instructions.

3. *Program structuring facilities*. The solution to a problem expressed as a computer program is *structured* to correspond with the algorithm that has been expressed. During program design one decomposes the problem into sub-problems and so on. The grammar of a high-level language usually provides language constructs that allow one to structure the solution in terms of solutions to problems, and in a *nested* fashion. Procedural high-level languages usually have constructs to directly support sequence, selection and iteration. Assembly languages normally provide little in the way of structuring facilities.

4. *Fixed symbolic names within the programming language*. In both high-level and assembly languages the names and symbols provided for basic operations and structuring facilities are often given symbolic names. These names are often given a mnemonic significance to act as an aid to the programmer's own memory. For example many programming languages require the programmer to specify how data will be stored in computer memory, for example as characters (ASCII), or for numeric only data, as integers or in a floating (decimal) point representation for real numbers. High-level and assembly languages provide built-in type definitions with mnemonic names; see Fig. 2.2 for a set of typical examples and Fig. 5.17 for Pascal examples such as `integer` and `real`. Figure 6.1 has assembly language examples of mnemonic names (`load`, `add` and `store`) for machine instruction operation codes.

   Fixed symbolic names (such as `begin` in Pascal) are known as *reserved words*.

5. *Symbolic names for the programmer—symbolic data naming*. In high-level and assembly languages, addresses of locations in the computer's memory are given identifiers with symbolic names; the programmer typically would provide names

with a mnemonic significance. This capability avoids the problem of the programmer having to associate a numeric address with each data item. Furthermore, consider for example maintaining a program in which memory addresses are in their numeric form. Suppose for example a new instruction or data item is inserted in the program; many of the memory addresses will no longer be correct and will have to be manually altered, a very unsatisfactory state of affairs.

6. *Modular and object-oriented programming.* The programming language typically allows the programmer to designate individual structural units of program to have symbolic names. The units may be data structure definitions (type definitions), or they may be processing units in which case they include interfaces that also define the types of the input and output data. Structuring of programs in this way which assists both in the design process and in the ability to *reuse* programs is sometimes called *modular* programming. Such reusable program units are called modules. Most high-level and assembly languages provide modular programming facilities. *Object-oriented* programming languages provide further benefits (Fig. 6.19).

7. *Portability.* There are several good reasons why a program should be able to execute on different designs of CPU, which have different instruction sets. Not only is this convenient but in commercial terms it means that the investment in producing a program is maintained. Programs are not cheap; as artifacts they are labour intensive to produce. High-level languages assist in ensuring the portability of programs because they enable programs to be written that are independent of CPU design. Different designs of CPU can have very different instruction sets. Thus a program written in the assembly language of one CPU design may have no meaning for another CPU design.

There are several disadvantages in respect of portability of programs written in assembly languages—or for that matter high-level languages that have been designed for a specific CPU (not unknown, but perhaps not so common as in the past)—for example:

- A program written in assembly language will not execute on another CPU which has a different instruction set.
- The user can get 'locked-in' to a single supplier.
- Programmers, who are skilled persons, get 'locked-in' to a particular type of CPU.

Portability of both programs and programmers between different CPU designs can be achieved by providing a common high-level language but different translators for different CPU designs.

8. *Detection of errors.* High-level languages, as distinct from assembly languages, typically have a rich syntax, arising from the need to provide structuring capabilities. The syntax enables the detection and location of any syntax errors in the program. As well as errors arising from, for example, the use in Pascal, of a begin without a corresponding end, the syntax of types can ensure we do not attempt nonsensical operations—for example a statement in which a number is to be arithmetically added to a set of alphabetic characters (as in

adding a person's age to their name). The importance of syntax as opposed to *semantic* errors for programs that are compiled is that they can be detected during the compilation process, without executing the program.

8.4.2 Disadvantages

1. *Translation process*. It is particularly important that the translator programs, both compilers and assemblers, be fault-free.

   In comparison with a compiler, the translation of assembly language programs to their binary machine language program equivalents is reasonably straightforward. An assembler is structured very much like a compiler. However the grammar of assembly languages is usually simple. As one assembly language instruction statement corresponds to one machine language instruction, the code generation process is also straightforward.

   On the basis of relative complexity, it can be argued that for high safety and security applications there may be a case for using an assembler. In any case, if a high-level language is used for such applications, then a *validated* compiler should be employed.

2. *Unavailable functionality*. Because high-level languages are general purpose as far as the CPUs on which the translated machine language program is to execute, some features of specific CPUs are typically not available. Examples are input and output. Instead *separate* procedures are available to do such functions; these separate procedures may themselves be written in the assembly language of the relevant CPU and provided in a library. Portability is maintained by virtue of having a standard *interface* from the programming language to each of these procedures; e.g. in the case of C++, <stream.h> (see Fig. 7.5).

NINE

PROGRAMS AND HARDWARE

The objective of this chapter is to describe how the very great majority of stored-program digital computers work. We start by describing computer hardware in terms of the various physical functional units in a computer and how these are organized internally and with respect to each other. We then describe the representation of data and then of machine language programs within the computer's hardware. Finally we describe how the computer hardware interprets the machine language program.

The explanation of the detailed hardware functions of specific input and output devices (e.g. keyboards and screens respectively) and how data is transferred between these and the computer is deferred to Chapter 10.

9.1 COMPUTER ORGANIZATION

Stored-program digital computers, since their early days in the 1940s, have been organized in essentially the same manner with reference to the various *hardware functional units*.

Figure 9.1 shows the main hardware functional units of a computer and how they are *logically* related. The directions of the arrows indicate the direction of data flow. The *central processing unit* (CPU) is at the 'centre' and is in control of the input interface, the memory and the output interface. The input and output interfaces shown in Fig. 9.1 represent the logical boundary between the computer and the potentially very varied input and output devices.

The way in which computer programs are organized and executed by the computer hardware is essentially the same now as it was in 1949 when the 'Manchester Mark I' stored-program digital computer (built at the University of Manchester), first operated. In 1946 John von Neumann laid down the principles for the architecture of computers that apply to nearly all stored-program digital computers today (Burks, Goldstine and von Neumann, 1946). These are summarized in Fig. 9.2.

Memory

↕

Input → Interface → CPU → Interface → Output

Figure 9.1 Logical organization of a computer's main hardware functional units.

1. The machine language *instructions* that make up a computer program are stored in the same hardware functional unit, the computer's *memory*, as the program's *data* (hence the term *stored-program* digital computer).

2. The instructions are *executed* by the hardware functional unit called the Central Processing Unit.

3. The instructions are normally executed in the order that they are are present in the memory. This last requirement corresponds to the sequencing of steps in an algorithm.

4. Instructions are provided that allow different sequences of instructions to be executed.

Figure 9.2 Principles of the von Neumann machine architecture.

The von Neumann architecture implies that the computer memory is structured in such a manner that individual instructions and data items can be accessed by addressing, either *explicitly*, as is the case for data, or *implicitly*, for instructions executed in the normal sequential manner. Thus the memory is structured so that every *location* in it that can contain either an instruction or data item has a unique numerical address. Each address is denoted by a unique integer—0, 1, 2 etc.—up to the number of locations in the memory less one (in computer internals, one numbers from 0 rather than 1). Thus the memory of a computer that is directly accessible to instructions is a sequence of unique memory locations. Because each memory location can be accessed with the same effort and in approximately the same time, this type of memory is sometimes called *random access memory* (RAM).

Each memory location is of the *same* size. Usually the size of each location is sufficient to hold the representation of a *character*—e.g. a letter or a digit. This is why the size of a computer's memory is sometimes quoted in terms of 'the number of characters'. Depending on the design of the computer and the particular item that is to be stored in memory, there may not be a one to one correspondence in size between the item (e.g. an instruction or data item) that is stored in the memory and the size of a memory location. In this case, if the item is larger than a memory location, it will occupy a whole number of adjacent locations. To provide for selection and iteration in a program (derived from an algorithm), instructions are provided which, when executed, cause the *next* instruction to be *fetched* from a specified location in memory, rather than from the location with the next sequential address.

Figure 9.3 is a diagrammatic illustration of a sequence of memory locations. The current contents of each location is shown as a pattern of *bits*, a bit value being a 1 or a 0. Against each location is shown the location's address, again as a bit

address		contents	
(decimal)	(binary)	(binary)	(character)
146	10010010	01000011	C
147	10010011	01101111	o
148	10010100	01101101	m
149	10010101	01110000	p
150	10010110	01110101	u
151	10010111	01110100	t
152	10011000	01101001	i
153	10011001	01101110	n
154	10011010	01100111	g

Figure 9.3 Example of a portion of memory and contents.

pattern. Human representations of the bit patterns, both the memory locations' contents and each location's address, are also shown. The contents happen in this example to all be interpreted as characters (in another example some or all could have been numbers or instructions). The addresses are also shown with the equivalent decimal value. The coding between the bit pattern representation, the character representation (ASCII) and the decimal number representation is explained later in the chapter.

In general, the data contents of memory locations can be changed. This can either be by means of instructions (contained in memory locations) that are executed by the CPU, that is by a program directly, or by input of data from an interface to particular memory locations, again by execution of instructions, but in this case usually indirectly. Most memory is *volatile*, that is, the data contents are lost on the removal of power. In some applications permanent memory is required. Furthermore these same applications do not change the contents of the memory; they are limited to just 'reading' the data values or executing fixed programs. Memory which can only be read, and is permanent, is called *read only memory* (ROM). Clearly it is necessary that such memory initially can be written to.

9.2 HARDWARE DESIGN

Computer hardware functional unis may use different types of energy, for example electricity, light and magnetism. Control signals and data values are usually distributed within and between the different hardware components by electricity.

The requirement for the combination of a very large number of electronic circuits in a typical computer, together with a need for a small physical size, has led to specialized technologies for their design and manufacture. Small physical size is clearly attractive since bulky equipment incurs costs by virtue of the space occupied. Small physical size is also important because electronic circuits expend heat in use. Less heat will be expended with smaller circuits. Some large mainframe computers have to be water cooled! Small physical size is also of importance for the speed of processing. It takes a finite time to transfer control signals and data between and within components.

The basic electronic circuits that provide the elementary logical capabilities required by a computer are *packaged* to make up the basic components, the 'building blocks' of the computer. The circuits making up the components of a computer, and thus eventually the CPU, the memory and the input/output interfaces, are integrated on individual *chips* of semiconductor material.

The size of a chip is in the order of a centimetre square and is 'wafer' thin. Semiconductor materials, for example silicon, are so named because their ability to conduct electricity lies between a conductor (for example copper) and an insulator (for example glass). What makes certain semiconductor materials of use in computers is that when 'doped' with very small amounts of other particular materials, the doped semiconductor, under the influence of small electric currents applied in a specific way, can be switched between acting as an electrical conductor, or as an insulator. Using this property, one can construct controllable on-off electronic circuits. Using this controlled switching ability, it is possible to build the electronic circuits that provide a memory capability, and other circuits that emulate logical operations. The manufacturing technologies are called *large scale integration* (LSI) and *very large scale integration* (VLSI). VLSI design, because of the very large number of circuits and their interconnections needed to achieve some design (a whole computer—CPU, memory and input/output interfaces—can be present on a chip), requires a specialized approach. There are sophisticated software systems which are used by design engineers to produce the VLSI chip designs.

9.3 DATA REPRESENTATION

Information may be represented in physical form in many ways. We can distinguish the sense used from the representation used. Our senses of sight, hearing, taste, smell and touch are used to receive information. We can transmit information using the appropriate physical phenomena such as speech or writing. But information, to be such, requires common standards of representation and methods of interpretation. Between two agents communicating there must be a common understanding of the basic units of which messages are composed, and a means of understanding input messages and composing output messages using these basic units.

In computing we shall refer to the basic units by which information is represented for communication and for processing purposes as *data*. Computers have been applied in the very great majority of cases to information divisible into single units that can be processed. Text, composed·of characters, and numeric data can be readily processed. Images, pictorial information, can be represented in a computer. Much data in the real world is present as continuously varying quantities; for example temperatures and the colours in the rainbow. The input and output of data and any necessary conversions to digital form between the real world and the computer is described in Chapter 10.

In everyday life we frequently represent data by *characters*; for example letters of the alphabet to represent words, digits in numbers and the various punctuation marks. Words are made up of sequences of letters, numbers of digits. We assemble

letters	A, B, . . . , Z, a, b, . . . , z
digits	0, 1, 2, . . . , 9
punctuation marks and special symbols	! , " , & , . . .
layout	BEL, CR, SP, DEL, . . .

Figure 9.4 Characters.

text, whether literary or numerical with the aid of punctuation and layout, for example horizontal space and vertical space.

Characters are provided on a keyboard, word-processor or typewriter, by means of keys. Further keys provide for example horizontal space, backspace, carriage-return and line-feed. When we wish to represent data for input to, processing within, and output from a computer, the usual method is to use the characters found on a keyboard. Examples of these characters are shown in Fig. 9.4, in their *graphic* form where appropriate. Some characters have no graphic form, for example the equivalent of a typewriter's bell which is shown as BEL, the carriage-return which is shown as CR, the space bar by SP and the back-space key by DEL.

Suppose we associate a unique *integer* (i.e. a whole number) with each character. It is straightforward to store and manipulate numbers in computers, as will be explained shortly. There is a recognized standard for a specific set of characters and their numbering, the American Standard Code for Information Interchange, ASCII. Fragments of the ASCII character code table are shown in Fig. 9.5. Carefully note that the ASCII characters that are decimal digits do *not* have the same value as their ASCII character code. For example the ASCII character 7 has ASCII character code 55 (decimal), whilst the ASCII character code 7 (decimal) is the layout character BEL.

We have to deal with a finite set of characters. Each character has a number, its ASCII character code, in the range 0 to 127. It is thus possible to code any sequence of characters as a sequence of numbers. For example 'Cat.' can be coded as the numeric sequence 67, 97, 116, 46. An ASCII character code table can be used in reverse. For example the numeric sequence 68, 111, 103, 33 is the character sequence 'Dog!'. Thus it is possible to translate, in both directions, between keyboard characters and their numeric equivalent.

But how are the individual ASCII character codes to be represented in a computer? Calculating machines, whether the abacus or the mechanical devices now superseded by electronic calculators, typically represent numbers using the *base* ten. Mechanical calculators had a special representation for each of the digits 0 to 9. This means that numbers go from zero to nine and ten is formed from a 1 followed by a 0. For example the numbers zero to twelve are represented as:

0, 1, 2, 3, 4, 5, 6, 7, 8, 9, 10, 11, 12

Suppose instead of ten fingers we had eight. Our numbers might then be to the base eight. We might then have the following numbering scheme, called *octal*, for the numbers zero to twelve:

ASCII Character	ASCII code Decimal
BEL	7
CR	13
SP	32
!	33
"	34
	46
0	48
1	49
2	50
7	55
A	65
B	66
C	67
D	68
Z	90
a	97
g	103
o	111
t	116
z	122
DEL	127

Figure 9.5 Fragments of ASCII character code table.

0, 1, 2, 3, 4, 5, 6, 7, 10, 11, 12, 13, 14

In this case 10 is eight, 12 is ten and 14 is twelve! Note that we have to be careful in distinguishing the *representation* (e.g. 8, 10) from the value in words (e.g. eight, ten). Eight is eight irrespective of the number base, 10 might denote any number greater than one and is governed by the number base. In computing, programmers and computer hardware engineers sometimes use the base sixteen to represent values (for reasons that will become apparent). The number scheme with base sixteen is called *hexadecimal*. The numbers from zero to sixteen using hexadecimal are as follows:

0, 1, 2, 3, 4, 5, 6, 7, 8, 9, A, B, C, D, E, F, 10

Number	Base	
	Ten	Two
Zero	0	0
One	1	1
Two	2	10
Three	3	11
Four	4	100
Five	5	101
Six	6	110
Seven	7	111
Eight	8	1000
Nine	9	1001
Ten	10	1010
Eleven	11	1011
Twelve	12	1100

Figure 9.6 Numbers from zero to twelve to the bases ten and two.

Eleven is represented by A, twelve by B and so on up to sixteen which is represented by 10. 100 to the base sixteen is two hundred and fifty six (sixteen squared).

A much simpler scheme of numbering is to use the base two, *viz*:

0, 1, 10, 11, 100, . . .

The number scheme to the base two is called the *binary* system; the conventional system to the base ten the *decimal* system. Numbers from zero to twelve, to the bases ten and two, are shown in Fig. 9.6. Figure 9.7 shows an example of addition in binary. Notice that there has to be a 'carry' just as in conventional decimal addition.

```
  1  0  +
  1  1
------
1  0  1
```

Figure 9.7 Example of addition in binary: *two + three* gives *five*.

Using the binary system it is possible to represent the ASCII character codes using seven bits, see Fig. 9.8. However, computer memories are normally organized in eight bit units, known as a *byte*. Many computers have the byte as the unit of a memory location. Eight bits are used for two reasons, for data transmission checking, and because the hardware design is simplified. First, however, it is necessary to know the range of numbers that can be represented by one, two, three, etc. bits. Figure 9.9 shows the ranges for numbers of bits from one to eight. The range (denoted to base ten) is given by the following formula:

$$0 \ to \ 2^n - 1$$

where n is the number of bits. 2^n means 2 multiplied by itself n times; thus 2^3 is $2 \times 2 \times 2$, that is, 8.

| ASCII | ASCII code | |
Character	Decimal	Binary
BEL	7	0000111
CR	13	0001101
SP	32	0100000
!	33	0100001
"	34	0100010
.	46	0101110
0	48	0110000
1	49	0110001
2	50	0110010
7	55	0110111
A	65	1000001
B	66	1000010
C	67	1000011
D	68	1000100
Z	90	1011010
a	97	1100001
g	103	1100111
o	111	1101111
t	116	1110100
z	122	1111010
DEL	127	1111111

Figure 9.8 Fragments of the ASCII seven bit character code table—including binary codes.

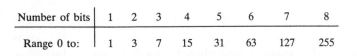

Number of bits	1	2	3	4	5	6	7	8
Range 0 to:	1	3	7	15	31	63	127	255

Figure 9.9 Ranges of numbers that can be represented by sets of bits (all values decimal).

ASCII Character	ASCII code		Parity		
	Decimal	Binary	Bit count (decimal)	Bit	Binary
SP	32	00100000	1	1	10100000
!	33	00100001	2	0	00100001
0	48	00110000	2	0	00110000
1	49	00110001	3	1	10110001
g	103	01100111	5	1	11100111
o	111	01101111	6	0	01101111

Figure 9.10 Examples of even parity.

Eight bits will represent numbers in the range 0 to 255 (decimal). However seven bits giving the range 0 to 127 (decimal) are sufficient for all the keyboard characters including the characters like BEL, see Fig. 9.8. The extra 'bit' is typically used when data is being transmitted, for example down a telephone line. Its purpose is for the *detection* of errors during transmission. This bit is called the *parity* bit. The idea is that, for *even* parity, the parity bit is set to be a 0 or 1 such that for any character, the sum of the 1 bits in the character—including the parity bit value—is even. For *odd* parity, the converse applies. Figure 9.10 shows some examples of the application of even parity. For example take the character '!'. Its eight bit pattern (from Fig. 9.8) is 00100001. The sum of the 1 bits in 00100001 is two, which is an even number. Therefore the parity bit for character ! is a 0, and thus its bit pattern with even parity is 00100001. Conversely, in the case of the character g, the sum of the 1 bits in 01100111 is five, an odd number, so the parity bit is a 1.

Suppose that in some computer system, or for some particular input or output device, even parity is assumed. If a character is input to the computer and it has an odd number of bits, this indicates an error has occurred during transmission, and software in the computer can act accordingly. Similarly, if an output device such as a screen receives a character with an odd number of bits, it may, depending on its sophistication, take action. Thus one reason for using the eight bit byte is that it affords parity checking.

9.4 THE BINARY SYSTEM

Digital computers use the binary system for representing programs and data, for executing programs, inputting data and outputting data. The binary system is simpler for computers because it is far easier to represent numbers using physical phenomena

Bit value	Electric current	Electric charge	Magnetism	Light
0	No current	No charge	North polarity	Absence
1	Current	Charge	South polarity	Presence

Figure 9.11 Physical attributes that could be used in a binary system.

by means of just two digits, 0 and 1. Some examples of physical phenomena used in computing are given in Fig. 9.11.

If we equate 0 with the `false` of logic, and 1 with `true`, it is possible to build circuits (typically electronic) that emulate the *elementary operations of logic* and their associated operators—and, or and not—together with an extra operation that proves useful—'not and' with the operator nand. Figure 9.12 gives the logical operations for two binary digits. One can then use these basic electronic circuits as building blocks to build more complex electronic circuits. An example of a more complex circuit is one to compare data represented in binary. Another frequently used circuit is that of the *adder* to do arithmetic addition on numbers represented in binary. So, for example, in arithmetic addition we need an electronic circuit design that will handle a 'carry' when the data values so require it (the nand is useful for this). The example of binary addition in Fig. 9.7 involves such a carry.

A further advantage of the eight bit byte is that eight, being a power of two, 2^3, simplifies the design of the computer's hardware.

Because numbers denoted in binary are so tedious to write down, and awkward to comprehend due to the multiplicity of 0s and 1s, and the lack of variety with just two digits, when computer programmers and computer engineers have to use explicit binary numbers, they usually represent them using their hexadecimal equivalents. Often, programming languages have a method of representing hexadecimal constants. In the C programming language, a leading OX or Ox represents a hexadecimal constant. Thus OX3A (or Ox3a) is 58 (decimal).

Binary digits		*Elementary Logical Operations*			
		conjunction	disjunction	negation	negated conjunction
A	*B*	*A* and *B*	*A* or *B*	not *A*	nand *A*
0	0	0	0	1	1
0	1	0	1	1	0
1	0	0	1	0	0
1	1	1	1	0	0

Figure 9.12 Elementary logical operations for two binary digits. 0 corresponds to `false`, 1 to `true`.

9.5 HARDWARE REPRESENTATION OF PROGRAMS

For a computer program to be executed by the computer hardware's central processing unit (CPU), the program must be in its machine language form and present in the computer's memory. In Chapter 8 we have seen how programs formulated in a high-level language, or an assembly language, are translated to their functionally identical machine language form.

The computer's memory, as has already been noted, is organized in individual locations, each of the same size, and each with a unique numeric address. The size of a location can vary between different CPU designs. Typical sizes are one byte, two bytes and four bytes—that is, respectively, eight, sixteen and thirty two bits. Sometimes locations of one byte in size are called *characters* and locations of two or four bytes in size are called *words*. Every machine language instruction and data item in a program, present in the computer's memory, is at a unique address in the memory. When the program needs to treat memory addresses as data, the addresses are also represented in binary.

9.5.1 Data formats

In this section we describe how individual data items are represented in the computer's memory. If we have to manipulate in memory, a data structure or a sequence of values, then we must rely on the high-level language compiler to have already generated instructions to split these down to their 'indivisible' constituents. This is because the instructions available with most CPU designs only operate with individual data items; for example an individual character or an individual number. There are CPU designs that recognize larger units than individual characters and numbers but we shall not discuss these.

Characters and numbers We have seen how character data is represented as ASCII character codes. There are various ways of representing numbers. For example 12 (decimal) can be represented as two ASCII characters, 1 followed by 2. The ASCII codes in binary are 00110001 followed by 00110010. Alternatively, the binary representation of 12, as a sequence of bit values, is 1100.

In mathematics we can have *integer* (whole) numbers, and *real* numbers (which when written in decimal notation can have digits after the decimal point). Indeed with recurring decimals and transcendental numbers like π and e there may be an infinite number of such digits. Furthermore, numbers in general may be positive or negative. When numbers are to be represented in a computer there is a finite number of bits available to hold a number. This imposes a restriction on the maximum size of a number and the *accuracy* of what the number represents. A byte will handle *integer* (whole) positive numbers in the range 0 to 255 decimal. Two bytes will handle numbers in the range 0 to 65 535 decimal ($256 \times 256 - 1$). If we also wish to have negative numbers, two bytes will handle negative and positive numbers in the range $-32\,768$ to $32\,767$ decimal (-256×128 to $256 \times 128 - 1$).

When we are dealing with the internals of computers, numbering starts at zero rather than one. In the case of decimal numbers, these can be stored as integer numbers together with an implied decimal point. For example, if we are satisfied with three decimal places, two bytes can hold decimal numbers in the range 0 to 65 535. The representation of negative integer numbers (for example −32 768), and of real numbers (by means of floating point) is beyond the scope of this book. You may wish to consult Anderson (1990) or Graham and Loader (1989).

Number representations The choice of which representation to use for numbers depends on the application. For example, provided no arithmetic is intended, the character representation may be used. Arithmetic, however, is much more efficiently done in terms of *speed* by the CPU with numbers in the binary representation. This is because the electronic circuitry is far simpler if the number is in its integer binary representation than if the number is represented as a sequence of ASCII digits. Furthermore, unless dealing specifically with low valued numbers, say up to 255 decimal for positive-only numbers, the binary representation is more efficient in terms of *space*, that is the amount of computer memory occupied. This is because a given byte that is used to hold numbers in the binary representation can hold a number in the range 0 to 255, whilst if the byte is used to hold a decimal ASCII digit then the range of the number that can be held is from 0 to 9.

Memory addresses The addresses of computer memory locations, which are unique numbers, are represented in binary. Binary is used for the advantages outlined in Sec. 9.4—the CPU frequently has to perform arithmetic with addresses, and address values can be comparatively large. Addresses themselves are required as data—for example, the address in memory of the start of a program, where within a program a selection operation instruction is to transfer to, and the address of an item of data. Irrespective of the value of an address, it occupies a fixed size in the memory of the computer, just as do individual characters and binary numbers. The amount of memory occupied by an address governs the maximum address possible; this therefore puts an upper limit on the overall size of the memory that might be accessed by a CPU. An address occupies usually two or four bytes giving, respectively, maximum possible memory sizes of 65 536 (2^{16}) and 4 294 967 296 (2^{32}) locations.

Memory sizing units When the size of memory is quoted it is sometimes given units of *kilobytes* or *megabytes*.

A kilobyte is 1024 (decimal) bytes, and a megabyte is 1 048 576 (decimal) bytes. Kilo, abbreviated to K, is *not* a *kilo* (1000 decimal). Mega is abbreviated to M. 1024 is 2^{10}, and 1 048 576 is 2^{20}. Thus a (small) computer with a memory size quoted as 64K bytes (or 64Kb) has a memory of 65 536 (2^{16}) bytes in size ($64 = 2^6$, $2^6 \times 2^{10} = 2^{16}$). A personal computer with a memory size quoted as 2Mb has a memory of 2 097 152 bytes.

There are further size units, and these too are based on powers of 2, the powers being multiples of 10 as is the case for kilo and mega. The units and their composition are shown in Fig. 9.13.

The memory available for application programs is usually smaller than the physical memory size. This is because there are normally already present in the

Unit	Abbreviation	Power of 2	Decimal size
Kilo	K	10	1 024
Mega	M	20	1 048 576
Giga	G	30	1 073 741 824
Tera	T	40	1 099 511 627 776

Figure 9.13 Memory sizing units.

computer's memory other programs before the user's application program is loaded. For example the operating system is already present in any but the most specialized fixed-application computers.

9.5.2 Instructions and their formats

Following the principles of the von Neumann machine architecture (Fig. 9.2), machine language instructions, when executed by the CPU, operate variously on data, and the selection and iteration of instructions. The CPU *executes* instructions in the sequence that they appear in locations in memory, unless the result of executing a selection or iteration instruction causes the next instruction to be out of sequence. Thus calculating the address of the location in memory containing the next instruction to execute, if it is in sequence, is a simple task for the CPU to do. Instructions themselves can be classified in a manner similar to the operations possible in an algorithm, see Fig. 5.12. However, instructions are normally very simple in their individual operation. If there is not an instruction that manages iterations of instructions, iteration in an algorithm is accomplished using an instruction that executes a selection, 'looping back' to an instruction in a memory location at a 'previous' (lower in value) address to the current instruction, until the iteration is complete.

Individual instructions have a binary representation made up of distinct parts represented as *contiguous* (that is, adjacent with no gaps) sequences of bits. An instruction typically occupies one or a few adjacent memory locations. One part, or *field*, is fixed for a given type of instruction—the instruction's *operation code*. The operation code specifies what the instruction does. Another field, the *operand*, is typically either the address of the memory location containing, or to contain, the data associated with the instruction, or the number of a *register* in the CPU. Registers are used as 'work areas'; they are each a small number of bytes in size. The CPU can access a register more quickly than it can access a location in memory.

Figure 9.14 shows the general format for an instruction. In fact, instruction formats are not usually as simple as this. For example, an instruction might have more than one operand, or there may be another field to indicate whether an operand address is direct or indirect (indirect meaning 'the address of an address').

Operation code	Operand

Figure 9.14 Instruction format.

The set of instructions, that is the set of valid operation codes and operand values for a particular CPU, is known as its *instruction set*. There happen to be several different CPU designs in use, each with its own instruction set. However instruction sets provide essentially similar basic functions, see Fig. 9.15, each instruction being elementary in operation. An add instruction, for example, adds two numbers together. One of the numbers will be at the memory location specified by the address in the instruction's operand, the other number might already be present in a register in the CPU—the result of a previous instruction execution.

1. Memory instructions

   - load—Copies the contents of the memory location at the address specified in the instruction's operand to a specified register in the CPU, overwriting the previous contents of the register.
   - store—Copies the contents of a register in the CPU to the memory location at the address specified in the instruction's operand, overwriting the previous contents of the memory location.

2. Arithmetic and logical instructions
   These operate on the contents of a CPU register, normally getting any other value from the memory location at the address specified in the instruction's operand. There are operation codes for both arithmetic operations, and logical operations. Examples of arithmetic operations are for example add, subtract, multiply, divide. The subtract instruction is sometimes absent; instead there is a complement instruction which causes a negation of the data, and the negated data is then added using an add instruction. Examples of logical operations are instructions to carry out and, or and not over a byte or a word (a small number of bytes) of data (see Fig. 9.12 for these operations on individual bits).

3. Branch instructions
   Branch instructions cause the CPU to execute the instruction (and typically those following) at the address specified in the branch instruction's operand.

4. Test instructions
   These instructions carry out a test, for example that the data defined by the operand is zero, and the result of the test, true or false, is stored in a register. true and false are usually implemented by a single bit which can take the value of 1 or 0; compare this with Figs. 2.2 and 9.12. The result of the test can be used by a *conditional instruction*. Examples of tests are whether the value in a CPU register is zero, or whether greater than zero, or whether less than zero.

5. Conditional branch and branch instructions
   A conditional branch instruction is one whose method of execution depends on the value set by a test instruction (which value will have been stored in a register). If the value is false, the next instruction is executed, as is normal. If, however, the test value is true the CPU executes the instruction (and those following) at the address specified in the current conditional instruction's operand. Thus test and conditional branch instructions are used by the programmer to cause the program to make *decisions* as to what part of the program is to be executed, typically on the values of data, input or calculated, at the time the program is executing. Conditional instructions are used to implement selection in procedural programming languages.

6. Input/output instructions
   Instructions are provided to input or output data between a memory location, or a number of locations at contiguous addresses, and an input device (e.g. a keyboard) or an output device (e.g. a screen). Input/output instructions and how they are used are described in further detail in Chapter 10.

Figure 9.15 Instructions found in a typical CPU's instruction set.

What is evident from Fig. 9.15 is how primitive individual instructions are in respect of what they do. They are rather remote from the operations that one programs in high-level programming languages. You may find it interesting to compare Fig. 9.15 with the basic procedural programming operations used in implementing algorithms shown in Fig. 5.12. The code generation stage of the compiler generates a sequence of such instructions in order to model the high-level language program. The instruction sets of different CPU designs can vary. Complex instruction set computers (CISC) have instruction sets in which the instructions are designed with (particular) high-level languages in mind; thus there might be a single instruction to implement a procedure call. The code generator step in the compiler is thus relatively straightforward. Reduced instruction set computers (RISC) have instead small instruction sets in which each instruction is very simple. A compiler's code generator step is therefore more complex. The proponents of the RISC approach argue that with a small number of simple instructions, a simpler and faster CPU can be made. The argument goes that the overall execution speed of a given high-level language program is faster than with a CISC CPU, given a sophisticated code generator that can take advantage of a given RISC CPU's instruction execution timing characteristics.

9.6 EXECUTION OF INSTRUCTIONS

In this section we explain how the CPU executes a program.

Figure 9.16 illustrates the same simple high-level language (Pascal) program fragment and its translation to the equivalent assembly language representation and binary machine language representation for a very simple hypothetical CPU as shown previously in Fig. 6.1. The purpose of this example program fragment is to program the mathematical formula:

$$z = x + y$$

This has been programmed in Pascal which includes the statement:

$$z := x + y;$$

This Pascal statement specifies that the memory location with symbolic address z is to have stored in it the sum of the data at memory locations whose symbolic addresses are x and y. (Note that the Pascal symbol $:=$ does *not* mean mathematical equality. It means 'copy the value on the right hand side to the memory location whose symbolic address is given on the left hand side.) Thus this single high-level language statement translates to *several* machine language instructions; this behaviour is not atypical.

Figure 9.17 illustrates the same binary program fragment as *loaded* (by the loader program) in the memory of the hypothetical computer, together with the CPU. This CPU has within it a *register* called the *program counter*. The program counter contains the address in memory of the current instruction being executed.

Pascal program fragment:

```
var x, y, z : integer; { define data representation }


begin



        z : = x + y;




end.
```

Translation to assembly code and binary machine instructions

assembly code			binary	
label	op code	operand	address	contents
x	integer		..0010	....
y	integer		..0011	....
z	integer		..0100	....
.			......	....
.			......	....
.			......	....
	load	x	..1001	0001..0010
	add	y	..1010	0100..0011
	store	z	..1011	0010..0100

Figure 9.16 Simple program in a very simple hypothetical computer.

The CPU also has within it another register called an *accumulator* which is used to contain the result of the current instruction. More sophisticated CPUs often have several such work registers. So, in the program fragment, the accumulator is used in building up the sum of the values present in the memory locations designated by the symbolic names x and y, for the result to be stored in the location with symbolic name z. The meanings of the load, add and store instructions for this hypothetical computer are as follows. A load instruction copies the data present in the memory location with address defined by the instruction's operand to the accumulator register. An add instruction adds the value of the data present in the addressed memory location to the value currently in the accumulator. A store instruction copies the value in the accumulator to the addressed memory location.

The CPU contains other registers but these are not available, at least directly, to the programmer; for example the *memory address* register which contains the address of the memory location specified in the program counter or the current instruction's operand.

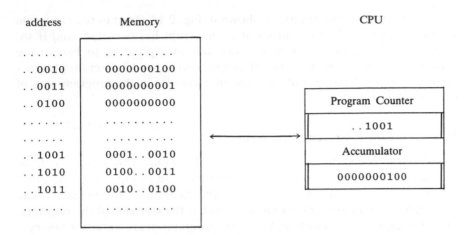

Figure 9.17 Simple program fragment in a hypothetical computer.

In Fig. 9.17 the program counter indicates that the computer is executing the load x instruction. The memory address register contains the address of the memory location symbolized by x that the CPU has extracted from the operand of the load x instruction. At this point in the execution of the program the values present in the memory locations with symbolic addresses x and y (*physical* addresses . . 0010 and . . 0011 are four and one respectively); this has occurred due to previously executed instructions (not shown). At the point of execution shown in Fig. 9.17, the CPU has just copied the value from the memory location with symbolic address x to the accumulator register by execution of the load x instruction.

9.6.1 Interrupts

The CPU must respond to asynchronous events as well as executing instructions. In responding to such an event, the CPU is interrupted. Hence such an event is

- Input or output transfer complete
  In all but the most primitive computers, input data and output data can be transferred between the device (for example keyboard or printer) and the computer's memory at the same time as the CPU is executing a program. This type of interrupt is to inform the CPU that the data transfer has completed.
- Input or output device attention
  If an input or output device's status changes, for example it is powered on or off, an attention interrupt occurs.
- Interval timer
  This interrupt is used so that the computer can be programmed to perform actions that are time dependent. An interrupt occurs at regular time intervals. An example of the use of the interval timer might be the transfer of a file of data to another computer at a time when the tariff to use a communication service is low. Another example might be in a chemical process that requires temperatures, pressures and flow rates to be input as data at regular intervals.

Figure 9.18 Examples of interrupts.

called *interrupt*. Examples of interrupts are shown in Fig. 9.18. Prior to the execution of each instruction, the CPU checks to see if an interrupt has occurred, and if so, suspends execution of the current program, switches to a program to handle the interrupt, and then normally resumes the interrupted program. Chapter 10 provides a further description of interrupts and their use in particular in the programming of input and output data transfers.

9.6.2 CPU instruction execution algorithm

The computer's CPU works by means of a fixed algorithm. This is shown in an informal manner in Fig. 9.19 and expressed in JSP notation in Fig. 9.20. The input to the algorithm is the contents of memory, and the contents of the registers. The output is any changes to the contents of memory and to the contents of the registers. The CPU is an interpreter for machine language programs represented in binary.

The CPU continuously iterates the following steps:

1. Process any pending interrupts. An interrupt is an asynchronous event, i.e. 'outside' the program being executed.
2. The CPU *fetches* the instruction from the memory address indicated by the program counter.
3. The CPU increments the value in the program counter so that it contains the memory address of the next instruction.
4. The CPU *executes* the instruction by extracting the operation code from the instruction and does as indicated by the operation code. This may involve loading data from memory to a register in the CPU, or storing data to memory from a register in the CPU. The address of the location in memory for the data is indicated by the instruction's operand. In the case of a branch instruction, the instruction's operand is the memory address of the instruction that is the next to be executed—the CPU places this address in its program counter.

Figure 9.19 CPU instruction processing algorithm expressed informally.

```
execute  iter
        instr seq
                    interrupt       iter
                            Process any pending interrupt

                    interrupt       end
                    Fetch instruction from the memory address
                    indicated by the program counter;
                    Increment the value in the program counter;
                    Extract the operation code from the instruction;
                    opcode      seq
```

Figure 9.20 CPU instruction processing algorithm—JSP notation.

```
                        Extract the operand from the instruction;
                        operand select        load
                                              Load data from the
                                              memory address whose
                                              value is that of the
                                              operand to the register
                                              specified in the
                                              instruction;
                                  or          store
                                              Store data from the
                                              register specified in
                                              the instruction to the
                                              location n memory with
                                              address that of the
                                              operand;
                                  or          arithmetic/logical
                                              Apply data from memory
                                              address to contents of
                                              the specified register;
                                  or          branch
                                              Place the value of the
                                              operand in the program
                                              counter  register;
                                  or          test
                                              Apply the specified test
                                              retaining the result —
                                              true or false — in a
                                              specified register;
                                  or          conditional branch
                                              If the test result in
                                              the specified register
                                              is true, place the value
                                              of the operand in the
                                              program counter
                                              register;
                                  or          input/output
                                              Perform the input or
                                              output of data between
                                              the specified input or
                                              output device and the
                                              specified address
                                              sequence of memory
                                              locations;
                        operand end
           opcode    end
      instr end
execute  end
```

Figure 9.20 (continued)

TEN

INPUT AND OUTPUT

In this chapter we describe how input and output of data is achieved, what input and output devices are, how they are accessed by the computer to achieve data transfer, how they can be classified, and finally we examine representative devices in more detail.

Data to be processed by computers exists in very many forms. Some of these forms are the result of computer generated output. In order that the computer can input data for processing, and then output the processed data, computers are provided with a variety of input and output devices.

Input and output devices, collectively called *input/output* devices, are the items of equipment from which a computer obtains its input data and to which it sends its output data. Examples of the more visible input and output devices include keyboards for input, modelled on the 'qwerty' typewriter keyboard, and screens for output, modelled on printing on paper. A keyboard with screen, used in conjunction with a computer, is called a *terminal*.

Somewhat less visible are disk drives and their associated disks for both input and output (unless read-only disks) modelled on, respectively, filing cabinets and their contents. We use the US spelling 'disk' rather than 'disc' as most software systems require this spelling when used as an identifier in programs. Less visible input and output devices include communications links to, for example, other computers, for both input and output, and a clock for the interval timer (some computers have their clock built-in, but the clock is still usually treated as an input device).

In some cases the form of the data to be input or output is that of continuously variable physical quantities, and is called analogue data (discussed in Chapter 1). To deal with analogue data, digital computers require it to be converted to digital form on input, and to its physical form on output.

A keyboard is an example of an input device and a screen is an example of an output device. In both these examples, the data is *character data*, thus the items of data will be ASCII characters in their binary form. A disk drive and its associated disk comprises a device in which data can be both input to, and output from the computer. The disk is where the data is stored. The form of data representation, whilst binary, depends on the application. If the data is a word-processing file, then *character* data represented as ASCII character codes would be apposite. Numerical data is possible, for example for storing the geometry of an aircraft wing. The disk is normally an *erasable* memory medium, one can *over-write* existing data. Compact disk—read only memory (*CD-ROM*) disks, which are the computer equivalent of CD-audio, are non-erasable.

Because the speed of communications is generally limited, and it does take time to transfer data, devices such as disks, which are frequently used and for which both the data rates are high and the *response times* must be low, are usually situated close to, or packaged within the computer cabinet.

10.1 HOW INPUT AND OUTPUT IS ACHIEVED

In previous chapters the notion of a computer has been introduced with the model:

data input → process → data output

To provide for input and output of data, hardware is required both in the computer itself, and also externally as devices to communicate in some fashion with either the real world (via analogue to digital converters (ADCs) and DACs for analogue data) or for data storage and retrieval purposes. The various input and output devices, such as keyboard and screen, are connected at the computer to hardware components within the computer called *input/output interfaces*. An input or output device may be housed within the computer, or be outside. For example see Fig. 1.10 which shows the packaging of a typical personal computer. Such devices may be geographically remote from the computer, a matter discussed in further detail in Chapter 12.

Physically, computers are usually organized so that the various hardware functional units are plugged into *slots* in a *bus*. A bus (short for the word 'bussbar—carrier of electricity') is effectively a channel along which control signals and data are transferred between the various functional units within the computer, see Fig. 10.1. Compare Fig. 10.1 with Figs 1.10 and 9.1.

The CPU is in overall control of the input and output of data, between memory locations and the input and output devices. This is because the CPU itself is under the control of one or more programs. The CPU instruction set includes input/output

		Keyboard	Screen	Printer	Disk
		↓	↑	↑	↕
CPU	Memory	Interface	Interface	Interface	Interface
↕	↕	↓	↑	↑	↕

Bus

Figure 10.1 Example of physical organization of main hardware functional units.

instructions (see Fig. 9.15) which enable the programming of the transfer of *binary* data between the input/output interfaces and the computer's memory. Input and output interfaces, and thus devices (such as keyboards, screens and disks), have unique numeric binary addresses. In programs one normally refers to a device with a mnemonic symbolic address. The operating system translates the device's symbolic name to the device's binary address.

In respect of the bus and the various hardware functional units, Fig. 10.1 might suggest that the various hardware functional units bid for the bus. At the level of the actual transfer of bytes or words data between the functional units, this is normally the case. Thus the bus can be used in a time-shared fashion so that several data transfers are apparently in progress at the same time. For example, on a personal computer, a document may be being printed at the same time as one is using a word-processor program to edit another document using the screen and keyboard. The ability of input/output devices to transfer data to or from memory locations in an autonomous manner is called *direct memory access* (DMA).

1. The CPU executes instructions that specify:
   - The address of input or output device;
   - The address of the first memory location of a sequence of ascending addressed memory locations;
   - The number of memory locations whose content is to be input or output;
   - Whether input or output is to be done (some devices can be both input from, and output to, for example a magnetic disk).

2. The CPU executes an input/output instruction. This instruction uses the data from the previous step to work out what to do.

3. The following bulleted steps are carried out *at the same time*:
   - The addressed input/output interface performs the following steps in sequence:
     – Data is transferred from the input device to the memory locations, or from the memory locations to the output device. This continues until all the data items (the number of memory locations) have been transferred.
     – The input/output interface *interrupts* the CPU and waits for a response.
   - The CPU carries on executing the same, or more usually another, program. This means fetching instructions from memory locations, loading data from memory locations into CPU registers, and storing the contents of CPU registers in memory locations.

4. When the input or output has completed and the input/output interface has interrupted the CPU, the CPU stores in dedicated memory locations sufficient data (called the *CPU context*) to enable it to resume at some later time the program it was executing. The minimum CPU context is the contents of the CPU's program counter register.

5. The CPU then loads the CPU context of the input/output interface's *interrupt handler* program, from another set of dedicated memory locations, into the CPU's registers. This operation may be done by the CPU's hardware, or the CPU may have to execute a program that determines which of the input/output interfaces has interrupted it.

   The storing of the interrupted program's CPU context and the loading of the interrupting program's CPU context, treated together, is called *context exchange*.

6. The CPU executes the interrupt handler program in order to do any processing as a result of the completion of the input or output data transfer.

Figure 10.2 Device driver algorithm for input/output using DMA and interrupts.

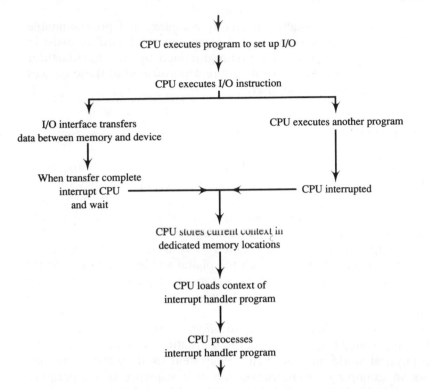

Figure 10.3 Diagram of device driver algorithm for input/output using DMA.

However, as has been said, the CPU is in overall control. In all but the most simple computers, there is delegation of local control by the CPU (by programmatic means) to the input and output interfaces, and thus to the devices. The way that input or output is programmed is by means of the algorithm shown in an informal manner in Fig. 10.2 opposite, and in a diagrammatic form in Fig. 10.3. This arrangement means that the various input/output interfaces and the CPU can be carrying out their tasks *concurrently* and thus provide a higher throughput of work.

The input/output algorithm shown in Fig. 10.2 is difficult to implement, requiring skilled *systems* programmers. For example, in general what will the 'another program' be? Furthermore, what if the input or output device is itself complicated? We shall see for example that disk devices are themselves addressable. Because of this, such input/output programs are usually provided as part of the computer's operating system.

In Chapter 11 we shall introduce two concepts to simplify input/output programming. Firstly we shall introduce the concept of the *process*, in which one can have more than one program appear to execute at the same time. Processes provide an easy way to take advantage of the ability of having the CPU and the input/output devices operating at the same time. Secondly, for each type of device, the operating system provides a device driver, a program that implements the algorithm shown in Fig. 10.2 with the specifics for a given type of device.

Input and output devices are usually sufficiently complex, and programmable to various extents, that they themselves use small computers 'on-board' to assist in their functions. These small computers are preprogrammed by the manufacturer and are packaged with the device. However the more sophisticated of these devices can often be further programmed by the user.

10.2 ANALOGUE DATA

Much data in the real world is present as continuously varying physical quantities. Computers may be required to output to devices that manage continuously variable quantities; for example the lighting intensity control in a green house. In computing, such continuously variable quantities are called analogue rather than digital; cf. the analogue computer described in Chapter 1 (see the figures starting with 1.2).

Many input and output devices can be deemed to be analogue in nature, and these provide the necessary conversion between the digital and analogue data forms as part of the device. In some applications, it makes sense to separate the conversion between digital and analogue form (particularly when the latter is electrical in nature) and the physical phenomena.

Hardware input devices called *analogue to digital converters* (ADCs) and hardware output devices called DACs carry out the translation between the analogue quantities of the physical world and the digital equivalent used by the computer. Figure 10.4 shows an example of ADC conversion of a sequence of temperature values recorded by a thermometer to digital data values (those that have appeared in Fig. 1.7).

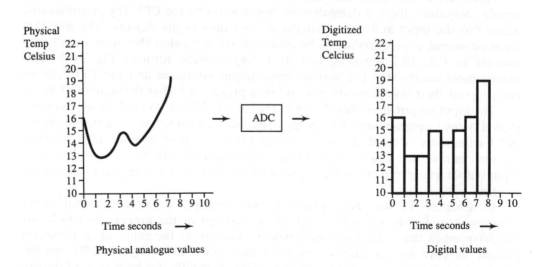

Figure 10.4 Analogue to digital conversion.

ASCII Character	ASCII code		Parity		
	Decimal	Binary	Bit count (decimal)	Bit	Binary
E	69	01000101	3	1	11000101

Serial data transfer
(by convention the least significant bit is usually sent first); thus

10100011 $\longrightarrow$

Parallel data transfer

1
1
0
0          $\longrightarrow$
0
1
0
1

Figure 10.5 Serial and parallel data transfer of the ASCII character E with even parity.

10.3 DIGITAL DATA TRANSFER

Digital data are transferred between the computer and input or output devices either *serially* or in *parallel*; see Fig. 10.5. In serial transfer, the data bits are transferred one after another. A parallel transfer involves the transfer of a sequence of bits, typically a *byte* (eight contiguous bits representing a character) at a time. Serial transfer requires simpler electrical cabling compared with parallel data transfers. However, parallel transfer speeds can be faster than serial transfers by a factor of the *data width*—the number of bits in the sequence. For these reasons, serial transfer is typically used for slow devices, such as keyboards and *serial printers*, whilst parallel transfer is used for fast devices, such as disk drives.

10.4 CLASSIFYING INPUT AND OUTPUT DEVICES

We classify input/output devices according to whom or what is immediately concerned with the data.

10.4.1 Human computer interaction

Human computer interaction (HCI) involves conscious human interaction with a computer. HCI thus requires motor activity by the human for input of data to the computer, and the use of a *sense* to receive data output from the computer. Thus computer data input is data output by a human, and vice-versa. The user interface with the computer has been described in Chapter 3.

Computer typesetting The representation of text on the screen or paper can be of importance. The restricted set of ASCII characters and their graphic representations is sometimes insufficient; for example where documents of publication quality are to be produced.

The computer equivalent of typesetting such material may dictate the use of various *fonts*, both in style and size; Fig. 10.6 shows examples of fonts available in the L^AT_EX documentation preparation system, see Lamport (1986), used during the writing of this book. We use the US spelling *font* rather than *fount*, due to the use of the word with the former spelling in computer document preparation software (cf. disk rather than disc). There is also the need to provide *diacritics* (e.g. circumflex as in rôle) and provide *special sorts* (e.g. dipthongs, as in dæmon).

10.4.2 Data acquisition and control

In this instance the data may be input with either no direct human involvement, for example temperature and flow rates in a chemical process, or the use of an interval timer to control the timing of the washing-cycle steps in a washing machine. There may be indirect human involvement; for example a light pen used to read bar codes on merchandise in a retail shop. Outputs typically involve no direct human involvement. Instead the output is used to *control* some device; for example a valve in a chemical process or the spin-dryer motor in a washing machine.

Font styles: roman, **bold**, sans serif, *slanted*, SMALL CAPS, typewriter.

Font sizes: tiny, scriptsize, footnotesize, normalsize, large, Large, LARGE,

huge, Huge.

Figure 10.6 Examples of font styles and sizes available in the L^AT_EX document preparation system.

10.4.3 Data storage and retrieval

Data storage involves output of data by the computer to a storage device and thence to a storage medium; data retrieval involves the input of data from the storage device and thus ultimately from the storage medium.

The memory directly (randomly) addressable by the CPU via the computer's bus might be used to hold such data but there are various problems associated with this approach:

- The memory is usually of a limited size. This is principally in consequence of its cost 'per bit' (however memory costs are decreasing as technology improves).
- The memory is normally *volatile*; that is it requires electrical power to maintain its data contents. Power is sometimes provided by a battery in the event of an unforeseen interruption in the supply.
- The memory is not normally designed to be removed from the computer with its data contents intact.

In consequence, data storage devices have been developed. An example of a data storage device is the magnetic disk drive and its associated storage medium, the magnetic disk. The following are points that affect comparisons between different types of data storage devices:

- *Logical size*. The logical size—as distinct from the physical size, itself a matter of consideration—is usually measured in bytes, or (because the values are usually unmanageably large), in K, M or G bytes (see Fig. 9.13).
- *Speed*. We need to distinguish between *seek time* and data *transfer time*. Seek time is the time it takes to get to the particular place on the medium at which the data resides.

    Seek time is typically small on disks, because, as is explained in detail later, the head (equivalent to the pickup on a gramophone) can be moved directly to a particular part of the disk. Hence we refer to such devices as *direct access* devices. On the other hand, tape based devices such as cassettes have, on average, a comparatively slow seek time, the access being *sequential*.
- *Fixed or removable media*. Fixed media cannot be removed from the computer, whilst removable media can. Fixed media devices are usually faster than removable devices, and a given device can normally store a larger amount of data than removable media devices. However removable media devices enable the transporting of data and the backing up of data. Backing up of data is discussed further in Chapter 11.
- *Cost*. Sequential access devices for data storage are in general cheaper than direct access devices. The mechanical components are simpler.

10.4.4 Inter-computer communication

The input/output devices so far described have been 'unintelligent', though (as will be explained in the next section) they are often in themselves programmable to a certain extent but in a very specific fashion—to make them more flexible devices in themselves. However, one can have as an input/output device another computer. In this case the 'first' computer is an input/output device of the other computer and the other computer is an input/output device of the first computer. One might wish to do fairly straightforward things like transfer a file of data from one computer to another one. Clearly if the other device is a computer, programmable in its own right, more sophisticated things can be done. We discuss these matters further in Chapter 12.

10.5 SPECIFIC DEVICES

In this section we describe some common input and output devices. The first two devices, keyboards and screens, are usually physically adjacent, and are used together by a user. However screens are also used alone, for example for displaying information in public areas.

10.5.1 Keyboards

Keyboards represent the typical input device for human use. They may be based on the typewriter 'qwerty' keyboard (named after the sequence of alphabetic keys at the top left of the keyboard), usually extended with extra keys such as function keys and a numeric key-pad. Specialized keyboards are used for specific applications; for example on a cash till.

Keyboards are designed so that each key or key combination (for example upper case letters require the simultaneous use of the shift key) generates the appropriate ASCII character code. The code is sent to the computer serially. For example for E, whose ASCII binary code with every parity is 11000101, the binary digits 10100011 (see Fig. 10.5) are sent one after another to the computer (by convention the least significant bit is usually sent first). The computer must reassemble the incoming bits into the byte containing the ASCII code and validate the parity of the transmitted character. This is usually done by *hardware*, except on primitive personal computers and primitive embedded computers where a program inputs each bit and assembles the resulting byte. Thus there must be a program executing in the computer that waits and then inputs each ASCII character code from the input interface and places the character in the computer's memory at particular memory locations. However the program may use an input character value to indicate something else is to be done. An example is the DEL character. The program in the computer that is inputting the input data must interpret this as a command to 'delete' the last character that has been placed in computer memory; the next character input will be placed at the deleted character's position.

When one sees the character that one has typed on the keyboard appear on the screen, it means that the program in the computer has, on input of that character, output it to the screen. This technique is called *echoing*. Echoing is not automatic; a program must instruct the computer to do it. This is because the keyboard and the screen are separate devices.

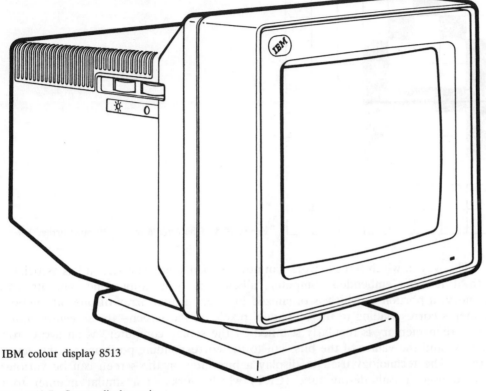

IBM colour display 8513

Figure 10.7 Screen display unit.

10.5.2 Screens

Screens are a common output device read by humans, see Fig. 10.7.

Close visual inspection of a computer screen will reveal that it is composed of a rectangular array of individual elements. These are called *pixels* (picture elements). In a monochrome screen, with no gradations from absence to presence of light (no 'grey' scale), a pixel is either off or on. If one inspects individual characters one observes that they are constructed of equal sized rectangular arrays of individual pixels. Figure 10.8 shows the character A occupying an array of 8×10 pixels. Note that the extra pixels at the right and base are needed to separate adjacent characters on the screen, and to handle characters with *descenders* such as g and q.

Character displays In this section we describe screens used to display ASCII character data—character displays. Each line on a screen usually has 80 character positions, and there are typically 24 lines. If each character occupies a rectangular array of 8 pixels in width and 10 in height, the whole screen will have 80×8 pixels in width and 24×10 pixels in height—a rectangular *array* of 640 *rows* $\times$ 240 *columns*, a total of 153 600 individual pixels.

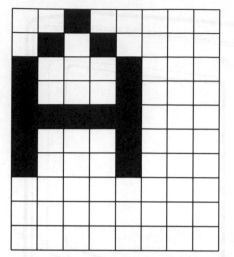

Figure 10.8 Character A in 8 × 10 pixel array.

The way in which screens work can now be explained. The screen has associated with it its own embedded computer, albeit usually a simple one, and its *own* memory, a portion of which is organized in a rectangular array of one bit memory elements corresponding to the individual pixels on the screen—the *screen memory*. The screen memory is regularly scanned by the screen computer, as an array, row by row, and the values of the bits sent to the corresponding positions on the actual screen. The technology used to display a bit value on the screen can be various; for example a cathode-ray tube (CRT) which works in a similar manner to a television tube or a liquid crystal display (LCD) as used with digital watches. Whatever method is used, the effect is to show a spot of light or be light reflective, for a pixel memory location containing a binary 1, and no light or be non-light reflective for a binary 0. To get dark characters on a light screen, *reverse video*, a binary 0 causes light or reflection and a binary 1 no light or non-reflection. The technology for implementing screen displays by scanning an array of pixels and displaying their bit values is called *raster* graphics.

The physical way in which the display itself presents bit values (e.g. cathode-ray tube or liquid crystal display) is normally independent of the application. Thus the same application can be used on a variety of different physical screen technologies.

Each character that can ever be displayed has an associated array (e.g. 8 × 10) of bits in a read-only memory (ROM) attached to the screen's computer. The bit values are permanently set to the required 0 or 1 value. Each of these character arrays has a unique identifier, its ASCII binary value. There is in the screen's computer a *register*, the cursor position register, which contains the position on the screen of the cursor as two coordinates—the horizontal (character position in a line) and vertical (line number). For example when the cursor is at the third character position and on the tenth line, the cursor position register will contain the numbers (in binary) (2,9) decimal (as noted previously, numbering in the internals of computers is from zero rather than one). When the computer outputs to the screen an ASCII character, the numeric value of the ASCII character is used to select the correct character array. The position of the next character (i.e. that following the last character input) is calculated using the current values in the cursor position register. Allowance must be made for the carriage-return character, and for *scrolling* when the lowest line on the screen has been completely entered. Knowing the bit values in the character array and knowing the cursor position, it is possible to set the relevant bits to the required values, 0 or 1, at the correct locations in the screen memory.

Graphics displays Raster graphics can be used to display computer typeset text and pictorial information as well as ASCII characters, provided that the *resolution* of the screen pixels is sufficiently fine, and that there is the necessary software in the computer to achieve this.

In the case of character data in computer typeset material, the software in the computer will, for a given character from a particular font, directly set the relevant pixels in the screen's pixel memory (rather than send to a character display device an ASCII code). A fine resolution is needed to distinguish font styles, to cope with small font sizes, and to handle formulae and diagrams. Because of the range of fonts, diacritics, special characters and so on, the pixel settings for characters are dynamically constructed by software rather than being obtained from a ROM as is the case for character displays. A common reason for displaying computer typeset material on a screen is to *preview* it during editing prior to committing to printing (typically on a laser printer described below).

Standardized software has been introduced for graphical user interfaces: the window system and window-manager functions; see Chapter 3. X-Terminals are terminals (screen, keyboard and mouse) which have an embedded computer with the X-Window system software permanently in place.

Because software to deal with fonts and pictorial information is both difficult and tedious to produce, special programming languages have been produced to alleviate this burden, one such being *PostScript* (a procedural high-level programming language, Adobe Systems Incorporated (1990)).

Pictorial information is represented as binary information associated with the pixels making up the screen. Pictorial information so represented is known as *graphical information* and there is an associated branch of computing known as *Computer Graphics*. The pictorial information may have been produced wholly by the computer, or it may be a *digitized* image from, for example, a digitizing camera (see Sec. 10.5.5). Pictorial data typically requires that each pixel has an *intensity* (black through greys to white), for example in the range 0 to 15 decimal, and possibly a colour. Sixteen grey scales means that each pixel will require four memory bits (0000 to 1111 binary) to indicate the intensity. The extra memory and electronic circuitry clearly adds to the cost. For each pixel, the data from the computer has four bits rather than one (to specify the intensity value for each pixel). (Intensity can also be implemented by software techniques. For example *dither* uses a higher pixel resolution. In a given area of the image, the proportion of 0 and 1 pixels governs the intensity.) The amount of data (in bits) transferred from the computer to the screen for raster graphics is considerably greater than if characters are to be displayed—for example 80 times for monochrome, 320 times for 16 grey scale levels compared with a screen full of 8×10 pixel characters. The use of colour requires each pixel to have further bits to indicate its colour. Because of the large amount of data associated with screens used for graphics, such screens usually require higher speed parallel data transfer links with the computer to prevent them from being unsatisfactorily slow in responding to changes in the information to be displayed.

Where a computer has a dedicated screen, as in, for example, personal computers or in computers designed for graphics applications, an alternative method to output data to the screen is often used. *Memory mapped screens* are ones in which the screen memory is the computer's memory. To update the screen display, the CPU alters the appropriate memory locations in the computer's memory.

10.5.3 Printers

Printers vary in the technology used to effect the actual printing; for example a print head and ribbon as with a typewriter, *ink jet* and *laser printers* that use a printing technology similar to that used by copiers.

The way characters are formed can be either whole characters (in the same way as a typewriter works), or the characters are formed from a set of elements using techniques similar to raster graphics. Data transfer is serial for the slower printers, for example *serial printers* which include those print head and ribbon printers in which the print head prints a character at a time and moves across the paper. Parallel transfers are used for faster printers; for example *line printers* in which a line of text is printed by having a print hammer for each character position over the width of the paper.

Dot matrix printers An example of character formation from a set of elements is the *dot matrix printer*, see Fig. 10.9. This is a serial printer in which the printer head is moved relative to the paper. As with raster graphics, each character is formed as a rectangular array of bits, for example 8×10. The print head has separate *print units* each capable of printing a dot. The dots so printed lie one above another in a vertical line. In this example there would be 10 such units. The printer head itself can be stepped to the different vertical columns making up a character, in this example 8 columns. Thus a character is formed by stepping the printer head from left to right within the boundary of the character and activating the relevant print unit. A dot is formed by the relevant print unit causing its needle to be pressed against the ribbon interposed between the print head and the paper. The translation of an ASCII code for a character to the relevant print needle units and the stepping of the print head is accomplished by software/hardware in the printer.

Dot matrix printers can produce various fonts for character material and pictorial information employing raster graphics techniques. However their relatively coarse print head resolution limits their application in these areas, especially with the advent of laser printers.

Laser printers Another example of character formation from a set of elements is the *laser printer*, also known as a *laser writer*; see Fig. 10.10. The way these work in respect of the organization of data for printing is similar to the method used by

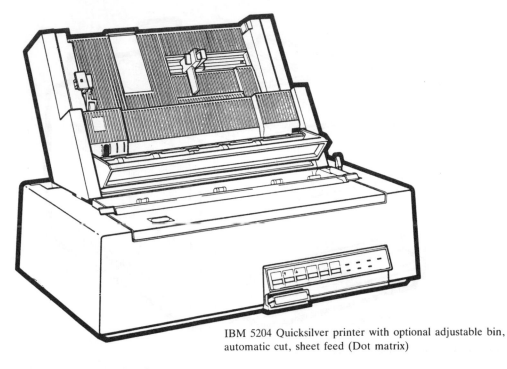

IBM 5204 Quicksilver printer with optional adjustable bin,
automatic cut, sheet feed (Dot matrix)

Figure 10.9   Dot matrix printer.

raster graphics screens. They have some advantages compared with dot matrix
printers. For example, they are comparatively silent in operation and this is an
important consideration when there are humans in the vicinity of the printer. Laser
printers can have a much higher resolution when compared with dot matrix printers.
Laser writers can thus produce publishing quality output with a range of fonts.

As with raster graphics, laser printers can be used to print computer typeset
material and pictorial information, providing the necessary software is present in
the computer, and the printer's own software (for example PostScript) and hardware
can manage this.

10.5.4 Disks

Disk drives and disks use magnetic or optical means as the recording technique.
Magnetic disks are normally erasable, whilst some optical disks (CD-ROM) are not.
Both magnetic disk drives and optical disk drives operate on essentially the same
principles, apart from the physical techniques of the data output (done once for a
CD-ROM disk) and data input.

The surface of a (magnetic) disk is coated with a magnetic medium. Small areas
can be magnetized as north or south poles (when data is output) representing the
area's bit value. When data is input the magnetic polarity of the area indicates its
bit value. In the case of optical disks, pits are formed on the surface of the disk

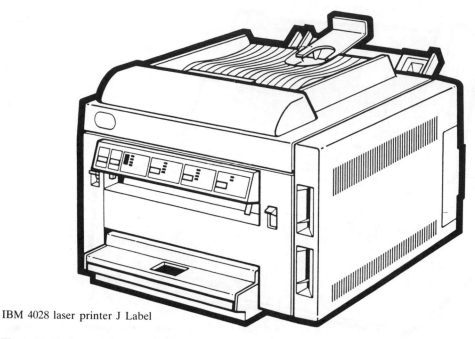

IBM 4028 laser printer J Label

Figure 10.10 Laser printer.

when the data is output. A pit or its absence at a given small area on the disk indicates an individual binary bit value. Pits are detected by means of reflected light generated by a laser that points at the relevant areas on the surface of the disk.

The surface of a disk is divided into a series of concentric circles called *tracks* over which an input/output *head* can be positioned, see Fig. 10.11. The disk is rotated at a constant speed, as in a gramophone. However, unlike a gramophone, the tracks are concentric circles, *not* a single spiral. The tracks represent just positions on the surface of the disk. Each track is divided itself into a set of *bytes*— each byte being eight bits. Each track has the same number of bytes—so clearly the bits in an inner track are physically closer than those in an outer track.

When a program within the computer outputs data to the disk, it first instructs the disk drive as to which track, and which byte in that track it is to commence outputting to. The head is positioned over the track, and the data as a sequence of bytes is transferred from *contiguous* locations in the computer's memory to the track under the disk's head. The value of each bit (0 or 1) in each byte causes the head to physically record the bit value on the area under it. For example, for a magnetic disk drive, the appropriate magnetic polarity is set in the magnetic coating on the disk surface below the head. Inputting of data is done in a similar manner, except that, for a magnetic disk drive, the head detects the changes in magnetic polarity to form the bit values.

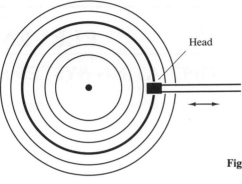

Head

Figure 10.11   Disk tracks and head.

10.5.5 Digitizing camera

The digitizing camera is a television camera which transmits data to the computer as a sequence of pixel values. Each pixel is as the pixel on a screen. The values indicate the intensity and the colour. The values themselves are binary numbers. Thus if four bits are associated with each pixel to indicate intensity, there will be sixteen possible intensity levels ($2^4 = 16$).

Because the picture, when transmitted to the computer's memory, will be in a well structured form—a rectangular array of data structures, each representing intensity and colour—one can have computer programs to *process* that data. The applications, *image processing*, are varied, for example:

* *Image enhancement*—in which one might manipulate the contrast, reduce 'noise' (for example pictures from inter-planetary space probes), and sharpen boundaries.
* *Recognition*—of shapes (for example a robot looking for say a nut or a bolt) and of features (for example to assist in medical diagnosis).

CHAPTER ELEVEN

OPERATING SYSTEMS

For other than the simplest applications of computers, for example those embedded in washing machines, there exists a set of programs collectively called an *operating system*. These programs provide the base facilities that make feasible the programming and running of application programs. This chapter explains what operating systems are, how they are organized, what facilities they provide, and how they coexist and interface with application programs.

The term 'operating system' is derived from the fact that in the early days of computers, many of the operational aspects of computing (those now carried out by operating systems) were carried out either manually or with considerable manual intervention.

As we have seen, computer systems comprise hardware and software. The software at first sight would appear to be just the programs to solve particular problems—for example a program to act as a word-processor. Unfortunately it is not that simple. If we consider the word-processor example we soon find out that if we write a program for a word-processor, then a lot of the programming is involved not with the specifics of word processing (such as justifying a paragraph) but with programming functions that will be present in many of the other programs. Such programming tasks include reserving locations in memory for the program's instructions and data, input from the keyboard, output to the screen and the printer, and input/output to files on disk.

An operating system provides facilities to simplify the use of the computer by all the users of the computer (see Fig. 13.1). Many operating system facilities act as a 'layer' between the user and the internal aspects of the computer system, for example the bare hardware, the format of data, the addresses of individual input and output devices, and the interfaces between and to programs. The user should have a consistent and uniform *logical* view of the programs and facilities available on the computer and not be concerned how these are *physically* realized. Operating systems comprise programs that enable users to name and access the resources of the computer in a consistent manner. A good book on operating systems is by Silberschatz, Peterson and Galvin (1991).

11.1 RESOURCES

The resources managed by an operating system are both *physical*, for example the computer's memory and a magnetic disk, or *logical* such as a particular file of information (amongst the many files present). Physical resources are hardware, whilst logical resources are those perceived by the user via a program or programs. Thus a file of course information has, say, the logical name courses, but it is physically realized on a particular collection of tracks on a magnetic disk. The user refers to the whole file as courses, whilst the operating system supplies (for the use of programs accessing the file) the map or translation between courses and the specific disk tracks on the particular disk drive.

The availability of resources means that they require management. This is because resources are sometimes needed by more than one processing function at a time. For example, on a personal computer we might be printing a document *at the same time* as inspecting an electronic mail message. It seems that we are sharing the CPU and the memory as resources between two processing functions. We call these functions *processes*. A process is a program that is, or can be, executed. Processes may have to contend for the resources. Resources may be *indivisible* or *divisible*.

Indivisible resources, for example a CPU or a printer, cannot be split up. However, they can sometimes be *time-shared*. For example if one requests several files of information to be printed, and there is a single printer, one expects the print of each file to be separate. One does not expect the text from the various files to be jumbled together. Thus the printer is used on a time-sharing basis. In the case of a CPU, this can be time-shared between more than one process (executing program), as when printing a file at the same time as using a word-processor. The CPU switches between the processes sufficiently quickly that the output on the screen appears simultaneously with the output to the printer. This is possible because the CPU can execute the instructions of the process's program quickly relative to the slower data output speeds of the screen and printer. In any case output to the screen and printer can be simultaneous due to DMA.

Divisible resources are those that can have parts of themselves reserved; for example a magnetic disk can have several files stored on it; and the memory of a computer may have various programs present, each in a different sequence of memory locations.

Resources (both indivisible and divisible) rely on another resource, time. Processes may have to wait their turn for an indivisible resource, or, in the case of a divisible resource, until sufficient of the resource is available. We shall return to this subject in Sec. 11.9 after first describing the various operating system components.

11.2 AN OVERVIEW OF OPERATING SYSTEM COMPONENTS

Figure 11.1 gives an illustration of the various components of an operating system, the logical resources and facilities that they provide, and their relationships with the computer's hardware.

OS Component	Relationship with Hardware	
	Logical	Physical
Interactive Computing	Login, command interpreter, electronic mail	Encryption/decryption mail addresses
Graphical user interface	Window system, and window manager facilities	Screen, keyboard and mouse.
Filing system	Files, whole and contents, directories	Disk drives, disks
Operating System Services	Programmatic Interface	Physical (and logical) resources
Process Management	Separate asynchronous processes	(Usually) single CPU
Memory Management	Areas of memory for programs and data	Actual memory
Initializing the System	Command interpreter, system checks— e.g. filing system consistency	All physical resources established and checked

Figure 11.1 Operating system components.

Operating system facilities can be directly visible to the user—for example, the *filing system* and the various utilities for carrying out operations on the filing system (e.g. printing the contents of a directory or a file, or making a copy of a file). On the other hand, operating system facilities may be used in an 'invisible' manner, for example *memory management* which is used whenever a program is loaded into the computer's memory and when use of the program has finished.

11.3 INTERACTIVE COMPUTING

Interactive computing is when the user, most commonly using a screen and keyboard, gets the computer to do what is needed, there and then.

For other than embedded computers, or computers used for just display purposes, there is human interaction with the computer system by means of an input device and an output device. With general-purpose computers the interaction is normally by means of a keyboard and screen respectively. Interactive computing refers to this method of dialogue with the computer system, and the associated operating system facilities that are used.

A given computer may have one or more users. The computer may be used either simultaneously (in which case there may be several screens and keyboards) or it is used in a serial manner, one user after another. In such circumstances it is normal to provide a *login* facility, to protect the computer, and any data stored in it, from unauthorized access. The facility selects the *home* directory of the user in the filing system (where the user's own files are stored), and is often used to select the *initial program*, to be first executed when the user has successfully *logged in*.

During login, the user types a *login-id* followed possibly by a *password* that should be known only to the user—and to the computer system. The operating system has a password checking program and password file to ensure the correct login-id/password combination has been entered. The password is normally *encrypted* both when it is registered for the user, and when the user logs in. The encryption is a one-way process—one cannot 'de-encrypt'. Encryption of passwords means that one cannot discover passwords even by examining the password file.

The program to be executed by the CPU after login is usually a *command* interpreter. A command interpreter (or *command shell*) allows the user to execute arbitrary programs. The command interpreter executes *command lines* (see Sec. 11.10). Command lines are either typed on the keyboard, or are present in a file called a *command file*. The command interpreter starts by executing the commands in the *login* command file. Each user may have their own login command file. If, after login, the computer system is to enter a particular application program, this is accomplished by the necessary command lines in the login command file.

Command line execution is immediate, hence the term 'command interpreter'. If the command interpreter is obtaining command lines from the keyboard, it provides a prompt on the screen before each command line is typed (and immediately echoed, character by character, on the screen). Such use of the command interpreter in this manner is called interactive.

Command lines start with the name of the command followed by zero or more command *arguments*. Commands can be implemented in various ways:

1. *Built-in*. The command is one that the command interpreter itself carries out. In effect the command name identifies a section of program within the command interpreter program.

    Built-in commands are used for frequently used commands that are easy to implement. An example of a built-in command might be that to list on the screen a directory of files on a magnetic disk.

2. *Command file*. The command name is the name of a file. The file contains a series of command lines (in their simplest form these would be as one might interactively type in to the command interpreter) in which case the command program is called a *command file*. Indeed, because one might want to solve complex and *abstract* problems—certainly more complex than line at a time command lines—command languages have programming capabilities akin to procedural high level languages. Thus variables, and sequence, selection and iteration constructs, are provided for the programmer.

    A command file that users and installers of software systems frequently make use of is the login command file. Another example of a command file is one to call a high-level language compiler and then a linker, as might be done during program development (see Fig. 8.1).

3. *Binary program*. The command name is the name of a file. The file is just a program in binary (machine language) form. The command interpreter executes the loader program (one of the programs making up the operating system). The loader loads the binary representation of the program from the file into locations in the computer's memory. The binary program is then requested for execution and comes under control of a component of the operating system, *process management*.

While the binary program is being executed, the command interpreter program's execution is normally suspended.

When the binary program terminates, the command interpreter program resumes execution from its point of suspension. The command interpreter program then normally executes the next command from the keyboard or the command file.

There is no hard and fast rule as to how commands are implemented. So with one operating system command interpreter, the command to display on the screen the contents of a file may be directly executed by the command interpreter, and on another operating system command interpreter the command name may be that of a binary program that is loaded and when it executes, does the file display. What is of importance to the user is that at the level of typing in commands the user is unaware of the method of implementation. This is an example of where an operating system provides the user with a consistent uniform logical interface, in this case to commands.

Commands frequently name operating system *utilities* (for example file processing utility programs to copy and delete files) as well as packages, such as a word-processor, high-level language compilers and interpreters, and the user's own programs.

11.3.1 Graphical user interface

Where a graphical user interface (GUI) is provided, the operating system is often responsible for this. The GUI and its components—the window system and the window manager—are described in Chapter 3.

If the operating system supports multiple concurrent processes (often called 'multitasking'), that is, the ability to have more than one program executed by the computer at the same time, then this fits well with multiple windows. Each application active in the computer at the same time is associated with a window or a set of windows. Thus one might have on the screen a word-processor and a graphics design package at the same time.

11.4 FILING SYSTEM

How are programs and data saved for reuse at some later time? How do we name and organize *files* of programs and data? How do we ensure unauthorized people do not read, change or delete programs or data files? How do we organize sets of data to suit the way in which it will be usually accessed?—do we use a key as in an author index in a university library system, the author's name being a key? What about managing the space on the medium on which files are to be stored, typically a disk (cf. a book library's shelf space)? The media on which files can be stored are usually divisible physical resources, for example magnetic disks. The *filing system* is the component of the operating system that provides the facilities that these questions imply.

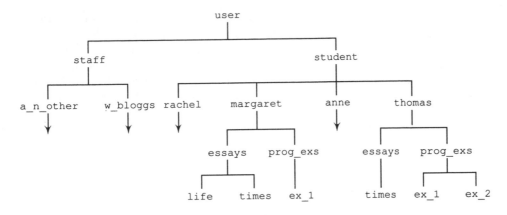

Figure 11.2 Example of an hierarchical filing system directory structure.

Consider files on disk. Each file has to have associated with it at least the number of the track and byte within the track where the file starts, that is, the *disk start address* of the file. If the file spills over a track, then there must be a scheme to find the subsequent track numbers reserved to the file. The filing system is responsible for the allocation of space (tracks) to files, and the release of space when the file is deleted.

If more than one file is to be stored on a disk we need a *directory* (itself a file!) to enable us to find the relevant file. A directory will have for each named file the disk start address, together with information to ensure only authorized users can access the file. Modern filing systems allow an *hierarchical* directory structure to be built; thus the *top-level* directory can obtain directories as well as files, and so on. This gives a 'tree-like' structure in which the directories represent branches and the files leaves. Hence the top-level directory is sometimes called the *root* directory. Each user has their own *home* directory in which they can hold their own files—and directories.

An example of a file directory system is shown in Fig. 11.2. This illustrates a directory hierarchy down to users' home directories. These in turn will typically contain directory hierarchies that have been created by the individual users to serve their own particular needs. This is shown in the case of Margaret and Thomas. It is usual to show directory 'tree' structures in the up-side down fashion illustrated in Fig. 11.2. A file is uniquely named by the names of the directories from the root directory down to the file. This sequence of directory names terminated by the file name is called a *full pathname*. Using the UNIX operating system and starting at the top-level or root directory user, in Fig. 11.2, the full pathname for Margaret's 'times' essay is the following sequence of directory names:

```
/user/student/margaret/essays/times
```

Using the MS-DOS operating system and assuming that the file hierarchy is on the A disk drive, the full pathname for Margaret's 'times' essay is:

```
A:user\student\margaret\essays\times
```

We shall use the UNIX conventions for file naming for the rest of this section.

Notice that the hierarchical structure allows different files to have the same names but within different directories; for example `times` and `ex_1`. As all files have unique full path names they are distinct. It is tedious to use full path names, especially if one is referring to files in a particular directory. Hierarchical filing systems thus enable each user to have a *current* directory. The name of a file can normally be expressed as just its name when it is in the current directory, or by a *relative* path name from some current directory nearer the root of the directory hierarchy. So, if Thomas's current directory is:

```
/user/student/thomas/prog_exs
```

he can refer to his 'Exercises 1' file by just:

```
ex_1
```

rather than:

```
/user/student/thomas/prog_exs/ex_1
```

The current directory is normally the home directory when a user logs in to the operating system. The user can change the current directory to an arbitrary directory providing that access is permitted to that directory—as defined by the entry for the directory in the hierarchically preceding directory. The root directory is a special case as it does not have an hierarchically preceding directory.

With several files, several disks, and in particular, on non-removable media, the user should not be concerned with physical matters like disk names, and 'where' particular files and directories reside. The filing system should provide a *logical* view and achieves this using the directory structure.

It is usually the case that many different applications will require many of the above filing system facilities. Rather than each application program containing within itself the programs to manage and access the file system hierarchy and the files within it, it makes good sense to have these facilities separated out and already present as part of the operating system. Advantages of this technique are that we obtain smaller programs (the filing system program occurs just once), standardization and consistency. For example one program might *output* data to a particular file, another can *input* data from that file. Each program need neither care nor know how and where the data is actually organized on the storage medium, and indeed what type of storage medium is used. Thus a program need only concern itself with the job in hand, not the minutiae of the precise organization of the data in the file and the layout of the file on the disk. We could alter the data organization on the medium and the program would not have to be changed. This example illustrates that characteristic of operating systems in which they act as a layer between the user and the hardware; the separation of the logical view and the physical view.

11.4.1 File back-up

To reduce the chance of losing data in a file, either by error, malpractice, hardware failure or physical loss or damage, operating systems provide *utility* programs to *save* individual files and also file directory structures. The programs copy the files or whole file directory structures to another, removable medium. The copy can then be archived, often at a different site. It is normal practice to create such *back-ups* in a regular fashion at intervals that reflect the value of the data.

Because operating systems normally record for each file (for example in the directory containing the file) the last time the file contents were changed, more sophisticated back-ups are possible. For example one might back up only the files that have changed since the last back-up.

11.5 OPERATING SYSTEM SERVICES

Most programs want to do common functions with standard interfaces like *input* of data, *output* of data, create a file, and get the current date and time. Writing programs to do these things again and again is clearly not sensible. Also it turns out that writing such programs is not easy, especially input and output device driver programs. Instead, a set of programs, operating system services, is provided as part of the operating system to carry out these basic functions. To enable application programs access to the operating system services, a library of interface programs is normally supplied with each high-level language system. For example, for C++ program libraries <stream.h> and libC.a provide access to certain of the operating system services (Fig. 7.5).

11.6 PROCESS MANAGEMENT

It is usually possible to organize the processing functions to be carried out by a computer so that these can be done in a wholly or partially independent manner. For example in an air-line seat reservation system, many of the transactions can be done independently of each other, whilst others are interrelated (consider simultaneously reserving seats for different clients in the same aeroplane).

In many cases then, whether one is using a single user personal computer, or is one of many *concurrent* users of a computer, the computer will apparently be executing several processes at the same time. Such processes are called *concurrent processes*. How is it possible for one computer to have more than one process being *executed* apparently *concurrently*? If one process pauses waiting for the transfer of *input* data or *output* data to finish, how is this pause effected? Should some processes have higher *priority* than others?

The computer's (usually single) CPU is an indivisible physical resource. Process management is involved in scheduling the CPU between the various processes sequentially. Because CPUs execute instructions at high speed, and for most of the time processes are held up waiting for input or output to complete (Figs 10.2 and

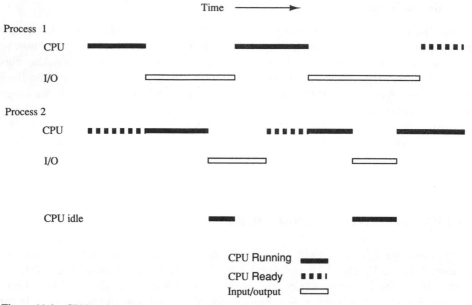

Figure 11.3 CPU and input/output overlap.

10.3), the CPU can be shared between processes with typically little degradation to the speed performance of each process. Figure 11.3 illustrates an example of the use of the CPU and input and output of data being overlapped in time.

11.6.1 Process states

We can show the (finite) possible states a process can be in by means of a finite state diagram as in Fig. 11.4. The diagram shows the possible states of a single process. Finite state diagrams are frequently used in computing. It should be understood that, in general, there are at any one time several processes in various states in a computer. Some of these processes are clearly 'user' processes, such as one associated with a current application like a word-processor. There are other less obvious processes such as an electronic mail receiver process and a process that is printing a document. There are also the various operating system provided input/output device driver programs which have a process for each input/output device, and an interval timer process which runs on a regular basis as a result of interval timer interrupts.

11.6.2 Process scheduling

Process scheduling is concerned with sharing the processor between processes. We shall introduce this topic for systems in which processes do not have priorities. The first scheduling method to be described is called 'round-robin'.

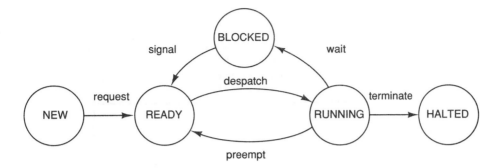

Figure 11.4 Process's states using a finite state diagram.

Round-robin scheduling A process starts in the **NEW** state (see Fig. 11.4) after the loader program has loaded the binary version of the program into an available sequence of locations in the computer's memory. A **request** occurs—by another process. For example, when a command line names a process, the command interpreter process creates a new process, and requests it to execute. 'Create process' and 'request process' are operating system services. The **request** causes the process to enter the **READY** state, where it joins the 'ready' queue (see below) of other processes also waiting to be executed by the CPU. Notice that such processes can normally be run independently of each other for some or all of their execution. Thus, there may be several processes in the **READY** state. If there is only one CPU, there can only be at most one process in the **RUNNING** state.

The process eventually gets to the head of the ready queue (as described below), is **despatched** and enters the **RUNNING** state. The machine language instructions in the process's program are then executed by the CPU, as explained in Chapter 9.

Eventually, the process in the **RUNNING** state either **terminates**, thus going to the **HALTED** state, or enters the **BLOCKED** state. The **BLOCKED** state is entered for example by the process requesting an input/output device driver process (provided by the operating system) and then waiting for input data to be read, or output data to be written from an input/output device. (Chapter 10 describes how input and output is achieved.) Alternatively, for a driver process the process is **BLOCKED**, waiting for an interrupt.

When the data has been input or output, or the interrupt has occurred, a **signal** occurs and the process re-enters the **READY** state queue.

Figure 11.5 illustrates the ready queue of processes (each in the **READY** state) at some instant during the use of a personal computer. If the user creates a window, the process associated with the 'create window' program would be *enqueued* (added to the *tail* of the queue). Similarly, if a facsimile process is **BLOCKED** on a data transfer, when this is completed, the fax process is enqueued on the ready queue. When the currently executing process (not shown) goes into the **BLOCKED** or **HALTED** state, the Mail Program is *dequeued* (from the *head* of the queue) and enters the **RUNNING** state. **READY** processes thus progress from the tail of the

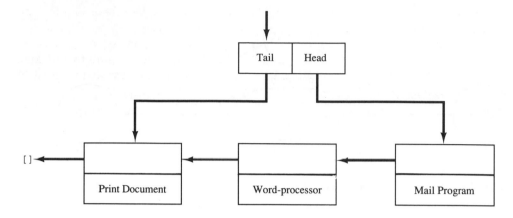

Figure 11.5 Ready queue of processes.

queue to its head; the queue stores the data, in this case the identifiers of the processes, on a first-come-first-served basis.

Pre-emptive scheduling Unless, as in round robin scheduling, processes voluntarily transfer from the READY state to the BLOCKED or the HALTED states, *pre-emption* of the current RUNNING process is necessary when either a higher priority process enters the READY state—event-driven scheduling—or because a process may take too much time in the RUNNING state—time-sliced scheduling.

Event-driven scheduling Blocked high priority processes (such as those responding to an interrupt), when they become READY, should be RUN in preference to a lower priority process in the RUNNING state. In this situation, *event-driven* pre-emptive scheduling is used. The lower priority process is transferred to the READY state, and the high priority process is placed in the RUNNING state. In a priority based, event driven scheduler, the READY processes occupy a stack rather than a queue.

Time-sliced scheduling Because a process may take too much time in the RUNNING state, thus holding up processes in the READY state that might be of higher priority, some operating systems *pre-empt* a running process, transferring it to the READY state and thus allowing the process at the head of the READY queue to be despatched. To provide time pre-emption scheduling, called *time slicing*, the operating system is itself run on a regular basis as a result of an interval timer interrupt to the (BLOCKED) interval timer process. The interval timer process itself pre-empts the currently RUNNING process, as too do other high priority processes (typically the input/output device driver processes).

Process priorities A given process may have a certain priority to be executed by the CPU. High priority processes are often ones that are to respond to an interrupt; or the user may have decided to mark a given process to be of high priority. Because of varying priorities, a single queue of READY processes, as described, is often not adequate. Various techniques can be used. For example, there can be a queue for each priority level, and an array of these queues. The next process to be selected to be transferred from the READY state to the RUNNING state is found by indexing the array until the first non-empty queue is found, and the process at the head of that queue is dequeued as the selected process.

Process context A process comprises the following:

- *Stored program*—the program that is present in the memory of the computer.
- *Data*—the data items associated with the program present in the computer's memory.
- *Resources* reserved by the process—for example input/output devices.
- *CPU context* the values in the registers in the CPU whilst the process is in the RUNNING state, such as the program counter and the accumulator register (see Fig. 9.17).

   When a process leaves the RUNNING state, its CPU context is stored in the computer's memory, at dedicated locations specific to that process. When a process enters the RUNNING state, its CPU context is loaded from where it was stored in memory to the CPU registers. As with interrupt handling (see Fig. 10.2), the storing and loading of the CPU's context are together called *context exchange*. In the case of a NEW process, the initial values of the registers (such as the program counter to indicate where in the program to start from) are placed in the process's dedicated memory locations for its CPU context.
- *State*—the location of the process on the state diagram as in Fig. 11.4.

11.6.3 Transaction processing systems

A common use of process management is in *transaction processing systems*, sometimes called *on-line* transaction processing systems. Examples are air-line seat reservation systems and bank cash dispensing systems. Such systems are characterized by having many simultaneous users (and thus processes) and shared data, subject to change. Each user performs one or more *transactions*. For example a clerk in a travel agency may make an air-line seat reservation for a passenger on the same flight simultaneously with another clerk at perhaps another travel agency. The process of seat reservation in the aeroplane requires that only one process at a time completes a reservation. To ensure the consistency of the changeable shared data (discussed in Sec. 11.9), the technical difficulties usually result in transaction processing systems running on a single powerful computer (i.e. a fast CPU or CPUs, large memory, many terminals) in which it is easier to program for consistent data access. The programming issues are discussed in Sec. 11.9.

11.7 MEMORY MANAGEMENT

The computer's memory, that is the memory directly accessible to the CPU, is a divisible physical resource.

How do we organize the space in the computer's memory into which varying sized programs will be *loaded* and for varying data size requirements? What happens if we need to fit more than one program in the memory? (For example, at the same time as the computer user is using a word-processor to edit a document, another program is printing a separate document on the printer.) What if the sum of the sizes of such programs is greater than the size of the available memory, or a given program is larger than the available memory?

Memory management is that part of the operating system that provides facilities to cater for some or all of these various resource requirements. In the simpler operating systems some of the requirements outlined above cannot be provided. For example if a given program is larger than the available amount of memory, this means that the computer programmer has to tailor the program in order that it can be loaded. One method is to split the program into separate programs or program parts (called *overlays*). Statements have to be added to the program to load the overlaid parts of the program when they are required. This is clearly a tedious matter and requires some skill. Furthermore, the available amount of memory is not necessarily fixed.

The more sophisticated operating systems provide *virtual memory* which relieves the programmer from the need to tailor programs to fit into the available memory. With virtual memory, the operating system manages the computer's memory space used by the programs in a manner that the programmer can be unaware of. In *paged* virtual memory (see Fig. 11.6), transparently to the programmer, programs are split into equal sized pieces called *pages*, and the computer's memory area that holds the programs' pages is also split into equal sized pieces called *page frames*. The pages of the programs that are being run on the computer (i.e. of the processes) are kept in a page file on a fast access data storage and retrieval device such as a disk (such devices are cheaper per byte than memory). Frequently only a subset of the program's pages may be present in computer memory at any particular time. Thus a program that is currently being executed by the CPU may refer to a location in 'virtual' or logical memory but whose address happens to be in a page of the program that is currently not in a page frame (for example a reference to page 3 in Fig. 11.6). If this happens the operating system places the process in the BLOCKED state (see Fig. 11.4), loads the required page from the page file into an unused page frame, and then returns the process to the READY state. If there are no available page frames, then an occupied one is chosen for replacement by the operating system and its contents (another page of the same program, or a page of another program) is if necessary output to the page file.

The reason that this technique for managing memory is called virtual memory will now be apparent. The programmer's view of the memory that a program uses is a 'virtual' or logical one; the operating system *maps* this virtual view to page frames in the computer's physical or real memory. The mapping is done by means of a page table; there is one of these for each process, and its content is maintained by the operating system. When, during instruction execution (Figs 19.19 and 19.20), the CPU refers to a memory location, its address is translated from the logical

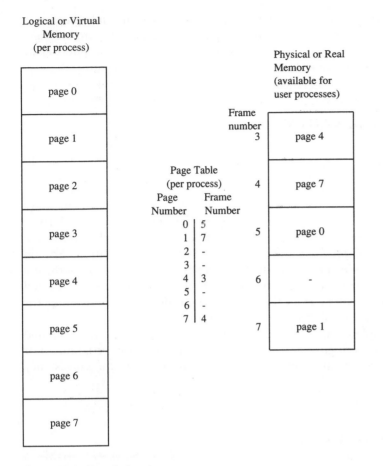

Figure 11.6 Paged virtual memory.

address to the physical address. This translation is performed by the computer's *memory management unit* (MMU) hardware; the programmer of the application does not have to do anything. The same hardware detects an attempt to access a memory location in a logical page not in physical memory. In this case the hardware causes the operating system memory management program to run. The MMU is both logically and physically situated between the CPU and the bus connection to the computer's memory.

Paged virtual memory relieves the programmer from organizing the use of memory, and it enables a given amount of memory to be shared between programs whose total requirements may be greater than the available amount of memory. However, paged virtual memory does require extra facilities including memory management unit hardware, a more sophisticated operating system and space on a fast access device for the page file. Because pages are loaded on demand, and loading takes time (both the output of a replaced page and the input of the referenced page), there can be delays in processing.

11.8 INITIALIZING THE SYSTEM

The computer system must be *initialized* when the computer is powered up. Computer memory is usually *volatile* in that without electrical power, any data is lost. Thus when the power is switched on, the operating system and then, perhaps, application program(s) must be loaded automatically into the computer's memory and executed. This process is often called *booting* the system. 'Booting' is derived from *boot-strap loading*. This loading process is itself potentially complicated so the idea is to have a series of *loader* programs of increasing sophistication. So, on power-up, a very simple loader program which is already provided by the *hardware* in read only memory (ROM) is executed and in its turn it loads a more sophisticated loader into the computer memory from the relevant input device. This technique is then repeated, i.e. loading by using its own 'boot-straps'.

It is normal to complete initializing by loading and executing the command interpreter—as in interactive login—and run any necessary checking programs. For example, an operating system utility program may be run to check the consistency of the filing system.

11.9 RESOURCE MANAGEMENT

The basic physical resources of disk space, the CPU and memory, have been introduced in earlier chapters, together with their operating system resource managers, namely the filing system, process management and memory management respectively. There are usually other physical resources that require management; for example the printer, and a communications link to a computer network. There are also typically many logical resources, both indivisible and divisible that require management. Examples of these are files (consider a file that can be changed by more than one user—how can consistency be maintained?), and the data structures that the user and the operating system use to manage both logical and physical resources.

When one studies the various resource management needs, it is evident that the following basic properties must be established for a given resource:

- Divisibility
  - *Indivisible*—e.g. a CPU, a keyboard, or a software package with a single user licence.

- *Divisible*—e.g. a magnetic disk medium, or a screen when used with a GUI system.
- Shareability
  - *Exclusive access*—e.g. printer when there may be several users or programs requiring a print at the same time, or a software package with a limited number of user licences.
  - *Concurrent access*—e.g. a file of air-line flight seat prices accessed by agencies throughout the world.
- Subjectivity to change—e.g. a file containing the seat reservations for a particular flight.

Thus a resource may or may not be subject to each of the above properties. Where a resource is shared between more than one process, then the management of that sharing may be non-trivial. The study of resource management is a considerable subject—we shall introduce just two problems by way of illustration.

11.9.1 Critical sections

Where data that can be changed is shared by more than one concurrent process, then the processes may not function correctly. For example, suppose there are two processes P1 and P2, which both access a shared variable integer data item whose memory location is named count. P1 increments count and P2 decrements count. The Pascal statements to do this are:

P1	P2
count : = count + 1;	count : = count − 1;

Thus, incrementing or decrementing can be achieved by a single statement. When the program(s) containing the above statements are compiled to a hypothetical machine language (simple, but not unrepresentative of machine languages), each statement translates to a sequence of several machine language instructions. These (using assembly language for representation purposes) are:

```
        P1                          P2

load    count               load    count
add     1                   add     −1
store   count               store   count
```

Suppose the CPU can be scheduled by a time-slicing scheduler between the two processes P1 and P2, and that the current value in count is 0.

The following two (of many) sequences of instruction execution are possible (the value in count before an instruction is executed is shown in the centre):

Sequence A

		P1	count		P2
1.	load	count	0		
2.	add	1	0		
3.	store	count	0		
4.			1	load	count
5.			1	add	−1
6.			1	store	count
7.			0		

Sequence B

		P1	count		P2
1.	load	count	0		
2.			0	load	count
3.			0	add	−1
4.			0	store	count
5.	add	1	−1		
6.	store	count	−1		
7.			1		

Sequence A provides a correct value for count after the two Pascal statements have been executed. Sequence B, however, results in an incorrect value; sequence B purports that incrementing and decrementing zero results in one!

A *critical section* is a section of program where a process changes the value in a location shared with one or more processes. The illustrations above show two critical sections, one for P1, and one for P2, because the location count is shared between these two sections of program each of which is to change whatever data value exists in count.

If critical sections occur, to guard against incorrect results, when one process is in its critical section none of the other processes should be in their critical sections. This was the case in sequence A, but not sequence B.

A combination of hardware techniques, operating system facilities and approaches to design can be used to manage critical sections. Further detailed discussion is beyond the scope of this book. However it is worth noting that one technique, *semaphores*, involves having a queue associated with each shared location. A process joins the queue if another process is in a critical section for that shared location. When the (other) process leaves its critical section, the waiting process at the head of the queue enters its critical section.

11.9.2 Deadlock

There are two non-shareable indivisible resources, R1 and R2. There are two processes, P1 and P2.

Process P1 has reserved resource R1, and requires resource R2 (as well as R1).

Process P2 has reserved resource R2, and requires resource R1 (as well as R2).

As a result the two processes are deadlocked with respect to each other.

Deadlock is a potentially serious problem when we have a system in which there is more than one process competing for resources. Techniques exist to variously:

- *Prevent deadlocks occurring*. For example resources must be requested according to a total ordering (e.g. R1 always before R2).
- *Avoid deadlocks occurring*. For example, if the resource manager is previously told the reservation requests that are to be made, it can sequence the processes and avoid deadlock.
- *Detect a deadlock and then recover*. For example, on detection of a deadlock process P1 is forced to a previous state prior to reserving resource R1, thus releasing R1 and allowing process P2 to continue. Subsequently P1 continues from the previous saved state. Such schemes are complex; for example states at certain points must be saved in case they are needed for deadlock recovery.

11.10 OPERATING SYSTEMS AS PLATFORMS

Operating systems have developed into *de facto*, and now industry, standards as *platforms* on which application programs can be executed. All the issues and problems summarized above are abstracted out of application programs; for example a Pascal programmer just uses a read statement to read some data. The programmer does not have to be concerned with either how a read statement is *implemented* or, another useful feature, with what particular file is to be used or on what medium the file is stored unless these are particular requirements.

Consider for example the copy program. Using the command interpreter the user might type, using the MS-DOS operating system:

```
A>copy file_a file_b
```

where A> is the command interpreter's *prompt*, here indicating that one's current directory is on disk drive A. At the time of writing the program copy, the programmer does not have to know the names of the files or whether the files are on disk or whether one of the files is, say, the printer (file_b would then be prn).

These are important points as they mean that a program is more valuable by virtue of its portability between different computers, operating systems, and users of the program with their own files.

Many applications use specific operating services, and the interfaces to, and functionalities of, the operating services can differ between operating systems. In the case of programming languages, these differences can to some extent be hidden from the programmer by means of libraries which contain standard interfaces and which within themselves map to the particular operating system.

However, it is often difficult to guarantee portability between operating systems. There tends to be a plethora of 'mapping' software or conversions to be undertaken. For example, consider the problem of full pathnames between the UNIX and DOS operating systems for Margaret's essay file:

UNIX:

    /user/student/margaret/essays/times

MS-DOS:

    A:user\student\margaret\essays\times

The MS-DOS command language differs from that of UNIX; so for the file copy example:

MS-DOS:

    A>copy file_a file_b

UNIX:

    $ cp file_a file_b

where $ is the UNIX shell (command interpreter) prompt.

In practice, portability is often difficult to achieve.

TWELVE
COMMUNICATIONS AND NETWORKS

The data, the processing capability and the user may be geographically separated, and so communication is essential. *Communications* is the study of information transfer; note that with this meaning, 'communications' is singular in number. In order to connect the data, processing capabilities and users, *networks* of computers and computer terminals are used.

The data to be communicated may be input/output data, for example, a terminal comprising keyboard and screen remote from the computer. Stored data may be remote from the user and also the user's computer; a file of prices of items on another computer, or *electronic mail* messages from another user using a remote computer. The locations of the data, the computers with the processing capability, and the various users might be geographically distant—another town or country—or they might be 'local'—on the same university campus.

Where data is communicated we term the various *logical* connections between the computers and input/output devices a *network*. We can have a *wide area network* (WAN) for geographically dispersed communications. For a local and dedicated community of users of individual computers who require access to common facilities such as printers and shared files we can have a *local area network* (LAN). A good book on the subject is Halsell (1988).

12.1 LOCAL AREA NETWORKS

Figure 12.1 shows a small LAN comprising three computers in the form of workstations (see Sec. 13.4.1); a file server computer (it has at least one disk drive), and a print server computer. This example is an *open* LAN rather than a *closed* LAN as it also happens to have a communication interface to the external world.

On a LAN there are typically requirements to share *resources*, both logical (for example files) and physical (for example hardware such as disk drives and printers, and computers themselves). The connections to one or more WANs are also examples of resources. These requirements are for convenience and/or cost. To

Workstation	Workstation	Workstation	File Server	Printer Server
Keyboard and Screen Computer	Keyboard and Screen Computer	Keyboard and Screen Computer	Disk Communications Computer	Printer Computer
↕	↕	↕	↕	↕

LAN Communication Medium

Figure 12.1 Local area network example.

share resources, a given resource such as a filing system and its associated disk drive or a printer are attached to a computer called a *server*. The reason for using a computer is to provide a uniform logical interface to the *clients* of the resource. Thus, for example, even though several people on their own client computer request a print-out of their own file at around the same time, the printer server computer will accept these requests and queue them (usually in temporary files on the file server computer's disk) for subsequent printing.

Because LAN users are physically close together, for example in the same building and in the same organization, there is a resulting requirement for high speed communications using the LAN communications medium (see Fig. 12.1) to shared facilities such as disk drives (for shared files).

Each computer on the LAN normally uses the same operating system. When one does this one endeavours to make the use of the LAN 'seamless', so that the users, both programmer and package user, do not have to know where the physical resources such as file servers are located. Having the same operating system means that the same standards are employed on all the computers; for example all the computers will use ASCII character codes and files of identical format. It is not uncommon for all the computers on a LAN to have the same instruction set for their CPUs. This means that the same binary form of a program (that is the machine language representation of the program) can execute on any of the computers. Thus the file server need have just one file for each (binary) program that any of the LAN computers might execute. When a computer's operating system is to be initialized, it may be loaded from the file server rather than from, for example, files on the computer's own disk drive. Indeed, some computers on the LAN may be 'disk-less' with private files on the file server.

Where the filing system is seamless across the LAN, it is sometimes termed a *networked* filing system. If the operating system is seamless, allowing, for example, processing as well as files to be distributed over the LAN (so as to provide users with an optimum service), then we have a *networked* operating system. Networked filing systems are not uncommon; networked operating systems are more difficult to implement. The ability for a user to logon to any of the computers in a network is an example of a network service to be expected in a networked operating system. In short, the components of the LAN must be mutually compatible.

12.2 COMMUNICATION CHANNELS

Underlying all communications is the need for communication *channels*, the actual carriers of data. Various physical media are used, for example electricity in wires, microwave radio and light in fibre optic cables. Communication channels may be dedicated for the whole or part of a computer network—*dedicated lines*—or one might use the public switched telephone network (PSTN) or other shared channel system provided by a communications service organization. The data may travel over different channels between its *end points*, with 'relay' points or *nodes* in between—for example satellite links.

When we mail a letter to someone we only need to give their name and address; we do not give routing instructions. Similarly, in the case of computer communications the user does not normally wish to be involved in the *routing*, that is the various channels and intermediate nodes being used; the user is only interested in *logical names* of the 'end points' and the *virtual circuit* between them. However the people involved with supplying and maintaining the communication services do need to know these particulars.

Data is represented in binary form in the computer or in storage media, and is transmitted within the computer, and between its input/output devices, in this form. To use a PSTN voice system that uses analogue rather than digital data transmission, one needs to translate each binary digit value, 0 or 1, to be transmitted, to one of a pair of audible tones (like musical tones) for the telephone wires, and at the other end translate the tones back to the binary digits. To do this one uses a piece of equipment called a *modem* which stands for modulator-demodulator. A modem will work in both directions, that is, for both sending and receiving digital data over the PSTN voice system. The modem is attached to an input/output interface in the computer. The hand held part of a telephone (that incorporates the microphone and ear piece) is placed on the modem which has corresponding audio generation and input ports. Modems are available that function without a telephone hand-set.

The introduction of *digital* telephone exchanges means that binary data can be transferred on some telephone lines; integration of both voice and digital data using the same medium, the integrated services digital network (ISDN), is the goal of these advances.

WANs are *logical* entities that are implemented over typically heterogeneous communication channels; a mixture of PSTN, ISDN, microwave and other communication channels may be involved. Although LANs are also logical entities, they usually have dedicated homogeneous physical channels due to the high data *traffic*, geographical proximity, and speed requirements.

There are instances when the data representation of the information being transferred is different for the sender and the receiver and translation must be effected. If the information is of a confidential nature, then it can be *encrypted* by the sender's computer system, transmitted in encrypted form, and *decrypted* by the receiver's computer system.

Information can be represented in data in a variety of ways; previous examples include positive integer numbers that can be represented as ASCII characters or as binary integers. Where there are alternative data representations, for some given information, the various data representations can vary considerably in size. There is usually one representation that the user or computer program that uses the data for input requires the data to be in. Depending on the nature of the data, it can be *compressed* by the sender's computer system and decompressed by the receiver's computer system. This can result in communications costs savings. Examples of such information include graphical data (digitized pictures) and numerical data where a high proportion of values are the same (often zeros).

12.3 ADDRESSING

Addressing in the PSTN has been present for very many years and is achieved by means of dialing codes and subscribers' telephone numbers. Connections are established, routing through appropriate telephone exchanges in the process of setting up a *call*. In a WAN we might use telephone numbers at least to whole computers or to the computer that serves as a *gateway* between the WAN and the LAN. Individual human users of electronic mail on a LAN or a gateway computer normally have a unique *electronic mail* (email) identifier which is a mnemonic representation, rather than a numeric one as in telephone numbers. An email address identifies not only the user but possibly the department, the site and the particular WAN. For example:

    P. G. Greenfield©CS. BHAM. AC. UK

where CS stands for Computer Science, BHAM for the University of Birmingham, AC for the academic network, and UK for the United Kingdom. The various mnemonics in an email address correspond to numeric addresses, and numeric addresses are those that are used by the network software on the various computers along the route. Tables are maintained on these computers map mnemonic names to numeric addresses.

12.4 MULTIPLEXING

Over a particular *physical* channel, such as wires or a fibre optic cable, there may be the need to have more than one communications call in progress at the same time. The needs include cost, complexity (too many cables) and an unacceptable waiting time for a call. Even though the *data rate* in bits per second may be high, a communications *session*—the period of a call—may be characterized by brief periods of data transfer and long periods when idle. Consider for example the user of a bank cash dispensing machine (an example of a transaction processing system terminal). Whilst the user is thinking about and composing a reply for a request by the computer system for information, the communications channel can be used for transmitting other users' and computer messages.

Multiplexing involves the simultaneous sharing of a channel between several users. The method of multiplexing used by both LANs and also communications service organizations who provide such channels, is to break each of the individual units of data transfer (whether files, data for programs, documents to be printed or electronic mail messages) into discrete *packets*. The packets are sent separately, but eventually arrive at the relevant end point where they are reconstituted to form a copy of the original data unit. Thus, in packet-based multiplexing the channel is 'time-shared' between the various data users.

Communications service organizations provide packet switched system (PSS) services. Functionally a PSS provides data transfer like the PSTN except instead of the primary use being for telephony, it is used specifically for packets of digital data. A packet assembler dissembler (PAD) is a computer system that is the interface between the user's terminal or computer, and the PSS. It is used to dissemble a message being sent into packets and present these to the PSS. On reception of a message from the PSS, the PAD assembles the packets into the message. Within the PSS the individual packets are transmitted independently; the routing of the packets is also independently done.

12.5 OPEN SYSTEM INTERCONNECTION

Communications requires at least two communicators and thus communicators must agree on the *protocols* to be used, that is, the precise rules for communication. To enable communicators to communicate in an *open* fashion, standards have been developed that define the set of protocols.

In the foregoing sections of this chapter, we have introduced various concepts, such as communications channels, media, addressing, encryption and data compression. Each of these concepts, and others, requires to be implemented variously in computer software, hardware and at the level of the physical communications media. We need to ensure that each of these concepts is independent of the others, wherever this makes sense. For example if we use electronic mail, we are not interested in the physical medium or media used to transfer our mail.

If a communications service is analysed it is apparent that it can be decomposed into a series of levels, called *layers*. At the highest layer, applications dialogue with each other. At the lowest layer, physical media such as electrical wires (of which there are a variety including twisted pair and coaxial cable) and fibre optic cables are used. Between these layers one can identify several other layers, and these fit into a hierarchy. For example when one communicates, just as in a telephone call, one does this during a session, during which time the sender and receiver are 'connected'. At the start of a session, a virtual circuit is established and remains for the duration of the session. At a lower layer, multiplexing will be applied to the data being transferred for a particular message. Communications system software and the hardware are typically designed in the form of separate layers.

The International Standards Organization has formulated a particular layered model for communications, the open system interconnection (OSI) model, and has specified the standards for this model (see Fig. 12.2).

Layer	What it Does	Examples
7 Application	The user application	Electronic mail, Print a file (LAN)
6 Presentation	Translates the data between the application and how transferred	Encryption and decryption, Data compression and expansion
5 Session	Allows communication sessions with other users	Equivalent of a call in telephony
4 Transport	Provides a transparent link to network	Multiplexing
3 Network	Sets up, maintains and terminates connections and takes care of addressing and re-routing	
2 Datalink	Synchronizes transmission	
1 Physical	Deals with electrical and mechanical interface to the media	Twisted pair, fibre optic cable

Figure 12.2 The OSI layer model.

A given message has to traverse all the layers of the OSI model if the sender and receiver are associated with different distinct computer systems. However, for various applications involving communications, some layers may be omitted or 'collapsed' together. For example communications with another user on the same computer can dispense with certain of the lower layers, whilst a computer node in a packet switched network can dispense with certain of the higher layers.

PART
FIVE

APPLYING COMPUTERS

THIRTEEN

CLASSIFYING COMPUTER SYSTEMS

In order to classify computer systems it is first necessary to know the characteristics of computers. The next stage involves classifying the users, those involved in developing a computer system as well as the end users. We then classify computer applications and computer users, and then finally we classify computers themselves. The classification of potential computer based solutions is left to Chapter 14.

13.1 CHARACTERISTICS OF COMPUTERS

Suppose we have a problem which can be reduced to a form that can be solved by the application of a computer. This involves, amongst other criteria, being able to express the problem solution by means of a program. What are the characteristics of computer solutions (as distinct from the particular problem) that may make them preferable to *traditional* methods of solution?

- *Repetitive work.* Computers are adept at doing repetitive jobs, each of which may vary, but under some predefined manner. This is done by the computer *executing* a *program*. A program is a specification of a problem in a form that can be interpreted by the computer. Thus a program is an *abstraction* of the solution to a problem. If the job to be done varies within some predefined way, the solution must accommodate such variations and ensure that the input data fully defines the current extent of the variation. For example a program that works out the average of a set of numbers should cope with both arbitrary values of the numbers and it may have to cope with various sized sets of numbers. It may also have to guard against input data in which there are errors. For a program that is to calculate the average of a set of *positive* numbers, a negative number in the input data is in error; thus the program should include *validation* of input data.

    Executing the program causes the input data to be processed, to produce output data. In the 'averages' problem the output would be the average, and it might include data indicating an error(s) in the input data.

- *Consistency*. Computers are *deterministic*. For a given program and a given set of input data, the computer *always* produces the same output.
- *Reliability*. Computers can run continuously with the exception of *down time* for *maintenance*. In fact, true continuous running is possible with *configurations* involving replication of computers, or computers designed with specific components replicated. Such systems, which allow parts of the system to *go down* deliberately (as for routine maintenance) or accidentally (for example an electrical power failure or equipment failure), are called *resilient* or *fault tolerant*.

  Programs themselves may contain errors. The requirements program is itself *validated* against the problem it is to solve when the software is produced (Chapter 7). Program (or software) *validation* is an important issue, in particular for computer systems working with stringent safety or security requirements— for example, air-traffic control or nuclear power station control. Similarly the hardware components of the computer that execute the program and also those that manipulate data, for example data transfers within the computer, may not be correct; in the same vein as software validation, hardware validation is also of great importance. Hardware validation is more mature than software validation, for three principal reasons. Firstly, because it is more difficult to make the changes to existing computers than it is to supply and install corrected software, there has been effort expended in hardware validation techniques. The second reason is that because the complexity of software applications is typically high, the software validation process is difficult. Finally, there are few hardware designs compared with a multitude of software applications.

- *Speed*. Computers typically have a considerable speed advantage compared with manual or non-computer equipment methods. For example, with a personal computer an instruction to add two integer numbers together might take in the order of one millionth of a second to do. In fact, such apparent high speeds for particular operations quoted in isolation can be misleading. The figure quoted above is for the case with the numbers already present in the computer's memory. Input and output of data also takes time (usually a lot slower). The activity of *sizing* a computer to ensure it has sufficient processing speed and memory size to hold the programs and data is known as *capacity planning*.

13.2 CLASSIFYING COMPUTER USERS

Computer systems are used by *users*. Computer users can be direct or indirect users, and conscious or unconscious of being users of a computer system. All are users of the software and the hardware that make up the system.

A computer hardware system can, unless it is an embedded computer, usually support various different software applications. Computer systems may be used to produce computer systems. This feature applies both to the physical or *hardware* components of the computer as well as the programs and data (the *software*). Specialist computer applications are used in the hardware design process and in

People involved in developing a computer system

- The *Customer*, who will have produced the *requirements* for a particular computer system. The customer will classify the eventual *end users* of the system.
- The *Systems Analyst* who specifies the inputs and outputs and the processes (by analysing any current manual or mechanical system and synthesizing the needs of the intended computer system).
- The *Programmer* who 'writes' the programs.

People who use the computer system—*end users*

- *Direct users* are registered on a given computer system whenever there may be shared information susceptible to *update*, that is the information can be changed, or the data has some security or chargeable value associated with it.
- *Administrative personnel* are involved with the registering and maintenance of user information that a computer system requires. They use software to assist themselves in this task. In particular if shared data is present, access to this may be restricted to particular users. For example in a lending library system, acquisitions of new books are entered into the system only by the acquisitions personnel. Even if a computer system permits public access, for example that used in the lending library, the computer system still has the concept of an (usually) anonymous user for a person making say a catalogue enquiry.
- *Support personnel* are involved in duties such as regular *back-up* of data, and installing new application software systems.

Figure 13.1 Computer users.

the production of software. Because of this property of computers, and because the ability to produce new or improved software applications is usually possible, often with little or no changes to the hardware on which the application is to run, computer systems have lifetimes that include the definition of their requirements and, unless *packaged* software is used, the design of the software. Thus, independent of the purpose of a computer system, we can classify the users of the system (see Fig. 13.1).

We can distinguish two types of computer user. First there are those involved in the development of a computer system as part of the software life-cycle, and second there are the *end users*, those people who will use the developed and installed computer system. A different computer may be used for development of a software application; this is the case for applications that are products. Within each of these broad types, further subdivision of users occurs (Fig. 13.1).

In a computer installation we may find one individual involved in several of these user roles, and *vice-versa*. We may also find further division of labour; for example in the development and installation of software we might find project managers, communications engineers, capacity planning specialists, and so on.

13.3 CLASSIFYING COMPUTER APPLICATIONS

Any taxonomy is to an extent based on the needs of the users. Two user views are taken here, firstly that of the customer and end users of the computer system and secondly that of the developer.

13.3.1 Horizontal and vertical

From the perspective of customers and end users, applications may be characterized as to whether they are of use to a very wide number of such users, that is *horizontal*, or whether they are specialized to some particular user needs, that is *vertical*.

A common example of a horizontal application is a word-processor; many users of computers use a word-processor. Similarly one finds packages that provide some facility used frequently in industry and commerce; for example payroll or sales order processing. The idea is that most people and organizations wishing to do these things want them done in a standard way but need perhaps 'standard' customizing. A vertical package is one that has been produced for the needs of some particular user, for example a package to prepare restaurant menus.

13.3.2 End user to system building

From the developing perspective, applications are characterized as being either *end user* or *system building*. End user applications provide a specific user function such as a chemical plant control system. System building applications enable a user to construct a new application either wholly from scratch or by building an application from existing components. The reality with typical computer applications is that most end user applications permit some level of programming and at least some degree of tailoring when they are installed. Thus the personal computer user who purchases a word-processor product will typically find facilities for setting default values once (for example their preferred type fonts and, say, margin widths) rather than setting these for every document.

13.4 CLASSIFYING COMPUTERS

The classification we adopt is broadly based on names that are ascribed within the computer industry to physical configurations of computers.

Computers are intrinsically general purpose. A given computer may be used for a variety of different tasks, at different times, and even simultaneously if it has sufficient 'power'. By power we mean the amount of some specified type of work that a computer carries out in some given time. However a particular computer may be specialized by only being used for a particular application—for example word-processing, or by being physically embedded (and often 'invisible') in some other artifact—as for computers in medical body-scanners or washing machines.

13.4.1 General purpose computers

The classification we adopt here is more concerned with the physical aspects of the computer. There are several variables involved; for example the size of the computer's memory, the speed at which it can process information, and the number of keyboards with screens attached to the computer.

- *Personal computer.* An individual self-contained computer with its own keyboard, screen, printer and disk drive(s). A personal computer is sufficiently powerful for the typical applications needed by an individual, such as word-processing and data management.

  Personal computers can be classified physically according to CPU power and memory size, and the environment in which they are used; for example desktop (see Fig. 1.9), portable (but requiring a normal power source), lap-top (battery power source) and note-pad (battery power source). Logically, the intention is that all these computers are identical. Physically they differ, e.g. bulky hardware items, and high power consumption items. These restrictions apply constraints on, for example, the types of screen technology and the size and number of disk drives. Where logically identical, programs will operate independent of which type of computer.
- *Workstation.* An individual computer with its own screen, but sufficiently powerful in terms of speed and memory for applications that require considerable computing performance; for example computer aided design (CAD) as used in architecture and mechanical engineering. Workstations are sometimes *stand-alone* (with their own disk-drive and disk, but more often are *networked* in a local area network (LAN) in order to share file servers with disk drives—and thus programs and data).
- *Main-frame.* An individual computer or 'closely-coupled' computers with usually a large number (e.g. 100–1000) of terminals. A main-frame computer is sufficiently powerful in terms of speed of processing and adequacy of the size of the computer's memory that it can support many simultaneous users. The reason for concentrating the processing on one computer, rather than each user having their own personal computer, is that it is much easier to program the simultaneous access to files, especially if some users may change the contents of the files. The applications typically involve transaction processing.

13.4.2 Special purpose computers

The list that follows is not exhaustive.

- *Embedded computers.* Computers are intrinsically general purpose; they can be programmed to perform an unlimited variety of tasks. However for some applications it makes sense to pre-program the computer for the tasks associated with the application. Embedded computers are those which are built into artifacts, as described in Chapter 1.

  An embedded computer is specialized for a particular set of functions. This specialization is characterized by its being connected to the internal workings of the artifact and possibly with a display to provide user information, and a hardware facility for input of user data or programs.

- *Super-computers*. Super-computers are characterized by being able to process information at a very high rate—perhaps best suggested by quoting a common application they are used for—weather forecasting. Sophisticated weather forecasting requires a very large number of calculations, and clearly needs to be completed and output in good time.

FOURTEEN

VALUES AND ETHICS

Before we go ahead and apply a computer-based solution, it is necessary to classify potential computer-based solutions by characterizing the nature of real world problems that might be amenable to solution by computer.

In this chapter we examine computer-based solutions in the abstract, in order to derive criteria that may be used to argue the benefits and the disadvantages of a computer-based solution. We then discuss some ethical issues involving security and privacy.

14.1 EVALUATION OF COMPUTER-BASED SOLUTIONS

Computer-based solutions have both advantages and disadvantages. In considering whether to propose a computer-based solution we should be mindful of these. As far as disadvantages are concerned, we need to be aware of how each of these might be avoided, prevented or mitigated.

The implementation of a computer-based solution may require an understanding of the computer industry and Kavanagh (1988) provides an introduction to this subject.

14.1.1 Classifying (potential) computer-based solutions

Before we can determine if a computer-based solution is feasible for a new problem, one has to classify the various sorts of potential problem. Given such a classification, deciding on the feasibility is thereby assisted.

Computer systems acquire and process information, in the form of data, in order to provide information, again in the form of data. The acquired *input* data is information created directly or indirectly by humans or by data acquisition from sensor devices. The *output* data is information that may either be for (possibly eventual) direct human use or alternatively the information may be used to control devices. An abstract model of a computer system is shown in Fig. 14.1.

REALWORLD → input data → process → output data → REALWORLD

Figure 14.1 Data processing.

Examples of hypothetical computer systems which are instances of the abstract model are shown in Fig. 14.2. In each system either humans or devices are involved in the *input* and *output*.

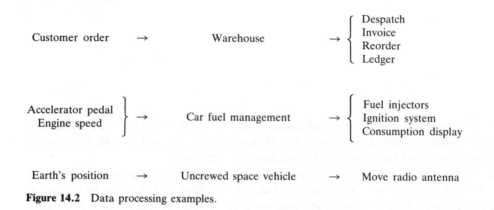

Figure 14.2 Data processing examples.

In the examples in Fig. 14.3, the technological evolution of the solution for the production of individual documents on paper is shown. Benefits in the form of *extra* functionality are apparent with the technology improvements and particularly so when a computer is present, as is the case of the word-processor. For example one can save documents or document parts, and later recall them. One can edit documents. A spelling checker program can be used to check text. Furthermore one can normally *preview* the document on the screen, and, only if it is satisfactory, print it on paper.

Pen and ink

Typewriter

Keyboard, Disk   →   Word-processor   →   Screen, Printer, Disk

Figure 14.3 Technological evolution.

From examples such as the above, the following characteristics are apparent in respect of the computer-based solutions:

1. One or more inputs.
2. One or more outputs.
3. In *some* instances replacement of manual or non-computer equipment systems

takes place, in *other* instances no previous manual or non-computer equipment system exists.

4. The computer-based solution normally has more functionality than the prior manual or non-computer equipment system. This extra functionality is ancillary to the primary purpose of the application. A car fuel management/fuel consumption display would have been expensive and difficult to provide with previous technologies. In providing such extra functionality, there may be further input or output data and devices, and certainly further programming over and above the basic solution so as to realize the extra functions required. Often, some of the extra functionality is in the form of extra output information and this may be used by other (computer based) solutions, either in the same computer system or by *communication* with other computer systems.

5. Computer-based solutions can be characterized by comparing them with traditional techniques. A method for doing such a comparison is by characterizing the nature of the work done:

- Work that could be done by people *given* the time to do so. For example:
  - Clerical work—accounts, order processing, etc.
  - Calculations arising from experimental data—e.g. survey results.
  - Engineering calculations in design—e.g. stress analysis of mechanical components.
  - Publishing assistance—e.g. word-processing integrated with graphics and layout design.
  - Seat reservation systems—e.g. for theatre tickets.
- Work that could be done with traditional equipment. For example:
  - Manufacturing engineering components—e.g. production of automotive pistons.
  - Controlling a chemical process—e.g. an oil refinery.
  - Laboratory analysis—e.g. blood samples.
- Work that cannot be done either by people or by traditional equipment. The reasons can, for example, be:
  - *Hostile or remote environments.* Consider for example an uncrewed space vehicle. Calculations and decisions need to be done on board the space vehicle itself using data acquired by sensors on the space vehicle; the speed of transmission of electromagnetic radiation for communication (e.g. radio) being finite means that they have to be done *in situ*. It is not feasible that the calculations be done on Earth, on data sent by the space vehicle and results transmitted back as the delays would be unacceptable. Also, the vehicle may become obscured by a heavenly body such as a planet or moon.
  - *Speed necessary to complete the work.* Consider the case of sophisticated weather forecasting—it is just not possible for human beings to do all the calculations in the time available for the result to be a *forecast*!
  - *Complexity.* To make up specialized equipment for perhaps a one-off job may be just too difficult. An example is the radio antenna control in an uncrewed space vehicle. Calculations need to be done based on

various sensor data. It is not feasible to build a special purpose piece of equipment which must include the ability to perform mathematical calculations, to take decisions, and to acquire data, and to control devices.

14.1.2 Advantages

In Sec. 13.1 and in the previous section, several advantages of computer-based solutions have been implicitly introduced: repetitive abilities, consistency, reliability, speed, extra functionality over manual and non-computing equipment solutions, and work that can be done neither by people nor non-computer equipment. To this list of advantages can be added:

- *Reduction in costs*. For example wages. However, computer-based solutions themselves have associated costs, both in setting up and in maintenance. (This issue is discussed further in the next section.)
- *Availability and timeliness of information*. Information, for example for monitoring an enterprise or a manufacturing plant, is considerably easier to provide, can be available *up-to-date* and *on-line* (rather than having to wait as is normal in a manual system, due to the slow speed of information flow). Up-to-date on-line information can assist personnel in decision making.
- *Flexibility*. The computer program (the *software*) specifies how the computer system will behave for given input data. Programs can be created and changed independently of the physical (*hardware*) parts of the computer system. An analogy for software and hardware in this respect is that of a cassette tape recording and a cassette and cassette recorder/player respectively.

14.1.3 Disadvantages

- *Opacity of solution*. Most computer software is opaque; that is, one cannot understand how it works unless one is a specialist and there is *documentation* to describe it. This is because most and typically the older and well established computer programming languages, the languages used by the programmer to state to the computer how it is to process the input data, require the programmer to explicitly state not the specification of the problem itself, but instead how the problem is to be solved by the computer. This means that such computer programs reflect how computers work. Thus we have opacity for two reasons— we use specialized languages which can be obscure and difficult to understand by the non-specialist, and we specify the 'how' rather than the 'what'. This point is expanded upon in Chapter 6.
- *Investment and maintenance*. Computer-based solutions themselves have a cost. There is the capital cost, and the maintenance costs of both the hardware and software.

    The training of the computer users, both the direct users of keyboards and screens, and also the indirect users whose work will be changed, is a cost to be borne in mind.

- *Invalidity*. The very flexibility and openness made available by having a programming language means that in practice errors are difficult to avoid. They can originate from, for example, an error in the initial requirements study for the system, or an error on the part of the programmer in translating the specification—usually written in a natural language, such as English, having a propensity to ambiguities—into a program. With thought one can see that there are several other points in the steps from and during the requirements to the installation of the program at which errors can be introduced in producing a software solution.
- *The potential for social dislocation*. The replacement of existing systems by computer based systems can lead to unemployment, a loss of work interest—for example a feeling of 'lack of involvement'—and the potential for the easier misuse of confidential information. Training of both direct and indirect users is of importance to mitigate these problems.

  Another consideration is the loss of personal skills. Once a program has been implemented to do something that was previously a personal skill, the program embodies that skill.

  Following on from the above considerations, the use of computers becomes a dependency; thus in various activities their continued use is essential. In many areas we have passed the point of 'no-return'.

  Where a computer system is a dependency, then it is necessary that it has high availability. For example the effects of power failure, flood and other forms of dislocation must be planned for. Preventive measures (for example emergency power supplies) and other contingency plans become a requirement.

  During the introduction of a new computer system, there is usually the need for a period of *parallel running* of the old and new systems to ensure consistency of operation and results. This must be borne in mind in the planning of the project.
- *Confidentiality and irresponsible usage*. Computing facilities, programs and data are artifacts and as such can be regarded as property and may also be subject to privacy. There is therefore the potential for irresponsible usage, both directly or by other means, for example *hacking* (improper access to a computer system), and malpractice by *virus* programs. To guard against irresponsible usage, legal and security procedures must be effected. These issues are discussed further in Section 14.3.

14.2 REUSING SOFTWARE—THE 'COMPONENT' APPROACH

Due to its labour-intensive nature, the production of software is a costly, complex and time-consuming process. Furthermore the job is a skilled one. When a particular software item has been produced there are several incentives to reuse it in other computer applications. To be able to do this requires firstly that this is a feasible proposition, and secondly that it is worthwhile.

At various steps in the software life-cycle the question must be asked: 'Do we use an existing item of software or do we write our own?'. Such a software item

1. Is the application area popular? Thus will there be a choice of software items at competitive prices?
2. Can all the requirements be met by a given software item? If not, can the missing requirements be programmed using, for example, either a high-level language or (less attractive) a programming language peculiar to the software item?
3. What is the commercial soundness of the producer of the software item? Will the producer be able to provide maintenance in the future? Is there an escrow for the software item whereby the software used in its construction is held by a third party?
4. Will the software item co-exist with other components of the computer based solution? For example can one easily transfer data between the software item and the other programs in the rest of the system? Does the user interface conform acceptably with that used with other parts of the system?
5. Can the contract with the supplier include maintenance arrangements in the event of faults being found—by others as well as the client? Will the supplier contract to provide upgrades. For example a payroll package may require amendment to conform to changes in taxation laws.
6. Are there training facilities? For example are there training courses available, and does the software item have a 'tutorial' mode?
7. Is the effort expended in searching for potential candidates and getting reasonable answers to the above questions worthwhile? Perhaps 'reinventing the wheel' is a better proposition.

Figure 14.4 Existing versus 'write your own'.

could be any of an object library, a package, a fourth generation language, an application generator and so on. The reasons for asking such a question include possible reduction in costs and lead-times that might occur. Relevant questions that might be asked in deciding which course to take are summarized in Fig. 14.4. Catalogues, books and journals can be referred to to identify potential candidates. Advice might be sought from a software consultancy.

14.3 SECURITY AND PRIVACY

The ability to obtain information from various sources usually using communication facilities, and possibly process this, raises issues as to improper usage that society has not had to deal with before. Whilst there has sometimes been the theoretical possibility that one could do such collection and processing in a manual fashion in the past, such exercises have usually been very tedious and difficult to accomplish. To date only state and industrial security and espionage services have usually bothered.

In response to concerns about the potential for the misuse and abuse of information, the UK Government has introduced the *Data Protection Act 1984*; see Data Protection Registrar (1989).

REFERENCES AND FURTHER READING

Ada Joint Program Office (1983) *Reference Manual for the Ada Programming Language*, American National Standards Institute, New York.

Adobe Systems Incorporated (1990) *PostScript Language Tutorial and Cookbook*, Addison-Wesley, Reading, MASS.

Anderson, R. (1990) *Computer Studies: a first year course*, Blackwell Scientific Publications, Oxford.

British Computer Society (1991) *A glossary of computing terms: an introduction*, 7th ed., Pitman, London.

Burks, W., Goldstine, H., and von Neumann, J. (1946) Preliminary Discussion of the Logical Design of an Electronic Computing Instrument. Reprinted in: Bell, C.J., and Newell, A. (1971) *Computer Structures: Readings and Examples*, McGraw-Hill, New York, pp. 92–119.

Cardey, S. (1990) Représentation de la Connaissance Linguistique: Grammaire Electronique et Didactique, Poster Presentes, Applica 1990, 2nd Congrès Européen Multi-media, Artificial Intelligence and Training, Lille, France.

Data Protection Registrar (1989) Guideline 1 to 8, Booklets 1 to 8, The Office of The Data Protection Registrar, Wilmslow, Cheshire.

Date, C. J. (1990) An Introduction to Database Systems, vol. 1, 5th ed., Addison-Wesley, Reading, MASS.

Diller, A. (1990) **Z**: *an introduction to formal methods*, John Wiley, Chichester.

Graham, J., and Loader, R. (1989) *A programmer's introduction to computer systems*, McGraw-Hill, London.

Halsell, F. (1988) *Data communications, computer networks, and OSI*, Addison-Wesley, Wokingham.

Howe, D. R. (1989) *Data Analysis for Data Base Design*, 2nd ed., Edward Arnold, London.

Jackson, M. A. (1975) *Principles of Program Design*, Academic Press, London.

Jensen, K., and Wirth, N. (1985) *Pascal: user manual and report*, Springer-Verlag, New York.

Kavanagh, J. (1988) *Alien's guide to the computer industry*, Computer Weekly Publications, Sutton, Surrey.

Kernighan, B. W., and Ritchie, D. M. (1978) *The C programming language*, Prentice-Hall, Englewood Cliffs, New Jersey.

Lamport, L. (1986) L^{A}T$_E$X: *A Document Preparation System*, Addison-Wesley, Reading, MASS.

Mandell, S. L. (1988) *Fundamentals of Information Processing*, West Publishing Company, St. Paul.

Meyer, B. (1988) *Object-oriented Software Construction*, Prentice-Hall, New York.

Nilsson, U., and Małuszyński, J. (1990) *Logic, Programming and Prolog*, John Wiley, Chichester.

Pereira, F., and Warren, D. H.D. (1980) Definite clause grammars for Language Analysis, *Artificial Intelligence*, vol. 13, pp. 231–278.

Pressman, R. S. (1987) *Software Engineering*, McGraw-Hill, New York.

Silberschatz, A., Peterson, J. L., and Galvin, P. B. (1991) *Operating System Concepts*, 3rd ed., Addison-Wesley, Reading, MASS.

Sterling, L., and Shapiro, E. (1986) *The Art of Prolog*, The MIT Press, Cambridge, MASS.

Stroustrup, B. (1991) *The C++ Programming Language*, 2nd ed., Addison-Wesley, Reading, MASS.

Trakhtenbrot, B. A. (1963) *Algorithms and Automatic Computing Machines*, D. C. Heath, Lexington, MASS.

Turner, D. (1986) An Overview of Miranda, *SIGPLAN Notices*, vol. 21, no. 12, December 1986, pp. 158–166.

INDEX